Conversations with American Women Writers

Conversations with

AMERICAN WOMEN
WRITERS

Sarah Anne Johnson

University Press of New England
Hanover and London

University Press of New England, 37 Lafayette St.,
Lebanon, NH 03766
© 2004 by Sarah Anne Johnson
Printed in the United States of America

5 4 3 2 1

Library of Congress Cataloguing-in-Publication Data
Conversations with American women writers / Sarah Anne Johnson.
p.   cm.
Includes bibliographical references.
ISBN 1-58465-300-0 (alk. paper) — ISBN 1-58465-348-5 (pbk. :
alk. paper)
1. Women authors, American—Interviews. 2. Authors, American—
20th century—Interviews. 3. Authors, American—21st century—
Interviews. 4. Women and literature—United States. 5. Authorship.
I. Johnson, Sarah Anne.
PS151.C675 2003
810.9'9287'0904—dc22   2003020646

"A. J. Verdelle: Managing the Whole Fictive World" is printed
by permission of The Wendy Weil Agency, Inc. © 2003 by A. J. Verdelle.
Many of these interviews previously appeared or are forthcoming
in *The Writers' Chronicle, The Writer,* and *Glimmertrain Stories.*
They are reprinted with permission.

For my Alice

*I am a writer who came of a sheltered life. A sheltered life
can be a daring life as well. For all serious
daring starts from within.*
—Eudora Welty

Contents

Acknowledgments

I thank the writers who've given generously of their time and shared themselves so willingly in these interviews, as well as the people who've contributed to this book in so many different ways: my editor John W. Landrigan for consistently providing good ideas; my family for always believing; Ailish Hopper and Randi Triant, my right and left hands; Jason Shinder, mentor, guide, and friend, for critical support and inspiration; Miriam, who keeps my eye on the heart of the matter; and Susan, my first reader, editor, creative consort, who lives with the making of the book, the making of the writer.

Conversations with American Women Writers

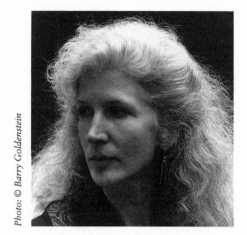

ANDREA BARRETT

The Hidden Map of the Story

Andrea Barrett received a National Book Award for her story collection *Ship Fever.* She is also the author of *The Middle Kingdom, The Forms of Water, Lucid Stars, The Voyage of the Narwhal,* and *Servants of the Map,* which was recently named a "Notable Book of the Year" by the *New York Times Book Review.* She teaches at the M.F.A. Program for Writers at the Warren Wilson College and has also been a visiting writer at numerous colleges, universities, and writers' conferences, including the Bread Loaf Writers' Conference. She is currently a Fellow at the Center for Writers and Scholars at the New York Public Library. In 2001, Barrett was awarded a MacArthur Fellowship.

I know that you were a biology student. How did you go from science to writing fiction?

By a long, confused road. I initially went to graduate school in zoology, which didn't work out at all. Later on I studied medieval history for a couple of years in graduate school, but I didn't stick with that either. In and around those two things I had about thirteen jobs in ten years, none of them related to each other, and none but the last two related to writing. It took me a long time to figure out what I wanted to do. It really wasn't clear to me. I kept trying awful jobs and fumbling around. I did finally just start writing, and I can't actually account for that, except that I've always been such a passionate reader. I loved reading and loved books and wanted to write, but I didn't understand how anyone became a writer. I didn't know any writers, and I didn't know about graduate programs in writing. But one day I started writing a novel. I worked on that for about six years and eventually had to throw it out, but in the process I learned something about writing and I began to meet other writers, and all that was helpful. It was a long road, though.

What did you do to develop your craft of fiction?

Mostly I wrote. I wrote and I read and I wrote and I read, which is still a way that a person can learn to be a writer. It's faster if you go to school. I teach now in the M.F.A. program at Warren Wilson College, and I visit other M.F.A. programs. I can see how much time it's possible to save if you have help and companions, but you can learn the same things by yourself. For a while, I did. As I got older, I began to go to writers' conferences and writers' groups and to make friends with other writers who I shared my work with and whose work I read. That was an enormous help to me.

It also helped me when I started teaching, for the obvious reason that before you teach something, you have to hurriedly go out and learn it yourself. I never felt more than a half hour ahead of my students. I've had wonderful students. They were often better read or farther along some paths than I was and I learned a great deal from them.

How did you decide to explore the possibilities offered in the world of science?

That's something that evolved gradually in me. Now, when I look back—at my early training as a biologist, all my friends who are biologists and doctors, and my husband, who's a scientist—it seems obvious that this is the world I know. It seems obvious to everyone now, including me, that I should write about that world, but in fact it wasn't obvious. It took me a while to find my way there. With my earlier books, it was so difficult for me just to do the basics of handling characters and trying to tell a story that I couldn't see my way into incorporating a lot of outside material into the work. By my third novel, *The Middle Kingdom,* I was able to begin to use some of that material. One of the chief characters is a freshwater biologist, but the book is not very much about his work. The work is in the background, more incidental. The work is not present in the book the way it is in my later books, but that's when it first crept in. In *The Forms of Water,* the fourth book, I began to use some historical material for the first time as background for a very elderly character. That's when I first started using a lot of research to build characters and to build material in the books.

Finally, in *Ship Fever,* something released in me. I think because I started trying to learn to write stories and left novel writing for a while, it suddenly seemed possible to reach into that older natural history material and see what I could make of it. Once I did, I felt really at home there. I loved it. I had that "Aha!" moment. I wondered why I wasn't always writing about this. I don't know what took me so long.

Were there any challenges you faced in incorporating science into your work?

Yes, and I still do. The truth is that I don't know science very well. I learned it as an undergraduate twenty-five years ago now, and I didn't learn it very well the first time. People often assume, and I'm grateful that they do assume, that I know a fair bit of science, because what I get on the page in the end is convincing, but the truth is that I don't know it very well. I do a lot of research to get it on the page, and I worry all the time that I've gotten things wrong. I have a flimsy understanding of it, and I'm always walking on eggs with it. Not so much with the older natural history material—that was written for a lay audience and anyone is capable of understanding it, even me. But when I'm working with contemporary science, I'm sometimes nervous.

Do you have readers who review your work for accuracy?

With certain stories I do. With "The Mysteries of Ubiquitin" in *Servants of the Map*—I got the idea for that particular field of research from a dear friend of mine who does research on ubiquitin. I asked her, when the story was finished, to read those sections for me and make sure that I hadn't done anything stupid. It was a great help.

Your work is often labeled as fiction about science, but it really strikes a balance between the science and the human story you're exploring. Is it difficult to strike that balance?

I'd propose that it's not really fiction about science, although it gets labeled that way and I often talk about it that way. It's fiction. Fiction is about people. Fiction is about stories. Those remain my primary interests. I use the subject matter of science as my "stuff." Any writer needs something to write about, and this is *my* stuff. But stuff is not what fiction is about. Stuff is what fiction is founded in and in part built by. But it isn't what it's *about*. Scientists are terrifically interesting people, and so the characters and the dilemmas that arise from people who are passionate about doing science can make for really interesting fiction. That's not exactly the same as fiction about science.

How do you go about conducting your research? What types of resources do you consult, and where do you find them?

I go to the library, nothing esoteric. I do read an enormous amount, but I'm not a great rummager in archives and lost papers and crumbling things, although I have friends who do that and I admire them enormously. I'm a reader of books, and of memoirs, and of diaries, and of collections of letters. I also look at a lot of visual material. If it's from a period when photography existed, I look at old photographs, which I find enormously helpful. I look at paintings. I look both at things about the time and things made *at* the time. It's interesting in one way to look at an etching made in 1857 of the things on Charles Darwin's desk, and it's interesting in another way to look at a painting or an etching made in 1930 about the things someone thought were on Charles Darwin's desk. They say two different things. Some of the things are about 1857 and some are about 1930, but it's all interesting. If there's music that I know from the period, I listen to the music. If I can, if the languages are available to me, I also look at novels and poems written in the period. Even though they may not be about what I'm researching, they tell me something about the tonality of the culture then, about what people are thinking, what things seemed important to them.

How concerned were you with getting the historical facts accurate?

I am pretty concerned. There are people who purposely bend historical fact in their fiction, but while that can make for interesting fiction, I'm not one of them. Because I spent a brief time formally studying history, it makes me nervous to bend what seems to be a known fact. There are people who would argue that there are no known facts, but again, I'm not one of them. If there's a historical person passing through a story or a novel, I won't have had him or her grow up in a place where they didn't grow up. I won't send a person to the Arctic when I know he went to the Antarctic. I won't have a woman living in Philadelphia when I know that during those years she was living in France. Those very basic things I will stick to.

Can you talk about how your research kindles your imagination and gets you writing?

Oh, in all sorts of ways. Sometimes things really do grow from the reading and the research, but it's always in such odd ways. Often it's a picture, a visual image. Sometimes it's an image in words, a sense of somebody on a dock or in a room holding a bandage. Sometimes a whole area of subject matter will seem interesting to me. That's what happened with "The Cure" in *Servants of the Map*. I used to drive through Saranac Lake a lot on my way to someplace else. I never stopped to look around, but it imprinted itself on me. I got curious about the porches, and then curious about the people who would've been on the porches, and then curious about the state of society that would've led everybody to be clumped in one place on the porches.

At what point do you stop your research and start writing?

Usually after the initial subject matter has suggested itself, I'll have to read pretty hard for a while just to get my feet under me. It's hard to write something about Gregor Mendel if you don't know what decades he lived in and you don't know what city his monastery was in. You have to get a sense of the period and the place in the most general way. But often I can start when I have only that general sense, because the research is very specific for the story or the sections of the novel. When I get to a part in *The Voyage of the Narwhal* where the men sail off on a ship, suddenly I realize that I don't know anything about how ships are built or where the stove is. I have to stop everything, and go learn about ships. As the ship comes up past Newfoundland to the edge of Greenland, I realize I don't know anything about Greenland. I don't know when the Danes went there or who administered what or what the Inuit peoples were doing or what the weather was like or what the coastline was like. The research lurches along stepwise.

It takes you on a journey of your own.

So much so. There's a hidden map of each story and each novel which exists beneath the story and which is the map of my own path through all these different areas of inquiry and exploration and learning.

How do you manage all of this historical information in a narrative, and what is the effect you want the history to achieve in the narrative?

I want the history to be correct insofar as it can be, but I also, ultimately, want it to be subordinate in the sense that I am writing a novel and not writing history. After the first draft or two, a lot of my efforts in further drafts and revisions are to take out much of the factual material I earlier worked so hard to learn and put in. I always put in too much. There are always long digressions and long ponderous passages and things that no person would actually say to another person.

Do you hate cutting them?
I do initially. I'm always glad in the end that I did. I always get used to it. I tend not to miss them soon after I've cut them, even though, each time, I think, "Oh, that was so interesting. I wish I didn't have to take that out."

But you asked how I managed all the information, and maybe you meant that in a more literal sense. It's evolved over time, and it's still evolving, and I don't have a perfect system. I keep thinking I'll find one, and I never do. For various books and sets of stories I've used various cumbersome, not very well organized combinations of three-ring binders full of notes, index cards, hanging files, smaller files, larger files, boxes, tubs, tins, maps on the wall. There's always a ton of paper around. It's hard sometimes to remember what's where and be able to get my hands on the stuff I need about, say, a ship's berth. I used to take notes on yellow pads, so there would be heaps and heaps and heaps of yellow sheets piled in folders all over. I'm trying to do some of this on the computer now, but I'm just learning to do that.

What's your process like when you're working on a story or a novel? What goes on through each draft or revision?
I do a great many drafts, no matter what it is. I'm a very clumsy writer. I've given up apologizing for it. It's the way I work, so it's the way I work. My first drafts tend to be unspeakably bad. I don't know how to express it: astonishingly bad, much worse than most student work. I'd never get into graduate school if I applied with those drafts.

I think all of you established writers should let us read your first drafts to renew our faith, to let us know that everyone starts at the beginning with each piece.
I gave a talk at the University of Michigan several years ago to the graduating students, the Hopwood Lecture. I was talking about exploration and discovery, but I talked some about *The Voyage of the Narwhal,* and I did actually read them the first three-quarters of a page of the first draft of that book.

Was it horrible?
Oh, it's amazing. Wrong in every way. It diverges from the final book in every way that it could. It's first person, not third. It's set thirty years

before the time I actually started the book. They went to the Antarctic instead of the Arctic. Reading the draft was fun; it gave the students some sense of how messy the process always is. It always is, no matter how long you do it.

So how do you get from those early drafts to the final, beautiful piece?

I write a lot of drafts. I draft and I draft and I draft. Some people can do more of this in their heads and not have to write it out so many times, but I seem to think largely on the page. This means doing it and letting it sit for a few days before looking at it, then doing it again and letting it sit, and doing it again. I let my friends read drafts after the first ten or twelve, when it's starting to get faintly coherent and you can faintly see the direction. My closest friend is Margot Livesey, a wonderful writer. Margot and I have shared our work for about a decade now. I let Margot look at it at various points along the way, although I try not to hammer her more than two or three times. Often she'll look at something like the tenth, the twentieth, and the thirtieth iterations: it's a huge help, to have a wonderful brilliant reader asking great questions. I cut a lot. It isn't as if I write very long the first time and cut in all the successive drafts, nor is it as if I write very sketchily the first time and add through all the successive drafts. Strangely, it's both. My early drafts are sketchy in the most important ways—everything vital is left out—and they're wordy in other ways—there's all this extraneous material that doesn't matter. So the revisions are in both directions. It's like building a house, if you don't know how to build a house and you're not very smart. You run around and you throw up some walls where you think the rooms should go, and then you come back in a week and you realize there's no bathroom and two kitchens, so you have to tear down some of those walls and put up others, and then in a week you come back and realize the attic is half the size it's supposed to be. The walls go up, the walls go down, the walls go up. Somehow a house gets built, but I don't exactly understand it. But that's what it feels like, putting up walls and tearing down walls until you get it right.

The more interesting question is, How do you know when you get it right? But I can't answer that one. I don't think anyone can truthfully. We all have feelings about that, but most writers, if we're honest, admit that that's what those things are—they're feelings, they're intuitions. Things *feel* right at a certain point. They assume a proportion or a shape that feels right. It's not an intellectual decision. It's an emotional or an intuitive decision.

At what point do you know if what you're writing is a short story or a novel? Do you know when you set out, or is it revealed in the writing?

Usually when things announce themselves to me, they announce themselves roughly in their form. Although I've made huge mistakes: I thought *The Voyage of the Narwhal* was a novella initially, but within thirty pages or so, I saw that I was wrong. I didn't persist in that very long. Again, I don't know what that is. It's a feeling thing, not a thinking thing. Some things *feel* like novels or novellas or stories. I've had stories get a good deal longer than I thought they'd be. I've thought I had a normal-size story on my hands and had it turn into fifty or sixty pages. But usually they arrive in their approximate shape.

Your most recent three books are concerned with the quest for scientific discovery during the nineteenth century and the complications, both difficulties and joys, that quest can bring to relationships. What draws you to this theme and this period?

It was such an interesting period both scientifically and in terms of exploration. It's an easy time and an easy place to make metaphoric sense from. If you're drawn to the shape of the journey anyways, and I am—the journey through our lives, the journeys we all make all the time—then that particular time and place is very rich in interesting examples. People made astonishing physical journeys for such complex reasons, some of which we now deplore, some of which we now admire.

How do your story ideas come to you?

All different ways. Sometimes I wake up in the middle of the night with an idea, but that doesn't happen often. Often they come to me through my reading. I see some little picture or some phrase that captures my fancy. I've been working with some of the same characters now through the last three books—you've probably noticed, in *Servants of the Map,* that there are things that hark back to previous books. Often these days, as I'm working on one story or novella or novel, I'll get a glimmer of somebody else in this gigantic family and what might have happened to them in some other time. Actually all the people are related, but you can't see it yet.

It's thrilling when they come back. I loved seeing Ned and Max again in "The Cure." It adds a new dimension to the work.

Most of the people in *Servants in the Map* and some of the people in *The Voyage of the Narwhal* are actually related, sometimes in complicated and distant ways, to the Marburg sisters in *Ship Fever.* They are various ancestors of theirs. The book I'm trying to start now will show more clearly how everyone fits together. I have a big chart in my office that's quite insane looking, all these wings and people through all these centuries over all these countries. But I don't think it's actually important to the stories. They stand alone, as do the novels, so it's not that it's some endless saga or set of sequels. More that this has been important for me as an idea-generating device. It's very fertile for me. When I'm writing something about Max, I can wake up one morning and think, "But what about Clara?" Then I'll be writing about Clara and her daughters, and I'll wake up another morning and think, "What was Gillian doing when she was eighteen?" And on it goes. And that's nice. I don't seem to run out of material.

Throughout *Servants of the Map*, *The Voyage of the Narwhal*, and *Ship Fever*, several characters recur, and their stories unfold in new and intriguing ways. For instance, Nora, Ned, and Denis Kynd first appear in the story "Ship Fever," then Ned is the cook in *The Voyage of the Narwhal*, and Ned and Nora are reunited in "The Cure" in *Servants of the Map*. What draws you to revisit your characters and continue to explore their lives?

They're alive for me. I spend so much time with them that when a book is done or a story is done, the characters don't disappear from my brain. I made them, and I live with them for a long time, and then I send the story or the book off, but they're still there. They seem, in some senses, to continue to live their lives without me. Sometimes, years later, it's as if I can go back to the barn in Pennsylvania where they have all been living and open the door and catch up with them. I don't know what that's about either. I seem unable to dismiss them. It does feel like death to me. Not to revisit them feels like killing them off. To lose those people from your life when you've had such an imaginative connection with them is too difficult. This way, I refuse to let them die unless I kill them off on the page.

The appearance of these characters throughout successive works, their individual growth and development as characters, gives them the sense of having a life beyond the pages of any particular story or narrative. It gives them a sense of individual existence that engages readers more deeply in their unfolding stories. How much of this is intentional?

It wasn't intentional at first. It surprised me and I went with it, and for a while I did it more or less unconsciously. But since the publication of *Servants of the Map*, which came out in February 2002, a lot of people have asked me about this. Inevitably, I've had to think about it consciously, to try to understand what that linkage does and what I'm doing. That's been interesting for me as a writer. It wasn't a planned thing, but I've been brought to consciousness about it, so I'm much more aware of it in what I'm writing now. I've had to admit to myself what I'm doing. That's often true for us as writers, not just with regard to this question, but with regard to all sorts of things we do, the characters we make, the themes we revisit. At some point in reviews or conversations someone will point out to us what we're doing. Often we're not conscious of it, and then we're forced to become conscious of it and to integrate that more deeply. That's interesting. I learned a lot this spring as people pressed at that point and made me think about it.

The story "The Behavior of the Hawkweeds" in *Ship Fever* interweaves the historic story about Gregor Mendel and his scientific quest with a contemporary love story. How did this interplay occur for you?
I initially wanted to write just about Mendel and the behavior of the hawkweeds, which is a true story. To hark back to one of our earlier questions, insofar as I was able, I tried to tell this story factually. But at that stage in my writing life, I wasn't able to tell it only about him. I didn't know how to manage the material. That was the first story where I used historical material to that extent, and the contemporary strand was like having water wings on when somebody throws you into the pool. I could tell the historical parts about Mendel and I could try to bring him and his life to the page, but I didn't have to commit myself fully because it was framed by the contemporary story, through Antonia's voice. There's a sense in which, as a writer, I can hide behind a first-person voice. If she makes a mistake in telling the story of Mendel, *she* did it. So, there's a level of security there—at least there was for me. I learned a lot writing that story. It was after that, where I had the blending of the contemporary and the historical and felt a little more secure, that I was able to write "The English Pupil," which is my first wholly historical story. I felt able to forgo the contemporary frame and the first-person, contemporary narrator.

What drew you to writing about the events of Grosse Isle and the Irish immigrants who suffered from fever?
That was one of those strange, wonderful serendipities. Two things converged. One is that I'm a great admirer of the Irish writer William Trevor. He has a beautiful story called "The News from Ireland," a long story, about forty pages, with multiple characters and multiple points of view, about the famine as the people on a Protestant estate in Ireland experienced it. It's a story I teach often. I was teaching at Warren Wilson and I had a student who wanted to write her critical essay on that story. As her supervisor, I asked her to read some material about the Irish famine so that she'd have a better understanding of both how well, and how extremely economically, Trevor had managed to work the historical

facts into that story. Then I had to read the same books because I didn't
know the facts either. This is what I mean about learning a lot when I'm
teaching. I assigned her a couple of books and then I read the same
books, which were largely about the Irish famine in Ireland. One had a
brief chapter about what happened at Grosse Isle, though, and it hit me
like a hammer between the eyes. I knew I had to write about it.

**It's interesting that you weave actual historical figures into the cast of
"Ship Fever" and other stories. What does a narrative gain from this?**
    A certain verisimilitude, I suppose. There were doctors and politicians
who were very important during the Grosse Isle epidemic, and any person invented or real might have brushed by or known of those people at
the time. It seems helpful to include those persons in the frame, not so
much in the center in the direct action, but to put them around the edges
so that the whole fiction will feel more real to the reader.

**Several of your female characters struggle to fulfill their intellect and tal-
ent while continually being held back by the societal constraints of the
time. In "Rare Bird" from *Ship Fever,* Sarah Anne Billopp conceals her
identity in her letters to Linnaeus. Alexandra in *The Voyage of the Narwhal* creates engravings and doesn't take credit. She wonders, "Why can't
my life be larger?" In "The Cure," Nora seeks to further her medical education by studying with a doctor, but doesn't have the option of becoming
a doctor herself. What draws you to the stories of these women?**
    When I think about the obvious things we all take for granted, as fem-
inists, the things that are open to us now, then I become interested, inevitably, in times when nothing could be taken for granted. I try to imagine
what it would feel like if I was the person I am now, or my friend was the
person she is now, and we lived a hundred or two hundred years ago with
these same interests and capabilities but were confined in this way or that
way. How would you make space, or find freedom for yourself? How
would you live? It's an interesting problem.

**How did you get interested in the disappearance of British explorer Sir
John Franklin and all of his crew on their voyage to discover the North-
west Passage [in *The Voyage of the Narwhal*]?**
    I was a little girl when I first got interested in the Arctic. I don't know
what it was that caught me then, but I gobbled up all these Arctic history
books. I was really mad for this. I loved it. Then it all sank away in the
emergency of puberty. When you're a teenager you're just thinking about
being a teenager. The material surfaced again when I was writing *Ship
Fever.* When I was doing the reading for the novella, I learned about one

ship that came from Ireland with a load of immigrants and hit an iceberg off the coast of Newfoundland. Everybody drowned. I wasn't able to use that terrible story in the novella, but it made me think about the coincidence in time between the immigrations from Ireland and the height of exploration in the Arctic, going on at exactly the same time. I thought I'd write a companion novella about someone exploring in the Arctic, but I turned out to be wrong about the size of it.

How were you able to create the setting of the Arctic region with such clarity and specificity? How were you able to conjure this place in your mind and in your senses?

Most of it was from reading. In those Arctic expeditions, everyone was keeping diaries: the ship's doctor, the ship's naturalist, sometimes several of the officers, almost always the captain, sometimes the crew. So there's a lot of material available from a lot of expeditions, and a lot of specificity in those materials, and also in the letters—descriptions of the weather, of the cold. Those were a huge help. I was actually able to go to the Arctic and see it for myself when I got a Guggenheim Fellowship between the second-to-last and last drafts. I went up to the north coast of Baffin Island for a couple of weeks and looked at the sky and the plants. It did help. The book was the better for that.

In many of your stories, and in *The Voyage of the Narwhal,* you use letters and journal entries to reveal the inner lives of your characters, and the journals become the real treasure and consolation of the expedition for Erasmus, especially Dr. Boerhaave's journal. Why did you decide to use journal entries to expose the characters' inner lives? What does the narrative gain from this?

Two things, I think. One is that these forms are utterly characteristic of the time. People kept diaries and journals so often among the upper, educated classes, the traveling classes, that the use of them seemed true to the time. I wanted to make a novel that had somewhat of the same shape and intent as a characteristically nineteenth-century novel, even though it was also a kind of critique of nineteenth-century novels, so I employed some of the forms that people employed then. Not only were diaries and journals common, but novels often employed diary and journal entries. Additionally, I like the texture of first-person diary or letter or journal entries juxtaposed to a third-person narrative. It breaks up the narrative and makes for a more interesting texture. It gives some contrast. So it's partly an aesthetic decision as well.

These journal entries also provide information that creates tension in the

narrative—information that we could not have if the point of view was limited to the men on the *Narwhal*. For instance, Alexandra reveals the fact that Kane has come back with relics. . . . This information casts a new light on the *Narwhal's* situation, and increases the tension. Were you aware of getting so much mileage out of the journal entries as you were writing?

Not initially as I was writing, but I was aware as I was revising that it was helping to do those things. I was consciously revising in those directions to let those entries carry some weight. Sometimes I could make a compact journal entry carry the weight of what would've been a lot of exposition in the main part of the narrative.

How did you decide to include the women back at home?

There didn't seem to be any way to write without them. Or, there was a way, but I didn't want to write that book. To not include the women at home would've been to write the nineteenth-century version of it: the boys go out on the boat, the boys find stuff, the boys come home, the boys are heroes. I couldn't see the point in replicating that story. The point seemed to be to re-create that story with the counterstory juxtaposed to it to show not just the face of the coin but the obverse of the coin at the same time. They're connected.

You often write about the inner conflicts and urges that drive people to search for things not known before and, equally important, to capture what they find. Zeke is a great example of this, and Erasmus, in a different way, but even Max in "Servants of the Map," and other characters. What draws you to this obsession?

I don't know that I have an easy answer for that, almost surely because it is connected to something deep in me. I don't have full self-knowledge any more than anyone else does, and that's why I can't answer that easily. Partly, the material just interests me. It's always dramatic when someone's searching for something unknown. There are always dramatic and metaphoric possibilities when someone is on such a search, so naturally a novelist is going to be drawn to those things. But it's also related to something in me.

Many of the frustrations and challenges your characters face remind me of artistic frustrations.

I think that's part of the link. Artistic discovery, the journey each of us makes as an artist, is nowhere near as dramatic or interesting or heroic, but it is a journey, and it can be a hardship and a trial. One is tested in certain ways. There are parallels, even if they're goofy parallels. We're sitting in a comfortable chair in a warm room and nobody's making us do this. So why do I think those things are analogous? Yet, clearly something about them *feels* analogous.

In "Servants of the Map," Max discovers his passion for botany and hopes he can make some contribution that will matter, that will save him from the futility of map making. "All he will leave behind are maps, which will be merged with all the other maps, on which he will be nameless: small contributions to the great Atlas of India, which has been growing for almost forty years." What draws you to his desperation to find something worthwhile to do that will distinguish him?

Because I feel desperate, too. We all feel that. Everyone is struggling to find something that makes meaning, that makes sense out of our lives. It's not easy for anyone.

When you started writing "The Cure," did you know in advance that you were continuing the story of Ned and Nora? Did you know that Max from "Servants of the Map" would show up as well?

I did know those things. The big surprise of that one was the form. The initial drafts are linear: I just plod ahead from Nora's youth through the time she meets Elizabeth and through their friendship. It was interminable and really boring.

How did you find the new structure?

Exasperation in part, largely because I couldn't write the middle. I knew where Elizabeth was at the end, and that Max would have to come back, and I knew that Nora and Ned had to have found each other, but while I could write with some ease about Nora in Detroit and also about Ned and Elizabeth later, the middle was endless exposition. At some point, I realized that I didn't need it. If you think of the story as a stick and you imagine snapping it in the middle and turning the second half backwards on the first half, that's what it felt like. I took what used to be the far tip of it and bumped it up against the original tip, then was able to excise the middle. That was a happy discovery.

What are you working on now?

I'm just starting a novel after a long time of initial research. It's a new period for me, set in 1916 and 1917 just before the U.S. enters World War I. It takes place in Saranac Lake, which is where "The Cure" is set, and it's about Leo Marburg, the grandfather of the Marburg sisters, who's in a sanatorium there. I've never written about the early twentieth century, and I know the period very poorly. It's taken me almost two years to move myself out of things Victorian and up a handful of decades.

What would you say to new writers working on their first stories or novel?

Try to be patient. It's so hard for people to be patient. It was really hard for me. It took me a very long time to get better, and a very, very long time to begin to publish. I wasn't very patient. It's painful. I think people now have even more motivation to be impatient than I did when I was starting out, because the culture is more impatient. Everything moves so fast. First novelists are pushed so hard to produce a second novel, and young people are pushed so hard right out of school to get the first novel done. It takes time to write well. You have to sit with it. You have to be patient with it. You have to trust in your intuition and in your own material and stay with it for as long as it takes. Writing isn't rocket science. A person can learn this if a person is dogged enough and spends enough time. If you throw yourself at it wholeheartedly and humbly and you read and work and read and work and try and try to get better and stay open to learning and growing, you will get better. People get better. There's so much that I can't do that I'm still learning to do.

It's a wonderful thing to think that you can get established in your career and still have room to grow and new things to get excited about.

There is a sense in which you can't get good at this in general, even though you can get good at the specific book or story you're working on. If you sit with it long enough, you will find a way through that has some integrity and that might be good, but when you start the next thing you're a beginner all over again. You may have a larger tool kit and a few more skills, but the project has its own new problems; it demands new thinking, and it's hard all over again. It's good that it's hard all over again. That's what keeps us challenged and interested.

Conducted: September 2002

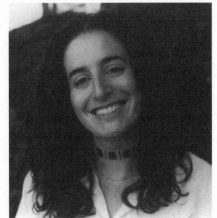

Photo: © Teal Minton

AIMEE BENDER

Somewhere along the Line,
I Ate Fairy Tales

Aimee Bender is the author of the story collection *The Girl in the Flammable Skirt* and the novel *An Invisible Sign of My Own*. Her stories have appeared in *Granta, GQ, Harper's,* the *Antioch Review,* and several other publications. She lives in Los Angeles.

How did you get started writing? What was your earliest recollection of wanting to write?

My earliest recollection harks back to second grade, when writing stories was part of the regular day. My teacher was a Ms. Jean Lamb, an extremely gentle encouraging woman who addressed the class as "my friends." It was my first sense of identity in elementary school, as a writer of stories, a feeling which I lost for years and years, and only recently remembered.

Who are some of the writers who influenced you in the early stages of your work, and who are influences for you now?

Earlier on (and still): fairy tales, Oz books, Roald Dahl all completely caught my imagination, and then writers like Anne Sexton, Eugène Ionesco, Flannery O'Connor took those imaginative leaps one giant step further, bringing weirdnesses into the worries of the adult world. These days: Haruki Murakami, Lynda Barry, Donald Barthelme, Italo Calvino, Steven Millhauser, Angela Carter, Richard Brautigan, Gertrude Stein—the Permission People! All are such big givers of permission, and are so incredible with language and deeply playful while still being very heartfelt and emotionally full. Murakami is endlessly interesting to me in terms of intuitive structure, and Lynda Barry's got such an amazing sense of voice, and Donald Barthelme's freedom and funniness and joy, and Gertrude Stein's no-nonsense feeling about nonsensical stuff, and Angela Carter's velvet sentences. . . .

You've been referred to as a magic realist. Do you agree with this, and how would you define magic realism?

I'm always honored by that reference, because I like the category so much. I even like how the words sound. Magic Realism. The way I understand it is as that combination of everyday mundane-world details alongside something magical, otherworldy, bizarre. The golden key inside a sack of barley. Also, there's often this sweeping sense of scope in magical realism that I don't know how to find as much in my work, though I want to push for that more, a feeling of a whole shimmering history beyond the pages.

Because your work is difficult to categorize or seen as edgy, I'm wondering what your early experiences were like when you were trying to get published.

It took a while for me to find a voice, and so early stuff I sent out was more copycatted stuff, but a poor copycat. When I started writing more magical or playful stories, it became clearer which places I should send to again and which places weren't at all interested. Those little notes on the margins were often really encouraging—even a penciled in "Sorry" felt like a small triumph. But also, I often got the comment "It doesn't add up," which frustrated me then and now is probably the wood that makes the foundation of one of my soapboxes regarding fiction. I just don't think it's a comment that feels toothy enough, and I definitely don't think a story needs to add up. What does that even mean?

What are you reading these days?

Right now, I'm rereading *The Bloody Chamber* by Angela Carter for my fairy tale class, parts of *Not Knowing* by Donald Barthelme, *Them, Adventures with Extremists,* and I just restarted *Huck Finn,* which I read when I was a kid and didn't understand at all. Oh, and book one of Lemony Snicket's series! Great fun that is.

How does your reading life inform your writing life?

Inevitably for a few days after I finish a book, I imitate the writer fairly consciously—I just loved *The God of Small Things,* and afterward I tried to make up shortcut phrases like she did, sort of rich playful phrasings, painful bonbons, but wow, that really did *not* fit with the stuff I've been writing, and it wasn't a very good copy anyway, and it didn't make sense either.

I've been thinking a lot about the idea of learning lately, and this question reminds me of that. How do people learn? When? Reading is clearly one of the best ways because so much of it happens in this secret underground way. The lesson becomes a part of the person, and they don't even know it's happening.

Does your teaching inform your writing life at all?

Yes—teaching forces me to state and restate what interests me about writing. And although the craft aspect is certainly a valuable part of a writing workshop, what engages me most is trying to keep the class open to a wide variety of fiction. Challenging the notion of a "story." I get frustrated by conservative viewpoints on plot or character! There are so many amazing possibilities! So all that helps me when I sit down with my own stuff, because of course I get conservative on myself and have to fight that all the time.

How do your story ideas come to you?

Mostly they happen during writing itself. It's rare that I'll think of an idea in my mind during the day and use it. Those ideas usually fall apart as soon as I put them on a page. Just today I had an idea for a story on a walk and now it's gone. Poof. Even if I write it down, it's hard for me to capture the feeling on the computer. But during my writing time, a sentence will pop out sometimes and interest me. I was writing a bad poem once that had one good line, about a girl who doesn't eat apples, and I found a short short in that; also there's a story in *Flammable Skirt* about a man who came home from the war without lips, and that came from a poem I was writing too. I'm a lousy poet, but I think the fragments are sometimes helpful as kernels.

What is your writing process like when you're working on stories? Do you work on more than one at a time?

I like to work on as many at the same time as possible. It seems like I do my best work when I have no idea that I'm working. Salon.com did an interview recently with Norton Juster, who wrote *The Phantom Tollbooth,* and he said that he feels some of the best work happens when you're playing hooky from what feels like the "real work." I thought that was so helpful—whenever I start to take myself too seriously, I can't seem to pound out what I want anymore. It's a constant act of humbling and rehumbling.

How many revisions will you do for a story, and what goes on in each revision?

In this here computer age we're in, it's so hard to tell. I'm revising constantly. Rereading constantly. I rarely will print out a hard copy until I've been through the story or chapter multiple times. The writer Carolyn See said once that she knows a story's done, or revision is done, when she can read it through without wincing. I thought that made a lot of sense. It's all about mediating the wince.

What do you look for in a story's beginning?

In my own or other beginnings? I suppose in a beginning I just want to be interested enough to read on to the next sentence, but what will bring me there is unpredictable. Some kind of tug or movement. Likewise, in my own beginnings that seem to work for me, I just want to find out what happens next.

And in an ending?

Endings are crucial, because once something has ended, the whole piece reshuffles. It becomes itself, or it makes the piece finite so it can then become deep. It's like the death of the piece and then the full life of it can begin. It can no longer be immortal. Uh-oh. I'm listening to Tori Amos as I write this, and I'm getting a little lofty. What I mean is just that an ending is the whole. And so I look for—something. Something has to be there. And mainly, I hope I don't know or can't predict what that something in the ending will be.

How is your process for writing and revision different when you're working on a novel?

I throw out tons. Hundreds of pages. I get impatient and have to remind myself that the middle is a long long haul. It just takes a while to figure out that what I'm writing has the wherewithal to last the length of a novel. Sometimes I'll catch a short story trying to masquerade itself inside the novel, wearing masks and scarves, and it tricks me for a while, but then on page 21 I have nowhere else to go. It's done. Unmasked.

Did you find the transition to writing a novel difficult? Was it harder to sustain a consistent voice through such a longer piece?

It was really hard. It still is hard. I thought, Now that I've done one, I can do two no problem! But of course each creature is its own evolutionary conundrum, and I don't know anything all over again. It's hard to sustain a voice, but more than that, it's just hard to trust the structure. I can tap into the voice on/off, and that's fine, I have patience for that, but sometimes the movement is absolutely static, and all I have to do is wait it out. For months at a time. One of the things I admire most about Murakami's writing is that he tells you the static times. He has the character experience the waiting along with himself and the reader. It's deeply relieving in some way.

Do you feel more comfortable with one form over the other?

I guess I do feel more at home with a story. It matches my style of talking more—to go the quicker route. But the novel is addictive. All that space! All that vast unknown!

How did *An Invisible Sign of My Own* first come to you?

I had Mona, and she was in a small town, and she was planning on leaving it. I like small towns. I grew up in Los Angeles. But the book was too sprawling, too unfocused, until I made her stay put in the town for the most part. It helped a lot to contain the space.

What drew you to the idea of Mona being obsessed with math and numbers?

I wrote the scene in the book where she sees all these numbers on lawns and they seem to indicate impending doom. The scene didn't fit with anything else I'd written, which, at that point, had been a lot about lemon trees and driving and a man who cuts his fingers into flowers. I was sure I'd have to cut the number scene, but I ended up cutting most of the earlier stuff. I liked writing about numbers. My wise friend Phil said, "Write what you're interested in every day," and when I did that, I seemed to be repeatedly interested in numbers.

How did you decide to open the novel with a fairy tale?

I was writing lots of little stories on the side, but I felt like I was cheating on my novel by writing stories. So I pretended they were all part of the novel. Sure, the swan story fits, and the cat story, why not? But of course those really were short stories, and once I just got less freaky about it, it was fine. The only one that fit was the king/executioner story. I wrote it and it immediately felt central, felt like Mona's story.

I also like how you end the novel with the same fairy tale, this time told in Mona's interpretation with an alternate ending where the people of the town, rather than lopping off parts of themselves, leave the town and swap their gift of eternal life for the gift of a life lived as a whole person—not unlike Mona, who decides to stop quitting things and stifling herself in exchange for the risk of living and all that living entails. How did you come to this as an ending?

I had those two together for a while, so I'd read them side by side, and I liked the way they switched. It meant something to me, that movement. I knew the second one would be last, but it took a while to realize the first could start the book; it seemed so grim and grotesque that at first I thought no way, which then seemed like the best indicator to do it.

What draws you to the fairy tale method of storytelling?

Everything. The imagination, the brevity, the violence, the sexuality, the humor, the great weird simple laden images like glass coffins, the melting feeling of being told a story. All of it.

What are some of your favorite fairy tales? Why?

I can't really think of any I don't like. I just reread "The Juniper Tree," which is a Grimm one, for this class I'm teaching, and it's the darkest of the dark—it involves a stepmom chopping the head off her kid and cooking him up in a stew for the dad, who eats it thinking his son is away on a trip. Whew! I love retellings, or other versions; the "Donkeyskin" version of Cinderella is wonderful, where she has gowns the color of the sky and the moon and the sun. Beautiful.

I've heard you say that fairy tales present plot as metaphor. What do you mean by that?

Mainly that a fairy tale character has no internal world, so the entire plot is a reflection of their internal life. Or at least it can be interpreted that way, to good effect. So suddenly the plot becomes wildly meaningful. Instead of the truth of regular life, where I don't believe in signs and symbols in the same way, in fairy tales everything is a sign for something, and the world is this strange blinking ordered universe of actions.

How else do fairy tales inform your writing?

I feel like somewhere along the line I ate fairy tales. I ingested and digested them, and now they're part of my whole person. The way they move plot, the settings, the imagery. I can't even tell very well how they inform my writing, because they're so connected to my original joy as a reader.

Many of your characters have some sort of physical deformity. What draws you to this?

In the story world, they're often showing physically an internal world that's hidden. It's different in the world of a mythic story, because in real life, if someone is deformed, it's generally not because of their internal world, unless they self-mutilate or something. But in a fairy tale, it can be. And you can show so much on the surface versus having to tell in detail what's happening inside the characters.

Do you think there is redemption in someone seeing the beauty in another's oddities or scars, like Mona thinking the science teacher's scars are beautiful?

Sure. I think we're all deformed in some way or other. Finding beauty in that seems like a good thing to me.

The father in the novel is slowly dying of a disease that he doesn't really have, and a father in *The Girl in the Flammable Skirt* develops a hole in his gut. Why is this a recurring theme—the fragility of the father?

If a father can be viewed as a stronghold of sorts in a family, then that fragility feels important to me—showing an inherent fragility in families, and in strong figures. Showing the flip side.

How did you decide to divide the stories in *The Girl in the Flammable Skirt* into three parts, and what were the unifying principles?

Actually that was my editor's idea, but it seemed a nice way to split it up to me too. I suggested "loss/rage/magic" to title the three parts, but they didn't really fit, and I'm glad we left them untitled.

In "Fugue" you interweave the stories of several different characters, and number and in some cases title each section. How did you develop this structure, or did it emerge as you wrote it?

I was feeling fragmented, and I was in a definite writing slump. Felt like I had nothing to work on. So it helped to have something in smaller pieces, and then it evolved on its own. It's so weird, but wonderful, when a piece feels like a terrible mess and then one day, even through the betterment of one sentence, it can suddenly feel like it has some unity. I think those are the moments I wait for, through all the mucky other days when it's murky and unclear.

Your stories deal with oddities and deformities—such as a man who returns from the war with no lips, a woman whose boyfriend is experiencing reverse evolution—yet you maintain enough of a sense of realism so that readers are drawn into these weird but emotionally moving worlds. How do you balance the more fantastic qualities of a story with the more realistic?

With all fantastical stuff, it's just keeping the rules of the universe believable. If one thing has changed, then everything relating to that'll change, but the rest is the same, needs to be the same.

Many of the stories explore how characters use sex as a way to avoid loss, deal with grief, boredom, or anger, express rage, or just plain escape. For instance, in "Quiet Please" a librarian sleeps with one library patron after the other to avoid dealing with the loss of her father. What interests you in exploring the many dynamics of sexual relationships, and what do you think it shows about character?

I think sex is a great way to write about character, because it tells a whole lot in a short time; it can be a distilled sense of a person in a way. What they are embracing, what they're avoiding. And I guess sex and loss have some weird connection in my mind, because they're sort of opposites and also not. It's hard to quantify, but there's something about intense closeness that both flies in the face of death while being acutely aware of it at the same time.

Your stories demonstrate in incredible attention to idiosyncratic physical detail that works to remind the reader of the mundane or ordinary in the midst of usually extraordinary circumstances or events. In "Call My Name," for example, a young woman follows a stranger home from the subway because she liked the way he looked at her: "He leans against the refrigerator and a magnet drops to the floor. 'You want to be tied up?' he says then. 'I'll tie you up.'" Why this juxtaposition?

Thanks. I don't know why, to tell you the truth. I just know that the magnet dropped.

Do these wonderful details come to you in early drafts, or are they something you work towards throughout revision?
Thanks. They seem to happen when I'm not thinking. Generally, as soon as I start to carve a metaphor in my head, it feels like a piece of lead on the page. But when they just occur along the way, they are much lighter, more like treats for me, while I'm writing.

The *New York Times* noted your pleasure in what they referred to as the "electric simile." For example, "a washcloth sprawled on his forehead like the limp flag of a defeated country." Again, I'm wondering if these just pop out as you write, or if they're cultivated through drafts.
Pop out. So much is about getting myself to not think. To hedge off any awareness of myself writing.

There's that saying about how there are people who want to write and people who want to be writers. It's a great line, I think, because the role of "writer" has this allure, but as soon as I start thinking of myself self-consciously, when I get sucked into that "ooh, writer" mode, then I have nothing to say anymore. The metaphors get sour. Everything goes bad. I'm immediately calmed when I remember it's not so lofty. That being a writer essentially means sitting down for some amount of time and hanging out with some words. And it takes all types.

What is the role of autobiography, if any, in your fiction?
Hmm. It's all autobiographical, and also none of it is. I wrote it, so it's coming from me. But the metaphors give me a lot of liberty to write about things many times removed.

Your sister, Karen Bender, is also a writer. That's interesting. Were you storytellers as children?
Karen was a great creative force to be around as a kid. I was inspired by her all the time. But I don't think of either of us as classic storytellers— or I'm not sure what that would mean. She did tell good stories. I felt pretty quiet a lot of the time. But we both wrote as kids—we were both writing independently of each other.

Do you read each other's work and offer critique?
Generally we wait until it's done, and then we'll read each other's work, once it's in the world. This is a freeing thing, I think.

feel and talk. I think I could've done that in another profession as well, but it helps to have that experience and training. I have a very good memory, which helps also. I was really trained as an old-fashioned social worker. I used to have to do what was called process recording, which was to write the entire verbal and nonverbal parts of an interview from beginning to end without a tape recorder. And I had to turn in dozens of those on a weekly basis. So that was good practice. Probably just being exposed to peoples' lives in that intimate way gives you the opportunity to see things that it might be difficult to see otherwise. Not that you couldn't see them if you were willing, but it's easier when you're invited into people's lives. So I'm grateful to those parts.

What role does empathy play in your writing? How does empathy work differently in writing than in your role as a therapist?
Writing and therapy have nothing in common. Writing is a narcissistic event. There's an act of emotional projection or transport in which you try to enter somebody else's soul, or make somebody up and breathe life into their soul, so that you can write the story you want to write. The act of empathy is critical to creating real and believable characters. But it's all in service of the art. Empathy for real-life people is quite different than empathy for people you've made up on the page. Writing is all about the writer and the writer's imagination. Therapy is not. I do think that if you cannot feel yourself to be in somebody else's shoes—which, by the way, I don't think therapy calls for at all, but writing does—if you can't feel yourself in somebody else's shoes as a writer, you can't write the character. You're writing from the outside.

Where do you get your story ideas?
I spend a lot of time looking out the window, walking around the house, watching daytime television, talking to my friends, going to the grocery store. There's probably material anywhere you look. Everybody's lives are full and mysterious and unexpected. It's just a question of whether or not you're paying attention, whether or not you want to stand around long enough to let them tell it to you, or imagine it.

We can see the beginnings of *Love Invents Us* in the character Susan in "Light Breaks Where No Sun Shines" and in Max in "Semper Fideles." What made you want to explore these situations in the larger context of a novel?
I don't think that that's what I was really conscious of doing. In the original form of the novel, that scene with the furrier, Mr. Klein, doesn't exist. When I finished the novel, I thought that there was a piece of

Elizabeth's history missing. Then it became clear to me that what was missing was that story about the furrier. I put it in the middle of the book, but that didn't work, so I put it at the beginning of the book. I didn't realize until after it got reviewed that it would look as if I had wished for the story to be the springboard to the novel. That's not how it was. When I wrote the novel, it began with Elizabeth and Mrs. Hill. There was no furrier. The use of Max's name is entirely an unconscious repetition. I was clearly not finished with that story. No matter how careful you are, you cannot control what you reveal.

When you originally wrote "Light Breaks Where No Sun Shines" and "Semper Fideles" in *Come to Me,* you had no idea that they would lead to something larger?

No, or not something longer anyhow. I always feel that there should be some small group of men and women carrying pom-poms on behalf of the short story. I don't actually see them as *smaller* than novels. I just see them as *shorter*. It's not the difference between Mount Everest and a large hill. It's like scaling Everest faster. So I want to say, "They're not smaller, they're just shorter." Obviously the short story is a form that I particularly like.

In *Come to Me,* you have a section called "Three Stories" that deals with the lives of David, Galen, Violet, and Rose from three different perspectives. "Hyacinths" is told from David's point of view, "The Sight of You" from Galen's point of view, and "Silver Water" from Violet's point of view. Each story is told during a different time in the family's life and serves to paint a portrait. What interests you about going into each different character's point of view, and what does the overall narrative gain from this?

One of the great pleasures of writing for me is to be God, to look at everybody as they stand there cupped in your hand. You actually can understand and be this person, and this person, and this person. And life is entirely different depending on who is seeing it. Even if you are empathetic, even if you are kind and observant, it is still unexpectedly different. I have a friend who has twins and one older single child. One of the things I love about this family is that what it's like for the two twins is a completely different family than what it's like for the older single child, and that's completely different than what it's like for the mother, who's on one hand the mother of a single child, with whom she forms a pair, and on the other hand the mother of twins who have already formed a pair. I love the fact that you can hold up anybody's family to the light and turn it around and see it differently.

Each story, though intertwined, stands on its own. Was this difficult to achieve?

No. To me it's exactly like family life. Of course you're interconnected, but you don't walk around with the other four people attached at the hip at all times. It's exactly like that.

You do this again with Henry and Marie in the stories "Faultlines" and "Only You," so that readers are drawn deeper into the lives of these characters who were introduced through their dealings with Galen and David. How do these stories come about? Do you meet the characters and then want to explore their lives more deeply?

Yes, I think so. The last story in that entire bunch of five stories was "Hyacinths," which is David's story. That's because I thought I would like to try to tell David's story, which wasn't clear to me until I had done everything else. I thought, What about David? He's not just a nice guy and a psychiatrist. I mean, how do you get to be a psychiatrist who's married to a lunatic? Not to mention, what's it like to be a psychiatrist with a schizophrenic daughter?

What order did you write those stories in? Do you remember?

The first story I ever wrote was "The Sight of You," which was the first story about Galen and Henry. The second story I ever wrote was "Silver Water," and then I wrote "Faultlines," which was the dinner party with all those people from everybody's point of view. No, sorry, here's the order: "The Sight of You," "Love Is Not a Pie," "Silver Water," and then I wrote some of the other stories, but then after I started learning a little more about how many points of view I could fold in, I wrote "Faultlines," and then I wrote the story about Marie and Alvin, and then I wrote "Hyacinths," which is David's story.

If those were the first stories you wrote, how did you develop your own way of writing a short story?

Ignorance is a wonderful thing. I read a lot of short stories. I didn't know any other writers. I didn't talk to any other writers. I didn't read any books on how to write a story. I guess the stories were taking shape inside of me, and I do read quite a bit. The voice was there. I don't understand it any better now than I did ten years ago. I'm grateful, but I have no idea. I don't like to write long. Even if I write a novel, I don't like to write long. Something about the arc of the short story always appealed to me, the swiftness. In any good short story, there's no slack. Almost every novel I read, especially every modern novel I read, could use a good edit.

By a short-story writer?

Or a poet, or just a good editor who happened to still be working for a publishing house who wasn't required to stop line editing in order to acquire and market. It's just striking to me. People could drop sixty pages without blinking, often a hundred pages without blinking. In a good short story you can't drop a sentence. I love that there's no room for error, no room for digression.

What's your process of revision like for a story?

I do twenty or thirty drafts. I'm a big reviser. I go back, and like a lot of people, it's easiest to polish the beginning; then I force myself to go through page by page from beginning to end, over and over again. You don't want something where the first three pages glitter and then it just falls off.

Do you find that when you write your early drafts, the beginning you start with is what ends up on the page? For instance, in "Silver Water" we see Rose singing, so that we're introduced to her gift before we're introduced to her illness. Is that how you originally began, or did the beginning grow out of the story once it was written?

"Silver Water" had been in my head for about a year. Each scene was pretty clear to me. Some of the middle was muddled, as it often is, but I knew that it would begin with her singing, and end with her killing herself.

Do you typically get the beginning and ending like that?

Well, more than I get the beginning, ending, *and* middle. Sometimes you just get the beginning, and sometimes you just get the ending, and sometimes you get two lines of dialogue that you carry around for a year wondering, Who's going to say that?

I've heard you say that you're interested as much in what people don't say as in what they say. You even have part of a story, "Faultlines," in which the dialogue contains what the character *didn't* say, or *should've* said. What interests you about this dynamic? Why is it important to show?

It's because I'm interested in people. I don't know anything more interesting than the difference between what people say and what they feel. There's a whole universe there below the surface. I'm always interested in the way that feelings underneath leak out and shape behavior. People try very hard to have them not show up or change anything or affect anything. But our defenses leak. That's how we know they're there. I love that.

You often use humor to diffuse an emotionally intense situation, and at the same time to create pathos, or a sense of the real sadness underlying the attempt at humor and the need for humor in a given situation. For instance, in "Silver Water," the scenes with the therapists, especially Big Nut, are funny in spite of the gravity of the situation. Are you aware of this as you work, or does it just come out at certain times? How does humor work in your fiction?

I don't see that much as diffusing the sadness of the situation. There is humor in grief. Funny things happen in hospitals. That's just how it is. I don't think that life is composed of sad moments, which are sad, in which bad things have happened to good people, and happy moments, in which good things have happened to good people. So for me, there being humor in the midst of difficulty and pain is not an attempt to either lighten the pain, or change the focus, or make a comment on it. It's the way it is. To me it's no different than the idea that there are both flowers and weeds in the garden. I don't feel like if I see weeds in the garden, I think, That's an interesting comment on the flowers. I think, That'd be because it's a garden.

How do you come up with the titles for your stories?

I read a lot of poetry, so periodically I steal from poets. I do give them credit. There are a lot of Dylan Thomas titles in that first collection. For instance, "Light Breaks Where No Sun Shines" is from a Dylan Thomas poem. In the latest collection, the title "Stars at Elbow and Foot" is from the Dylan Thomas poem "And Death Shall Have No Dominion." Sometimes they come from my imagination, or sometimes from things I've heard people say, like "A Blind Man Can See How Much I Love You." Mostly I like the titles. Usually I don't have to struggle a lot, though sometimes I do.

How did you decide to use hymns for the chapter titles in Love Invents Us?

I listen to a lot of gospel music, so that was just a labor of love. It meant another hour of Mahalia Jackson, and another hour of The Soul-stirrers. I do that all day for no reason at all.

Do you think of yourself as more of a novelist or a short-story writer?

I think of myself as a writer. Sometimes people introduce me as a novelist, and I assume what they mean is that they don't want to give me short shrift by saying you're *just* a short-story writer. I think of myself as a writer. I'm sure I'll write more novels before I die, and I'm sure I'll write more short stories before I die. To me, it's like being introduced as Amy Bloom, mother of a daughter. That's so strange. You just say you have kids.

What inspired you to write the title story in *A Blind Man Can See How Much I Love You*?
I had done all this research for a nonfiction piece of female-to-male transsexuals. It just stayed with me, particularly because I found myself thinking about how hard it would be for me if one of my daughters said to me that God made a mistake, and that she was supposed to be a man and she wanted to have the surgery. As devoted as I am to each one of them, and as fond as I am of them, I would support them, and do what they needed to do, but it would break my heart to lose my girls. And that's what I was thinking, and started developing this character Jane, the mother who wishes to do right in her own way. And her story is completely different for her than it is for the daughter/son. For him it's a story of liberation, and for Jane it's a story of loss.

In general, do you have to do research for your stories?
I usually don't write about things that require much research. If I have someone coming over from Paris, I like to get the street right, or the neighborhood, or the café there. If I say there's a garden courtyard at The Saints-Pères, I try to make sure that it has a garden courtyard.

In the section "Lionel and Julia" of *A Blind Man Can See How Much I Love You*, you pick up the thread on the lives of two characters introduced in the story "Sleepwalking" in *Come to Me*. Again, what inspired you to continue with these characters? Why have you chosen the linked short stories over a novel?
I have two more stories coming about this family. Things start to look up for Lionel; finally, he gets a break. But I think I work in stories here because I have to live my life and the characters have to develop and things have to happen for me to see what the next stories will be. I could've done it as a novel, I suppose, but I'm very happy with it being linked short stories. I hope that five years from now, when the stories are done and I have five or six stories from the same family, I can put them in one book.

In the final story of this collection, "The Story," you tell a story, and then the narrator tells readers of scenes omitted and names changed and places invented. She says that this is what writers do.
She outs herself as an unreliable narrator.

Right. Do you think this calls into question the reliability of *any* narrator?

It's clear to me from the way that people respond to the story that it set off all sorts of things for all sorts of people in terms of writing and telling the truth, the nature of fiction, and what it is that people chose to write about.

That the truth is not necessarily that which actually took place.

The truth is almost *never* what happened, not to mention that it doesn't really matter. I'm always telling my writing students that the fact that something actually took place is of no importance at all. On some level, of course any narrator is unreliable because *they're made up*! Somebody made them say those things and wrote it down to make you feel like it was really true, which is fun.

What are some of the responses you've gotten to that story?

There was a lovely review on Amazon.com about how I undermined my own reputation for Chekhovian decency. Of course, I'm glad to hear that I have a reputation for Chekhovian decency. But people will take that story sort of literally. In the last paragraph the character is talking about what she's done. There are people who say, "That's clearly how Bloom feels about fiction," but I would say that's the *opposite* of how I feel about fiction. But there's a wish for people to believe, especially in this modern age, that your characters represent your own opinions, and represent glimpses into your life and psyche. The narrator is summing up when she says: "I have made the best and happiest ending that I can in this world, made it out of the flax and netting and leftover trim of someone else's life, I know, but made it to keep the innocent safe and the guilty punished, and I have made it as the world should be and not as I have found it." That would not be what I understand the purpose of fiction to be. But that's fine. People found it interesting. I'm glad.

You tackle extreme situations in this book, such as a mother's experience with her transgendered daughter, a man with Parkinson's who wants his lover to assist in his suicide, and incest in the case of Lionel and Julia, yet you never rely on the sensational, but delve into the darker corners of the characters' lives. What draws you to the heart of these difficult narratives, and how do you not fall into the trap of letting the sensational aspects overwhelm the story?

It might be partially because I don't find them that sensational. Aside from the transsexual thing, which I think is unusual. Maybe there are a lot of other people over forty who don't encounter death, don't encounter divorce, don't encounter illness. Who has these charmed lives? No one's marriage ends, no one dies, no one is unhappy? Who are these people? I know what you mean, though. There are writers who pick a subject and think, That'll get them. But that's never how it seems to me. It's always about the people.

What is your process like when you're writing? Do you have a set time to work each day?

No not really. I tend to get really going later in the afternoon. But I can do a lot of puttering. I'm an expert putterer. Plus I have three children, so I can interfere in their lives. I have aging parents. I have plenty to do if I don't want to write. I can keep myself busy for a couple of days without going anywhere near my computer. But basically, when I have work to do, I usually buckle down in the afternoon. Sometimes I'll get a whole day in, but it'll be towards the end of the day. I'll work an eight-hour day, but never more than a couple hours at a time at the desk. I have to walk around, check the mail, make a cup of tea. So it's an eight-hour day that unfortunately starts around four in the afternoon.

In the *Boston Globe* on July 30, 2000, Gail Caldwell said that your stories "end most resonantly when left to the stony path of ambiguity." Do you agree?

It sounds good. I don't spend a lot of time reading reviews. I read them sometimes. But for me, I think a good ending hangs in the air like a musical note. It's just done. I don't think my endings are bound to ambiguity. I do think there's an avoidance of tying things up with a bow. But it's not the same thing.

Did your experience writing a novel teach you anything about writing stories? Does writing in one form inform the other in any way?

I think I've learned lots of things from writing the novel just because it was another book to write, and I had to learn new things, things I understand better now than I did then. I think I had to write the novel so that I could go on and do the next thing. The terrible thing about being a writer is that your entire learning process is done in public. If you're lucky and you get published, everyone gets to see you learn and fail and discover things.

What are you working on now?

I'm working on a nonfiction book *[Normal]* that I've owed to Random House for a while, which I guess is on gender, sort of, but is really about cross-dressers and transsexuals and drag kings.

How did you get interested in this?

The transsexual piece started because Tina Brown [editor of *The New Yorker*] said to me, "What are you interested in? I want you to write some nonfiction." And I said to her that I was just sitting at home one day wondering where all the male transsexuals were, and she said, "Great, that's the piece." So having explored that, I found myself interested in cross-dressers as well, especially heterosexual cross-dressers because that was baffling to me. Then I learned about drag kings, too, which are really different from drag queens. There's "Elvis-Her-Selvis." Then I thought I'd call it a day on that subject and work on the next collection of stories. That's what I have in mind for the next couple of years.

I know that you recently wrote the introduction to the Modern Library release of [Jane Austen's] *Persuasion*. In approaching the task of writing this introduction, how do you know what that introduction must contain? What part biography, what part literary criticism, what part a discussion of various elements of the story?

I wish I knew. I didn't know before I wrote it, and I don't really know now. The introduction is an essay, and every writer has to feel their way in terms of which elements they wish to focus on. For me, I love the book *Persuasion*, and there were these occasional moments in her various biographies that I was struck by in terms of parallels to the book and in terms of the way that Jane Austen was perceived at the time, which was as a gently amusing and frivolous lady writer. As is the case with good fiction as well, the character led me to the plot.

Did the folks at Modern Library give you any guidelines in writing this?

No. They said, "Please write an introduction to *Persuasion*." I said, "Okay."

What did you do to prepare for writing this introduction?

I read several of Jane Austen's biographies. I'd read all of her work, more than once. I read *Persuasion* several times, and a lot of literary criticism on Austen, and on this novel in particular.

Do you do a lot of teaching?

I teach a workshop at the Provincetown Fine Arts Work Center every summer, and I teach in the spring at Yale—I teach a fiction-writing class. Occasionally I do other workshops. I'm going to Napa to teach for a week, and then I'm going to Saint Petersburg because I really want to go to Russia. I like doing some teaching, but I don't have any wish to teach full-time. I feel very lucky that I'm not a writer who has to support myself as a teacher. I'd rather support myself as a writer. Different people feel differently about it. Some people don't want to spend their time writing magazine articles, but I'd rather do that than teach for a living.

What are some of the common problems you see in the work of new writers who you are teaching?
As I said to my students at Yale the other day, there were four major problems with the stories they just turned in. One was *I'm smart, you're dumb*. The other was *I'm smart, my characters are dumb*. Another one was *I have a secret,* in which the author tries very hard not to tell the reader what's actually going on. The final one was that complex emotions can only be expressed through complex and convoluted sentences.

What would you say to a writer working on her first stories or a novel?
There's no turning back. It's good news and bad news. The good news is that if this is what you really want to do, you will do it. The bad news is that however much you may want to do this, nothing more may come of it than the writing itself, so you'd better really prize that process, because maybe other people will read it and maybe only your writing group will read it. It's very difficult for people to do. There's that great line from Red Smith: "There's nothing to writing. You just sit at the typewriter until drops of blood fall." There's nothing to it but to do it. If you must write, you will. If you're lucky, maybe it'll turn out that you don't have to write. Maybe you could just garden, or do ceramics, or something else.
Conducted: January 25, 2002

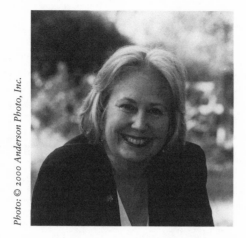

ELIZABETH COX

Putting the Pain in Straight

Elizabeth Cox is the author of *Familiar Ground, The Ragged Way People Fall out of Love, Night Talk,* which received the 1998 Lillian Smith Book Award for fiction, and *Bargains in the Real World.* Her work has been awarded the O. Henry Award and has been cited for excellence in *Best American Short Stories.* She grew up in Chattanooga, Tennessee, and received her M.F.A. from the University of North Carolina–Greensboro. Betsy teaches creative writing at Duke University and at the Bennington Writing Seminars.

When did you know you were a writer?

I don't think that I've ever thought of myself as a "writer." I had done so many other things before writing fiction. I was married, I had two children, and I taught special education for six years, so it just hadn't occurred to me to write until I was in my early thirties. By that time I was already somebody in the world: a teacher, a mother, a wife. My brothers published books of poetry, and I thought to myself, "I can do that." I wrote poetry first, published some poems, and returned to school to get my M.F.A. in poetry. While there, I tried my hand at some short stories. Writing stories felt more natural to me. I felt as though I had moved into a slot. I didn't think of myself as a "writer," I was just writing. "Writer" doesn't define me. "Teacher" defines me, but "writer" doesn't define me.

Why does teacher define you?

Because that's what I am. If someone asks me what I am, I say "a teacher." I tell people that I write, but I hardly ever say that I'm a writer. I do believe, though, that we learn how to live life through stories. I was raised in a boys' private school where my father was headmaster. Everyone in that community was a teacher—a huge family of teachers—talking about literature, not in a pretentious way, but in a way that made me love the stories of Shakespeare, or the tale of the *Odyssey* or the *Iliad*—letting me know these stories were real, and relevant. An English teacher who lived on the campus saw me reading Austen's *Pride and Prejudice*. I was very young, and didn't really know what I was reading, but he talked with me about it and made me confident about my reading. I began very early to learn that literature was a way of learning how to live your life. I think of writing as a way to deepen my life, teaching me to observe everything, every moment, more closely. Reading does the same thing. I put them in the same box, reading and writing. So I'm a teacher and a reader, and I write.

How does your teaching feed your writing life?

My reading teaches my writing life. My teaching takes away from my writing life. The effort I give toward a student's work is the same effort I give my own work. I read their stories more than once, live with it, so the energy is spent. I don't resent that. I can still work, but usually I have to wait for a time when I'm not teaching in order to write with focus. While teaching, I take notes, work with images and scenes, develop characters, but I can't get completely into a novel until I'm not teaching a course. So teaching doesn't feed my writing, though it feeds my life. It's a different part of my life that I have to balance with writing. Besides, it's my paying job.

How has growing up and living in the South influenced you as a writer?
My heart is in the South. Eudora Welty says, "Place is where the heart is." I'm beginning to develop a heart in Massachusetts, but when I go back to North Carolina or Tennessee, the air, the sounds, the smells, everything is familiar—it's what I write about. I've tried to write about New England and maybe one day I can, but I will need to live in the North longer in order to write about it. One aspect of New England that I am beginning to write about is the quality of light. New England light is sharper; it has an edge. In the South, the air is thicker and the light has a milkiness to it, has a softness that isn't in the northern air. At first, I thought I couldn't stand it; now I love it.

Do you consider yourself a southern writer?
Well, I'm southern. My stories are set in the South, the rhythm of the language, the plant life, the speech—all these are southern. I grew up reading the King James Version of the Bible, so that I know I use phrases and rhythms from that biblical background. I know that many writers do not want to be called southern writers, but I don't mind. It's the material I use, but the themes, I hope, are more than southern.

Where do you see yourself in the tradition of southern writers?
I don't want to presume to place myself among the great writers of the South, but I can say that they have been my teachers. I respond to the language in both stories and poems of Robert Penn Warren, to Eudora Welty's sharp humor, Faulkner, of course. I love the wordiness and the archetypal images Faulkner uses. I wish I understood more of Flannery O'Conner's way of putting a story on the page. I study the way she creates a story through three to five scenes. Ernest Gaines is someone I admire for the way he tells a story and the peregrinations that are taken, the labyrinthine way of getting to the final page—I see that as southern storytelling. I also see that truth is usually told with more complexity in the peregrinations. Paths which lead away from the main road, then come back, create more complexity, more truth, than a line that goes from beginning to end.

When someone suggested that I write a novel, I knew that I would not read a book on the novel, at least not at first. First I took a course in the sonata and symphony at Duke University. I studied the way a sonata develops the statement, development, and reiteration of that form, and how reminding phrases come back all the way through. I wrote my first novel, *Familiar Ground,* listening to symphonies and sonatas—Beethoven, Dvořák mostly. With my second novel, I took a course in astronomy and physics, and incorporated some of the astronomy into the book. At first I incorporated too much. When I showed it to a friend of mine she said that she "just skipped over those parts." So I took most of it out.

Did you find that the bigger idea of it gave you a lens through which you could look at what was happening in your story?
Yes. Exactly. I find that I understand complexities by looking at something larger. For my third novel, I read nature writing and biology, and I used much of my research in *Night Talk*. In this next novel, I'm reading about string theory in physics. Difficult reading, but Brian Greene, an expert on string theory, makes the ideas more accessible. Basically I love the idea that particles are divided into electrons, protons, and neutrons, which are made up of quarks, then up quarks, down quarks, neutrinos, then finally, strings. Everything in us and around us is vibrating. Isn't that a beautiful thought?

It goes back to the symphony idea that you started with.
Right. It goes back to music. I can't imagine how I will use any of my reading this time, but I'm learning something. The story I'm writing focuses on the violence young people do to other young people, and what kind of world we've created where that can happen. I keep wondering, What are we doing? I don't have an answer for it. I mean any answer finally seems presumptuous or trite, but I do want to present the problem in a way that makes the reader want to react. It was Rilke, I think, who said art makes you want to change your life. If I don't do it right, people will just be offended; if I do, then they will be encouraged to look differently at something vital.

In workshops, you often talk about "looking off to the side" when describing an emotional moment in the story. Can you talk about what that means?
It's a kind of peripheral vision. I used to go to the planetarium in Chapel Hill to observe whatever phenomenon that was happening in the sky, and one night I went to see a comet. You could see it without a telescope, and I was looking up to where everyone was pointing, but I couldn't see it, until the man behind me said, "You have to turn your head slightly and see it in your peripheral vision." When I did, I could see the comet and its movement across the sky. Stories are like that. Love and hope and hate and fear are best seen in this peripheral vision, and if you talk about them directly you can miss them. You have to offer an experience to create understanding.

For instance, in creating a moment of fear in a story where something dangerous is about to happen to a main character, you can increase that intensity by letting us hear something outside—a dog barks, a branch scrapes against the window—these details increase the intensity, even though they take us away from the moment. The author has made us look away, then come back. Hemingway does this in a bar fight: we'll hear a chair scrape or see somebody's foot beneath a table. The moment is prolonged, and it makes us more viscerally there to see or hear those seemingly disparate details.

You also teach the importance of drawing characters that are not stereotypical but are whole and real and inhabit an emotional world. Can you talk about how you achieve this in your own work?

When I first work with a character, he/she is flat. The character begins by speaking in ways that feel directed by the author. The dialogue is horrible, and no one seems to be speaking convincingly. I have to stay with these people until they come alive on the page, until they begin to speak and act in ways that feel more their own. But sometimes a character comes in whole. Anytime I write about a seven-year-old boy he comes in as a complete person. Seven-year-old boys are easy for me. Maybe I am (actually) a seven-year-old boy—disguised as a woman.

The more difficult characters have to be lingered with, like staying around people you know until you know something more about them. You might think you know how they would behave; then they surprise you, and your idea dissolves—they become alive outside your ideas of how they are. I create scenes and go with these characters to different places. Maybe we go to the zoo and I see something they are afraid of, or maybe they have an argument, or someone comes to see them. The more places (scenes) we go, the better I understand their behavior.

How do you keep characters sympathetic, that is, not too "good" or too flawed, but a realistic combination of both?

If a character is too nice, then I have to wonder what he/she would do to reveal selfishness, envy, jealousy, meanness in order to make the personality real. If a character is too demonic, I have to create vulnerability. I don't usually realize what needs to be developed until I get far into the story. For instance I'm working with a man now who is probably too good. I don't know when I will see a side of him that makes him a little more human—maybe something he fears. I always wonder what a character's secret is. I'm curious about people's secrets. Even sitting by someone on the plane I'll ask what their secret is, and often, to my horror, I am told. I don't ask that question as often as I used to.

Another interesting aspect of craft is the physical use of details, which can

be used to both deepen character and also to slow down a narrative. Could you say more about this?

When I'm writing a story or novel, I don't think about craft. When I'm editing I think about it, but not when I'm writing it. I use detail in order to see the moment. To be inside the moment we must use the senses, to see the cloth someone is wearing, to feel a breeze or the brush of a hand, to hear a door open, to taste an apple or a lover's neck. The use of the senses brings the physical experience closer. That ends up being craft, but when I'm writing I'm not thinking about the physical sense; I'm actually smelling, tasting, hearing seeing, touching. Later, during the editing process, I make the moments more clear.

How does compassion work in your creative writing and your teaching?

It is everything. I'm not sure we can write about characters unless we are compassionate, which means, of course, seeing everything. Compassionate, I think, means seeing all the sides of a person, all the capabilities, without judgment. If the author begins to judge, then he will begin to ask the reader to judge too, in the same way. The reader will balk when an agenda is felt. At least, I do. So if I'm judging a character I have to back up and look again in order to get myself out of it. A lot of writing, I guess, is trying to get out of the way—to get myself, my small-mindedness out, so that something else can be seen.

In teaching, as I see students create a character, I ask questions that require a different look at that character. Many undergraduate students will write something very judgmental about a father or a mother, with the young person being completely in the right. So I ask them to write from the point of view of the father/mother, and they are forced to get out of "themselves as victim" and see a different side. That's an obvious way, but also to ask questions about a character that keeps the author from creating only one dimension. That's the kind of compassion I teach: a way of looking that is not narrowly your own. Then of course, I'm constantly brought up short as I try to practice what I teach.

I think it must be difficult as a teacher to put aside your own ideas. When you read something, you automatically have your own thoughts about it, and to keep yourself constantly in check like that and tune in to what a student wants to do must be a constant challenge.

It is difficult. Sometimes (in my arrogance) I think I know what a student should do, but if I keep listening I can hear the way that student is trying to tell a story, and I try to help them toward that goal. I throw out possibilities and questions and challenges, but the student must do the work. Sometimes a student will come back to me and say, Do you remember when you said such and such? but I won't remember, because I was throwing out everything I could, and they took what was important to them. They catch what they need. If a student stays in one place and does not want to move, I challenge harder. I become fierce, I'm afraid. In the past few years I've tried to back off.

How do you become fierce?
I try to speak to the fear, or try to expose it. Sometimes I wonder if I should do this—a psychologist would probably say no. But because so much energy goes into keeping the fear hidden, when it's released a lot of energy is freed, and the student feels very alive. I must say that if the fear seems to be keeping something in place, I don't touch it. But if it is something the student can realize, that "everyone feels this way," "everyone is afraid of this," then they can give it to their character. Then they're working with human fear rather than letting it work them.

Your prose has a musical quality, a lyricism achieved through pacing, rhythm, and sound. How does music play into your writing life?
I do not apply music to my work in a deliberate way. I know other authors have done this successfully, but it isn't what I want to do. I learn something from listening to the structure of music, the changes, the return to a particular melody, and try to allow a story or a novel to move with that same rhythm. I hear how music moves off into a different direction before coming back, and I realize that my story needs to do the same. I'm listening to blues now. Sometimes when I listen to music, images come to my mind. The music itself, certain juxtapositions of forms in the music, will bring an image, and I get an idea from that image. For instance, in my first novel, as I listened to Dvořák, I thought of each character as an instrument, making a particular sound. One was an oboe, one a violin, one a cello. I actually imagined that what they said or did made a certain sound. I don't usually tell this because it seems too private to share. But there is a form that music has that strikes my imagination, that feeds me in terms of story. Other writers apply music theory more directly. There are stories written in the fugue form, for instance. I don't think I could do that. I don't imitate the music, but use it to inform my work.

What about the sentence by sentence lyrical quality of your work? Are you aware of it when you're writing?
There is music in my head that I try to put down on the page. Sometimes, in the first drafts, the music is stronger than the sense of the story. I hear the music first, and have to go back and find the story. Maybe I want to write music, but I cannot read a note or carry a tune. I have words. I

use words. The first draft has a rhythm in the words; then I have to go back and cut back the rhythm and work on story.

"Snail Darter" and "Biology" fit in nicely with the stories in *Bargains in the Real World*. What made you decide to include these excerpts from *Familiar Ground* and *Night Talk*? Did they already work as short stories or did you develop them as such for this collection?

"Snail Darter" was written for the novel *Familiar Ground*, but it was also published as a short story in a North Carolina anthology of stories. Even in the novel, I think, this short chapter seemed to step aside, to step into the life of one character whose life and difficulties were important in understanding why a particular violence was committed. "Biology" was reworked to serve as a story, not so much for this collection, but because I thought that this incident of a young girl's sexual awakening and regret had more to do with the fact that her father was gone, had more to do with the girl's longing for her father. The section ends with a letter to her father. As I looked at it, I realized it could be a story.

What importance do you place on the names of characters? What do you consider when choosing names? Warner James, or Warn, the preacher who seduces Evie, is particularly interesting, as are Josie Wire and Beckett.

Those names came quickly, without thinking. I laughed when the man said his name was Samuel Beckett. I like when names come in from the side like that, as if I were overhearing them, just learning them myself. I mean, I don't plan anything ironic or subtle, just want the name that fits the character.

Both "Saved" and "Biology" place a young girl's sexual desires, vulnerability, and innocence alongside fervent religious practice. What interests you about this juxtaposition?

The sacred and the sexual are close together. A young girl's desire for God, for that kind of passionate intensity that religion can offer, is mixed with her sexual desire. I wonder if the opposite is true, if the fear of God is connected to fear of sex. Passion is passion, right? In both cases, the girls were passionate. They were discovering God and sex, the sacred and the sexual, and they got in trouble. They got in trouble for going after their passions with a kind of abandon, and though I love their abandon, in both cases it brought them to the edge of danger. In the case of Evie ["Biology"], though she was hurt, her sense of herself was strong, and she was able to step back and go after "love" in a different way. In the case of Josie ["Saved"] the man learned something. He saw Josie's vulnerability and responded to it, rather than taking advantage of it. We also had, with

Josie, the added problem of her impending heart operation. She urged the man to take advantage of her, because she wanted to get her whole life into that moment.

In "Saved," Josie Wire wants to save Beckett by offering him the Bible, but it's only when she offers herself that Beckett is truly saved, in that he abandons his original intention and, instead, he is confronted with his own unwillingness to violate her. This is an unexpected turn of events. How did you arrive at this?

I did not know this is what would happen. I didn't know anything going into that scene. I love the position of ignorance. I love to approach a story or a scene as though I'm reading it instead of writing it. That's the fun for me—not knowing where it's going. I didn't know what Beckett was going to do until he did it. At the time I was merely watching them. He could've done anything. I was afraid he was going to hurt her; but I also knew he was not evil. I also didn't know he would tell her his real name or what his real name was until he said it. When I'm working in this way of discovery, I feel most located in my imagination.

By placing sexual danger against the backdrop of religion, you create a charged atmosphere of tension and mistrust. It's the age-old adage of good against evil, but deeper than that, is there something about sexuality and spirituality that are the same in your mind? Is there some way in which they work together?

Desire and wanting, the wish to abandon yourself to something larger, the feelings of letting go—all of this has to do with religion and sexuality, I think. I certainly don't think one is good and one is evil. Good and evil are alive in both, alive in *us*, finally.

In "Biology," the preacher uses his talk of eternal life and the soul to seduce a young girl, and she believes that he really loves her until he leaves for the next revival. She learns the difference between love and sex through her last shameful act with the preacher. What does his being a preacher bring to the narrative tension?

He's offering her something in terms of her soul, or he tries to convince her that he is. Though I don't know if she's as interested in the soul as she is in having the attention of this older man, because her father is gone. The fact that he's a preacher, that her mother encourages Evie to listen to him, then becomes suspicious, and that she comes back to tell her friend of her adventures—all these things make the moment more attractive to her. She wants the attention of her father, but her father isn't around, so she seeks the attention of this man. The story ends with the letter to her father. The story is about her longing for her father. It's true, psychologically, isn't it? We seek the love that wasn't given by our parents in someone/something else. Sometimes we seek love through religion, sometimes through sex, sometimes through our career choice. We seek some way to feel the connection we need to have.

I want to say that even though this preacher uses Evie in a despicable way, I did believe that his passion for religion was true—just misguided, just tied up with his own flaws.

When you're talking about the need to feel connected, I think about your new novel and the violence in it. Is that feeling of being disconnected a part of that story?

Absolutely. The novel focuses on regular families, parents and children who, for the most part, get along. Yet the children are drawn into violence. As I write I'm trying to observe, discover, what pulls them into a direction of violence. They are good people. In some simple way, it's about the way people don't have meals together, or about ways of being connected to a mechanical world rather than a personal one. It's about the rage of not having a connection. Many teenagers live in a home where love is evident, but the family is disconnected because of busy lives, or they find people outside of the family to love. Then children are left to create a world, a reality, before they know the difference between reality and illusion. As I write the novel, I try to clarify those distinctions for myself.

What does the fact that the preacher has sexual relations with a girl say about religion or about human sexuality?

Only that human desires are strong, and that they are in everyone. A preacher, a teacher, a mechanic—any of those men might have taken advantage of the girl. But to use a preacher combines the person's desire for religion—seeing how he uses religious fervor in a way that serves his sexual desires. He's a scumbag, but we don't really hate him, because Evie doesn't hate him. Evie is using him too, but she doesn't realize it.

Your stories have the quality of a tale told on the porch on a hot August night, luring readers in with lush descriptions and a country cadence that's hard to resist. How do you think your storytelling style has been influenced by the spoken word?

I grew up hearing stories, a lot of them on the front porch, or told in groups of adults sitting around. Children listened without adding anything. They stayed quiet. The cadence comes from whatever music is in my head from that oral tradition, and from the King James Version of the

Bible, southern rhythms, the rhythm heard by blacks in the South during the forties and fifties.

What do you look for in a short-story ending?

When I'm reading a story I look for some turn, some change, some event that gives a different perspective. In my own writing, I try to discover an ending, and I go a long while not knowing where the story is going. Sometimes the ending comes in the form of an image. In my first novel, *Familiar Ground,* the image was looking into the woods while driving somewhere and seeing a place that looked familiar—just a moment of imagining that you'd been there before. In *The Ragged Way People Fall out of Love,* the image was people sitting around a table at dinner in Halloween costumes. In *Night Talk,* the image was of one character who was mute, the one who had suffered the most probably, moving around between the two women—one woman was white and one black. The idea of his suffering and his inability to speak seemed an important aspect of the love and hate these women felt for each other. Sometimes an image offers a larger perspective.

What do you do when you have a place in a story that you know isn't working, but you're not sure why or how to fix it? Do you have any strategies for dealing with this?

I look away. I read something else, like science, or poetry, and often that helps me to become unstuck. I get the stuck passage in my mind; then I look away. I walk or go for a swim, or read; then I come back and see it differently. If I get to a place with characters where I don't believe something that is happening with them, then I'll have one of the characters express disbelief too. I incorporate the doubt to make it believable.

How did you arrive on the order for the stories in *Bargains in the Real World*?

First, I thought about putting them in the order they were written, but the truth is that the order had to do more with the material of the stories, or the rhythm of the stories. Some stories are told in a more straightforward way; some rely more on a rhythmical language. I tried to alternate both rhythm and material.

How is the process for writing short stories different from that of a novel?

A short story, when it begins, has a kernel that cannot be expanded. It has a set amount of time, and characters, and events. If it can be expanded, it becomes a novel, but I usually know very soon which it will be. The situation for a story is usually clear for me—a focus on a situation. A novel begins differently, without that kind of focus. With a novel I might have several situations, and some idea is driving me: the killing of a brother, the breakup of a family, the friendship between a black girl and a white girl and the difficulty they have bringing that friendship into their adult lives. So the novel form has a larger problem that drives me.

In each of your novels and in many of your short stories there is a mystery or a missing piece of information that creates suspense. In *Familiar Ground,* it's wondering what happened that night to Drue. In *The Ragged Way People Fall out of Love* there is the question of whether the couple will reunite, and then the real mystery surrounding the disappearance of their son. In *Night Talk* there's the question of who killed Turnbull, among others. Do you have this mystery in mind when you sit down to write, or does it come up as the story unfolds?

It comes up as the story unfolds, and very often what happens is a surprise to me. I did not know who killed Drue until the main character knew. When the young boy in *R W* was killed, I thought he was dead until he came back. I realized it as he walked toward the house. I discover as I go along, and it seems to be the best way for me. I know that people create outlines and write in an orderly fashion. Any fashion is more orderly than my own process. Secrets have power, and I discover the secrets along with the characters. I don't think about the "mysteries" occurring in my books, but I am aware of the importance of secrets.

What does the mystery bring to the narrative besides suspense?

It connects the reader to whatever secrets they have, and hopefully reveals the true hiddenness of things, or tells us something about the parts of ourselves we want to hide. I'm interested in what happens when what has been hidden is finally revealed, because with revelation often some new secret is unfolded. Maybe the secrets never stop revealing themselves.

In each of your novels and many stories as well, there is an outsider, a marginalized character who gets by on the kindness of the people around him. In *Familiar Ground* there is Soldier, in *The Ragged Way People Fall out of Love* there's the guy who lives in the cabin [Zack], and in *Night Talk* there's Capp. I love these characters, and they work to inform the narrative in many ways. Could you talk about this?

I always have these characters in my books. I think that the other characters might be defined by their relationship to these marginal people. I don't know—maybe I think that we are defined by this relationship, whether we ignore it or participate. These characters work more like an image, though I use them as characters. They come from a dream image

I've had, a recurring dream. The character was first an animal, mute but with enormous vulnerability, dependent on those around him. I'm glad I'm not a critic, because I don't know why they keep showing up.

How much of your work is autobiographical?
Probably all of it, but I change it, or else it comes from something I've heard about. I use events from my life, and then I revise them. My brothers comment on how strange it is to read names and places that are familiar, yet events have been changed, or to see a mixture of both brothers in one character. I take from everything I see and hear, from my own secrets and the secrets of others. I use everything; I just don't tell it straight. I don't use it in a way that is strictly autobiographical. The breakup of a family was written right after my divorce. Some of the things that the children said were from my own kids, but what happened in the book is not what happened to me. The pain of it is true, though. I wanted to put the pain in straight.

How do you handle recognizable characters in your fiction?
No one's recognized themselves, because no one character is based on any one person. They're always a combination of people. In *Night Talk,* for instance, the way that August taught his daughter about the world was very much the way my brother taught me about nature, but August is not like my brother, and my father wasn't similar to August. I use bits and pieces of people until a character comes alive in his own right. If I stay too close to a particular person, the character never develops completely.

When you use letters from one character to another, such as in *Night Talk,* what do these letters accomplish or solve in the narrative?
If you get inside, so close to the girl writing a letter to her father, you can expose what she wants and isn't able to say. She can be angry, and all the yearning, her love for him, can be shown—even more than she knows. Or the things that she complains about—her family, her friends, her brother—can reveal the ways she tries to build herself up to her father. Her relationship to her father, what she wants it to be and what it is, can be seen by the reader more clearly if we see what she's saying, and we know that there's truth in some of it, and not truth in some of it. We can see in the letters, in that first-person narration that is so private from one person to another, what she is hiding from herself, or hiding from her father. We can see how the father understands what she's saying more than she understands it. She can express anger or arrogance and we get a sense of her life as she experiences it, but we also see more than she realizes.

Do the letters help you, the writer, in any particular way?

Yes. I wrote the letters first and got to know her that way. I wrote all the letters in one group. I thought the novel was about a father leaving home. I didn't know it was about the appearance of Volusia and Janey Louise. Those two characters took over the story. Still, I got to know Evie pretty well through the writing of the letters.

What do you do to get to know your characters on and off the page?

Sometimes I eavesdrop conversations in public places, and I am struck by a phrase or a sentence that I know a certain character would have said in exactly the same way, or I'll see a gesture or some expression that I know belongs to a character. The more of those I get, the more the character is developed. Then I bring characters into different situations. The other day an argument took place between two sisters, and I learned more about them. One sister is having an affair with the husband of the other sister. They are arguing about something else, but the affair is always foremost in their minds. There's great anger and meanness in what they say to each other, but at the end the sisters are united against the man, and though nothing is said directly, indirectly so much is implied.

Seeing how people react to each other, what they lie about, what they admit or deny—these quirks tell us who the character is, and what is important to them.

There are several themes that recur in your work; one of them is forgiveness. In *Familiar Ground*, for instance, the narrator states that it doesn't matter what horrid thing happened. "What mattered here in this place, what mattered here on this day, not bright and warm, but covered with an early sodden light, was that all of this was but a subterranean rhythm. Something to be forgiven, consoled." Can you talk about forgiveness as a theme in your work?

I don't think I ever mean to write about forgiveness, but I think that every book so far explores that theme. I don't know if this next book has that theme or not. The first book was about self-forgiveness, the second about forgiving someone else, and the third was about asking for forgiveness. I wouldn't have said this before I wrote these books, but maybe I think forgiveness is the most important thing we can do. Theme arises out of the characters and their actions. A few years ago somebody asked my daughter what was the most important thing she would do. She answered, "Forgiveness." She was in her twenties. I said, "Good answer." She had to forgive her parents' divorce. There was a broken engagement early in her life. I hope I taught her that, but I'm not sure I knew it as well as she did. She teaches me.

Where did you get the idea for *Night Talk*? Did you have experiences similar to Evie growing up with black kids?

No. I grew up with blacks in my house, working, but I didn't know their kids. I think it's something that I wish had happened, but I didn't have that experience. I struggled with how I might get that experience on the page. I had seen racist incidents. I remember racism happening in more blatant ways when I was younger. I remember feeling puzzled about the mixture of affection and anger I felt from the black women with whom I came in contact.

Were you particularly close to the civil rights movement?

Not growing up, but later in my life I was. I went to Ole Miss at the same time as James Meredith. I remember the uproar of violence, the smoke bombs filling the dormitories, the sounds of gunfire. National Guardsmen stayed on the campus in tents for weeks. I'd been aware of the anger for a long time, but that was a wake-up call.

Some of the scenes depicting racism are written with such clear detachment that they truly make me cringe, or blush with embarrassment for the characters. How do you create such empathy in your readers?

I try to put down truthfully all the ways small and large that we are intolerant of each other. If the characters are human enough, the reader recognizes those places. I wanted to bring the reader close enough so that they could not see the character as racist, but as someone who was human and intolerant. Both girls were intolerant in certain ways. They had to figure out a way to be friends and still accept the difficult parts of each other.

In addition to the mysterious outsider, the derelict or mentally incapacitated, there is often a surprise revelation or turn of events or both at the end of your narratives. What draws you to this aspect of the story?

I love the moment when something turns in an unexpected way. I love wandering into a place, then having something happen that wasn't expected to happen. This process is part of the discovery, and keeps me from manipulating or creating an agenda. I have a note to myself on my desk lamp: Offer a life, not a text. I think this is a quote from a theologian—Niebuhr, I believe. Anyway, it sounded like a good one to remember.

Do the boys in your new novel have typical families?

Yes, though one has a troubled family and one boy struggles with his homosexuality. But yes, most of their families are typical, with struggles that are true to this millennium age.

Do you have a title for your next book?

I have about five working titles, none of which I will mention now.

What would you say to new writers? What advice would you give?

To pay attention! To look at the world around you as though every moment matters, because it does. To forget the wish to publish, and just write. Are you going to write the next book *whether or not* it will be published? The pleasure of writing is so different from the pleasure of publishing—can't hold a candle to it. And another thing: Read, Read, Read. Read everything—all the sciences, philosophy, history, poetry, folktales, plays. Read and study the thing that strikes your curiosity. Now, as a teacher, I have a story for you, an old story about a teacher who took his students out to see the night sky, and as he pointed upward he said, "Now I want you to look closely at my finger." The students got the point. So pay attention and be willing to be amazed with the day. God, what a way to live!

Conducted: October 2000

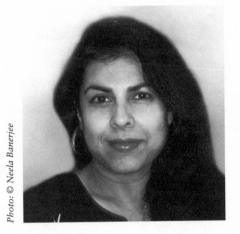

CHITRA BANERJEE DIVAKARUNI

Writers Are Great Eavesdroppers

Chitra Banerjee Divakaruni is the author of the best-selling novels *The Mistress of Spices* and *Sister of My Heart,* the story collection *Arranged Marriage,* which received several awards, including an American Book Award, and three collections of prizewinning poetry. Her work has appeared in the *New Yorker,* the *Atlantic Monthly, Ms., Best American Short Stories 1999,* and other publications. Born in India, Chitra lives in the San Francisco area.*

*Since the time of this interview, Chitra Banerjee Divakaruni has published the novel *The Vine of Desire.*

How did you get started writing fiction?

I started writing with poetry. After a few years of writing poetry, I discovered that my poems were becoming very narrative. I was using a lot of voice personae. I could see that my interests were shifting. I was becoming more interested in stories, in character, and in dialogue. I felt that I had to move to another genre.

How does your experience as a poet feed into your fiction writing?

I'm glad that I wrote and continue to write poetry because it made me more sensitive to language, particularly to the sound of words. I'm very aware of the rhythm of prose, which is very different from the rhythm of poetry, but it's certainly there. If you're not used to writing poetry, you're not as aware of it. I'm very conscious of the sounds of my sentences. I spend a long time reading sentences out loud to myself, and if something sounds awkward or not the way it should, then I'll work on it some more. It also has made me much more aware of compressing language and ideas into images. I think unless I had written poetry, I don't think I would've been as sensitive to that.

Who are some of the writers that have influenced you, and who do you admire now?

Maxine Hong Kingston really influenced me with *The Woman Warrior*. I'd been ready for that book when I read it, which was when I was doing my graduate studies at Berkeley. It opened up so many things for me, and it made me aware of the importance of her subject matter, and also gave me permission for my subject matter. I love the way that story plays such an important part in her book, and story plays a very important part in my books—telling stories, listening to stories, old stories out of our culture and how they affect us—all of those things.

How do your story ideas come to you?

Sometimes I'll overhear something. As you know, writers are great eavesdroppers. Whenever I'm at a gathering, I'm participating, but a lot of times I'm just being quiet and listening. I get ideas from things I see in newspapers and magazines, from other writers, from things that happen in my life, in the lives of other people I know. But ultimately the source of all writing is mysterious. It comes from some deep place. We call it the imagination, or we could call it the creative mind. The ability to transform these nuggets from life into art comes from the creative mind.

What is your process like for writing a short story?

A lot of times I'll start with an image. I'm a very visual person, and in some ways I have to see the character doing something before I start the story. It's the same way for my novels. For example, in *The Mistress of Spices* I got a series of strong visual images of an old woman in a little Indian grocery. It was a sensory experience: I could smell the spices, I could see the place, and I could *feel* it. That began the writing process. With many of my stories, it works in the same way. The image I get won't necessarily be the beginning image of the story when the story is complete. It could be the ending image. Sometimes I have to figure my way out backwards.

Having written both short stories and novels, do you prefer one form more than the other?
The joys and the challenges of each are different. I'm very glad that I work in both because the novel is like a tapestry. It's a long and painstaking process, and I have to work on the detail and create an alternative world, and it has to be as full and rich as I can make it. A short story is like painting a watercolor—the challenge is to have a lightness of touch. What I'm working with is nuance and subtlety and ellipses—what I'm leaving out is as important as what I'm putting in. I have to work with the power of suggestion, and I love the form because of this.

You've been very prolific, publishing a book every two years. How do you do it?
After my first son was born, I had a near-death experience. After I came back to life, I decided that I couldn't waste any more time. I had a sense of being driven. I had these stories and I had to write them, because who knows? We think we have forever, but I know that we don't.

When you're working on a novel, how do you know when you're done?
What I recently started doing was I'll finish it, then put it aside for about three months. When I say put it aside, I mean that I send it to my editor, my agent, and a few trusted writer friends, but I don't look at it while they're reading it. After three months, I get everyone's feedback, and I take a new look at it myself. Then I can make decisions because I have a much better perspective.

How many drafts do you do?
It depends on the piece. Some of the stories in this new book . . . I've been working on for ten years, because I just wasn't happy with them. I was convinced about the importance of the stories, but I knew that I didn't have the form right. "Mrs. Dutta Writes a Letter," for example—I must've thrown away ten completely different versions of it before I got the final

version. I knew that it wasn't ready until I got to this last version, and then I had a really good feeling.

It sounds like you work on your stories in conjunction with working on your novels.

Yes, when I'm working on a novel, I get to a certain point where I feel that I have to wait in order to process what I've written. That's when I'll work on a story.

Do you think that the years you spent working on *The Mistress of Spices* and *Sister of My Heart* helped you learn things that enabled you to finish the stories?

I've learned something from everything I write, and there are probably more things that I should've learned. I do feel that I'm at the tip of the iceberg in terms of craft. There's just so much to learn and to know.

Did each of your books pose different challenges for you as a writer?

With each one I was consciously working on different challenges, and then some unexpected ones came up also. For example, with *The Mistress of Spices,* I was trying to bring together very different kinds of things. I was trying to bring together the language of poetry and the language of prose. I was trying to bring together the old myths of India and the harsh realities of inner-city America. I was working with those very different genres, styles, almost different worlds that collide. Then with *Sister of My Heart* I wanted to work with the challenge of dual voices. I knew I would have two narrators and they would both be equally important, and they would alternate and they would give ironically different perspectives. With the short stories I wanted to express what I had to say through image. I wanted to get at things slantwise and not directly, and overall I wanted to write beautifully. The aesthetic level of the stories was a great concern.

What do you do to help yourself grow and develop as a writer? How do you develop the ability to deepen your work?

I wish I knew. Hopefully it just comes from keeping at it, and keeping at it, and keeping at it sincerely. With each book or story that I write, I'm learning to do something better, but I don't want to only do more of that same thing. I push myself by trying different things. In the novel that I'm working on right now, I'm trying to bring in other ways of telling the story. I'm using letters and the term papers of students in the novel. Finding alternative ways of telling the story is one of my main challenges.

What do you look for in a story ending?

Because stories are different they resolve themselves differently. Some stories lend themselves to epiphany, while some end with a question. Other stories end with a flash-forward of something that may or may not happen. Some stories will end with an inner realization for the character, not necessarily an epiphany, but an understanding or a reseeing of something that's been there all along. Sometimes a whole new image will come in that is only tangentially related, but thematically related. I'm always reading other writers and what they're doing. I came to writing fairly late after I'd finished all my formal education, so books have been my best teachers.

How is a short-story ending different from a novel ending?
The novel has a different pace. It's like a big wave that has been building up and up and up and now it has to crash, whereas the short story is more subtle. It's not that big dramatic crashing at the end but more like a dancer's movement, subtle and artistic.

What was it like to go from writing the short stories in *Arranged Marriage* to writing your novel *Mistress of Spices*?
One of the big things I had to learn moving from the short story to the novel was the pacing. The short story, to me, has a breathless pace. In the novel I had to learn the rhythm of a longer movement. I like the analogy of the wave, how before it comes to the shore, it crests and then comes down, crests and then comes down. Finally, it'll have that last movement. I really had to learn that pacing. I had to learn how to work with chapters and things that end in a different way than how a short story ends, like how a chapter ends.

The transformation of the individual that is an inevitable result of immigration is a central theme in all of your books, yet you approach it differently in each story. For instance, in *The Mistress of Spices*, Geeta falls in love with a Chicano, and her Indian parents are faced with what they consider a disgrace to the family. In "Mrs. Dutta Writes a Letter," you write about a grandmother who can't adapt to the life in America. Can you comment on this?
Immigration was a major transformative influence on my life. Immigration, in some ways, is what made me into a writer. Before I came to this country I had no idea of wanting to be a writer. It was after I moved so far from my culture and faced the conflicts that come with such movement that I had a subject that I felt passionate about. Immigration made me realize something that I hadn't thought about until I came here, and that is that we use the word "America," which really means something

different to each immigrant who comes over. And the experience of America is so different for each individual. For our children growing up here, who are the products of immigration, what does being American mean to them? *The Unknown Errors of Our Lives* is particularly concerned with the corresponding move back—immigration begins a movement that really only ends when there's a corresponding movement back to the home country. In this book, I'm focusing in a number of stories on that movement back.

In a way, your writing is like a movement back.
Yes, it's a way for me to revisit, to reconnect, to reunderstand.

Do you do any research for any of your books? *The Mistress of Spices,* **for example, contains so much information about the healing properties of spices. How did you pull all of this information together?**
For many years I've been interested in using spices and herbs for healing. I do a lot of that myself at home, so I had a lot of books already, and then I did some more research on that when I was writing that novel. Not only did I do research on the way in which Ayurvedic is practiced now, but I did research on how in our ancient texts a number of herbs and spices are mentioned which are lost now—we don't have them anymore or know where to find them anymore. In my book there are some of those spices, such as the spice that makes her young.

The Mistress of Spices **reads like a legend or fable. Is this story based on any real legend?**
No, but I drew on a number of legends and on the *feel* of legends. There are a number of legends about women healers in my language, and there are other legends about serpents who can guide you in your journey to light, who can act as a spiritual guide. There are other legends about the islands of spices, and other legends about islands where only women live. So I took a lot of different legends and wove them together depending on what the story needed.

Was the Mistress of Spices based on a real character from legends, or did you invent her?
I invented her, or I should say, she came to me.

What draws you to the fable-like narrative style that you use in varying degrees throughout your work?
I love the idea of the fable or the myth. It's a wonderful genre in literature. It gives so much to the reader in an apparently simple way. The old

fables and myths and folktales are very deep and very deep in us because they deal with many archetypal truths. I'm drawn to stories where the characters have no names, where they're just known as the mother, or the daughter. Those stories work on a number of different levels, and I like that.

How do you retain a sense of realism while incorporating this fable-like style?
That's through the use of very specific sensory details, which relate to the meaning of the piece.

Some reviewers have referred to your work as magic realism. Do you agree with this categorization?
I don't disagree, because I think that category can encompass a lot of things. I'm sure that I've been influenced by the works of people like Marquez and Allende, but I think what I'm doing, which is a little different, is drawing on the old fables and drawing on the legends of India to inform my characters, some of whom are legendary. That's the world that I want to juxtapose against the very real world of America. That makes what I'm trying to do a little different.

In *The Mistress of Spices,* Tilo, the one person who is purely Indian and segregated from America behind the walls of her shop, gives up her powers to become an ordinary Indian-American citizen. Do you think this says that the Indian must give in to integration at some point?
What was right for her was right for her, and not necessarily for everyone. Personally, I believe that if one has made the decision to come to this country, one cannot then create an artificial cultural ghetto in which to barricade oneself. What's the point, then, of coming out of their culture? I feel very strongly that some process of integration must happen, including your view of yourself and the relation of your culture to the larger culture. At the same time, you can use what you consider valuable. You don't want to give up the wrong things, or hold onto the wrong things. Nor do you want to promote old values that are not positive ones. Integration does allow us a wonderful opportunity to take the best of both cultures, and it would be a pity not to do that.

It's interesting, too, that if Tilo steps outside the walls of her shop onto the streets of Oakland, chaos will come to whomever she is in contact with. What does this say about the purely Indian mixing in with America? What does it say that can't resist leaving her shop?
She is responding to a life impulse, which is to move on and not to

stagnate. If she stays inside the door, the status quo is preserved, but she is stagnating as a human being. She is responding to a very necessary impulse. In terms of the old culture and the "promises" made through the old culture, stepping outside is a taboo, and she has to pay a price for it. For all our choices, even the ones that are important and positive and necessary, we do have to pay a price.

What drew you to the idea of this woman having to choose between an ordinary life and the extraordinary life of the Mistress of Spices?
That part comes from a number of Eastern and Western legends where healers have to give up the ordinary joys of life in order to keep their powers. Many times they have to give up romantic or sexual relationships.

The Indian-American immigrants in this story suffer a variety of dilemmas as a result of cultural differences or an inability to reconcile the Indian and American cultures within themselves. For example, Geeta's grandfather, who causes many problems for his family because of his inability to accept their Americanized ways. Comment?
The word "American" can mean different things to different people. For many people it's a wonderful word; to others it's a bad word—"You've become American." It depends on how secure you are with your own identity. One always responds to change from that place in one's life. If you're secure in your identity, the change doesn't bother you. But when you feel dis-ease like the grandfather is feeling—he's lost a whole way of life, just as Mrs. Dutta has lost a whole way of life, and in order to have family, both the grandfather and Mrs. Dutta have had to give up community—that's very difficult. On the one hand I have a great deal of compassion with their struggles, and on the other hand I realize that it can cause a lot of tension and bitterness within a family and ultimately break up a family and cause communication breakdowns between the generations.

You often use the descriptor of a metaphor as more than just a point of comparison. You use it to further paint the world of the characters that exists beyond the page. In *The Mistress of Spices*, for example: "But today the light is pink-tinted like just-bloomed *karabi* flowers," and "Saturday comes upon me like the unexpected flash of rainbow under a bird's black wing, like the swirl-spread skirt of a *kathak* dancer, fast and then faster." While the narrative isn't talking about the *kathak* dancer, or the *karabi* flowers directly, here they are adding a glimpse at the world of the characters. Are you aware of this as you work? Comment?
This comes fairly organically. What I'm trying to do is to think the way the character is thinking, and what are the connections the character will

be making depending on their background. Human beings often think by analogy and by remembering and by comparing. So that when we're faced with something knew, we think, not even consciously but subconsciously, This is like ———. And not every character will do that. Some characters don't think that way.

You also choose physical details that draw your characters quite distinctly and also serve to create an intimacy between the characters and the reader. For example, in *Mistress of Spices:* "Geeta's grandfather still walking like a military major though it has been twenty years. His shirt ironed stiff with pointy collars, his steel-gray pants perfect-creased down the front. His shoes, midnight-black Bata shoes spit-polished to match the onyx he wears on his left hand for mental peace." How do you arrive at these carefully placed details?

Often I get a very strong visual image of the character. I'm always happy and thankful that it happens, because it doesn't always happen right away. Quite a lot of the characters in *The Unknown Errors of Our Lives* don't have physical descriptions. In that case, what I'm doing instead is focusing on their mental habits. It's not so much their physical attributes that I'm concerned with but their mental states. This is another way of making a character come alive. In that book, I realized I was moving toward something different, not consciously necessarily, but I noticed that I was more interested in describing characters through their thoughts or internal habits. In this book, you're very aware of the *tone* of a character, and the whole tone related to the work. I'm thinking particularly of a story like "The Blooming Season for Cactii." Mira, the main character—we see everything through her eyes, and it's not until almost the end of the story, when she looks in the mirror, that the reader sees what she looks like. Yet, by then we very much know who the character is.

In *Sister of My Heart,* Sudha learns that her mother has lived all these years under a false identity, claiming to be a Chaterjee and denying her impoverished past. Similarly, in *The Mistress of Spices,* Raven's mother denied her past as a poor Native American. Both Sudha and Raven are left with the confusion of identity that results from learning the truth about who their mothers really are. What draws you this dilemma?

I've always been interested in a number of questions related to family, particularly parents. Who are we? How much of who we are is located in the past? In Indian tradition, the family is so important, much more so than in the West, and everything you do—good or bad—seems to reflect on your family's reputation. In some ways, I have difficulty with that thought, that who you are is related to who your family was. It's also true that how your family sees themselves has an enormous effect on you. I'm dealing with a paradox. Sudha and Raven must go beyond their mothers' weaknesses, denials, and falsehoods to find their own identities. But in between, before they can do that, they're in a very difficult situation, and they feel very helpless. When they realize that their mothers lied about who they are, they feel worthless, or they act out to overcome their feelings of inadequecy.

In *Sister of My Heart*, Sudha's father misrepresented his true identity and took Anju's father on a dangerous ruby-hunting expedition that cost them their lives. Sudha believes that it's her duty to repay the family debt to the Chaterjees, so when she learns that her elopement with her beloved will threaten Anju's match, she gives up her love and settles instead for an arranged marriage. What drew you to this idea of a child inheriting the karmic debt or unresolved burdens of the parent?

I wasn't consciously doing that, I don't think, but rather, I was still exploring this idea of how the past affects the world of the present, and how your understanding of the past can make you feel about who you are today. Again, in our Indian culture family is so important that the idea of family debt is a very important cultural idea. One of the things that children do for their parents is to repay their debts. This is considered honorable. In this case, it's not a physical debt but an emotional one. I hope that I've portrayed this ironically. I hope there are points where the reader is thinking, *No, no, don't do it.* I was definitely ambivalent about Sudha's choice. There's also the larger concept of the woman's role that I'm working with. All over the world, women are taught or brainwashed or conditioned into feeling that they have to be the ones who take care of others, the ones who give up things. Sudha's behavior is an extreme form of that, and I wanted the reader to feel that. On the one hand it's very noble, but on the other hand you just don't want her to do it. You don't want her to think that she has to make this sacrifice in order to be a good woman. For so many centuries this is what women have been told. I wanted to fight that. I also wanted to point out how important that is in the context of family.

In "Mrs. Dutta Writes a Letter," in *The Unknown Errors of Our Lives*, you render so clearly and with heartbreaking detail the difficulty of an elderly woman trying to adjust to life in America with her son and his family. Did you know when you started this story that Mrs. Dutta would decide to go back to India?

No. In fact, as I said earlier, I had ten different versions of this story, and in most of them she was going to stay in America, but then that just didn't feel right. In the final version of the story, she writes a letter to her friend, and in the writing of the letter, she makes her decision to go back to India. Throughout the story there had been many miscommunications between all the characters, but in the end, writing and clear communication is what saves Mrs. Dutta.

You also render the embarrassing moments in this story—Mrs. Dutta hanging her laundry outside and wrongly imagining the neighbor lady's thoughts, overhearing her daughter-in-law complain about her to Sagar—with excruciating detail and a clear-eyed detachment that makes readers cringe. How do you create such empathy in your readers?

Thank you for saying that. It is, of course, my constant aspiration. I think it happens when I'm really trying to see the story from two points of view, Mrs. Dutta's and her daughter-in-law's. That's one of the biggest challenges for me in writing. It's easy for me to focus on and get into one character, but to present conflicting points of view without creating stereotypes or making characters predictable is much more difficult. Also, it's so important not to be judgmental, that is, to present the details of the situation and to allow the reader to draw their own conclusions. I refuse to feel for the reader. The reader has to feel for herself.

In "The Lives of Strangers," Leela visits India to get in touch with her Indian identity. Why is it important that after befriending the outcast Mrs. Das, Leela must then reject her?

This isn't something that I'd planned on. The story developed in that way organically. In some ways I would've liked for them to have a wonderful, healing relationship. Leela has learned important things about how to connect with another human being, which she never knew before. But still, she couldn't give up that part of herself and embrace another person completely. She wasn't ready for it. On another level, she had to find in herself the genetic memory that she'd rejected. When she saw her aunt speaking about her superstition, Leela rejected that, until she discovered that deep down in herself there was a little bit of that, too.

Throughout your stories and novels there is a sense of the individuals trying to find home and what home means. They pendulum back and forth between their lives in America and their pasts in India, trying to find some truth that will help their lives make sense. Is this something that can ever be reconciled?

Some individuals might manage to reconcile this, but for many of us, this is the great dilemma of the twentieth and twenty-first century. Where is home? We've become such a mobile society, how many of us live in the homes where we were born? We've moved into a whole new way of life, and the question *where is home* becomes very important. It cannot necessarily be answered. Perhaps the only way to answer it is to create a sense of home inside of ourselves.

In your article for the *New York Times*, "New Insights into the Novel? Try Reading 300," you explain how reading three hundred novels in five months as a judge for the National Book Award gave you new insight into what makes a successful novel and what does not. After that experience you returned to your novel in progress, threw out two hundred pages, and started again. What did you discover that made you want to throw out those two hundred pages?

That was a painful experience. No, I was very happy, actually, as I restarted the novel because I knew it was going to be so much better. What I learned from reading so many novels is that the novel, as it goes on, has to expand. It has to give you a sense of a larger life, not just the story you're dealing with, no matter how well it's told. There must be a sense of resonance, a sense that in that story is the knowledge of a whole larger story whose presence is felt. I realized that my novel wasn't doing that.

How did you undertake the work of revisioning and rebeginning that novel?

I had to change the narrative structure. I had the novel in a multiple-narrator perspective, some who saw the story up close, but I had to add the omniscient narrative voice. I'd used this voice sporadically, but it hadn't been a big part of the narration. It's like changing the lens on a camera. Sometimes you're seeing it up close and sometimes from far. I hope this gives the novel a sense of opening up and expanding. I think it does.

To what do you owe the recent explosive growth of interest in Indian writing in the United States?

It's been coming for a while. People have been interested for a long time in writers like R. K. Narayan, Bharati Mukherjee, and Anita Desai—we're talking the last twenty years. One of the big things that happened was that India celebrated her fiftieth year of independence, and that drew a lot of interest. Also in the last twenty years, because of globalization, there's been a lot of moving back and forth with writers who live in both cultures, in terms of publishers who now have agents who are aware of Indian writers. There's a lot of great talent right now.

Where do you see yourself in the tradition of Indian writing?

That's very hard to say. Others will have to comment on that. I will say that I'm very proud of our literary heritage in my mother tongue. I read fluently in Bengali, so I'm in touch with a lot of wonderful writing being done in Bengali, which I know influences my own work. I see myself as part of that literary tradition.

Do you think the success of Indian writing has to do with the appeal of the exoticism of India?

I think if we're really talking about the well-known writers, I'd say not very much. The writers I'm thinking of are Amitabha Ghosh, Amit Chandhuri, and Jhumpa Lahiri, and they're not writing about the exotic at all. They're writing in a very deliberate way about the realities of the Indian-American experience. I think the interest is because of how well they're writing, and because these are such diverse voices presenting worlds within worlds.

In your teaching experience, what are the common problems you see in the work of new writers?

This particular problem sometimes occurs with very talented writing students. One of the things I tell my students at Houston is, "Stop! Don't read so much." Usually teachers are saying just the opposite, but there comes a time when you have to shut down all of the input channels, and you have to go into yourself and write what's in there. Sometimes students in writing programs are using too much of their logical and critical brainpower and not enough of their intuition.

What would you say to someone working on his or her first stories or novel?

I would say be very clear about where the heart of the story is, what is most important, what's at stake. Have you managed to stay focused on that? Is that where the energy is coming from? Or have you digressed onto other things which are easier or flashier?

Conducted: May 2001

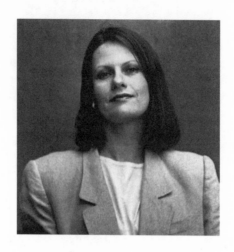

MARIA FLOOK

I'll See It When I Believe It

Maria Flook has published six books including *My Sister Life: The Story of My Sister's Disappearance,* a finalist for the PEN/American Martha Albrand Award for memoir; the novels *Open Water* and *Family Night,* which received a PEN/American Ernest Hemingway Special Citation; and the story collection *You Have the Wrong Man.* Her awards include a Pushcart Prize for fiction, fellowships from the National Endowment for the Arts and The Fine Arts Work Center in Provincetown, Massachusetts, and a North Carolina Writers' Award.*

*Since this interview, Maria Flook has published the nonfiction book *Invisible Eden: A True Story of Love and Death on Cape Cod.*

You have written novels and a memoir. How is fiction different from memoir?

Did you ever see the jacket of Exley's *A Fan's Notes*? They call it a "fictionalized memoir." No apologies. People expect a memoir to be about real events and real people and fiction is supposed to have invented characters. That's a basic expectation. But whether it's memoir or fiction, a story must come from a core anxiety or troubled heart if it is going to matter to the reader. In memoir, a writer uses the same devices used in fiction—scene, setting, characterization, dialogue, rising tension. In memoir, characters and events might be historically accurate, names, dates, etcetera, but it's not as simple as that. Why is the story important? It's not important because it really happened but because of what the writer is exploring and examining about the human grain. Characters come to life in memoir in the same way as characters in fiction. My fictional characters should, hopefully, be just as "real" as any in my memoir. They come from the same impulse as when I write about real persons. The seed of both must be this anxiety or heartache I mention.

People worry that if memoir uses invented material, that the story can't be trusted. But in art, I think it's the artist's first task to use invention for further discovery and to reach deeper levels of meaning. One of my favorite instructions comes from Matisse. He would tell his students in his painting classes, "Exaggerate in the direction of truth." One might ask, isn't it false to exaggerate the truth? I think what Matisse is saying is that one cannot reveal or portray the truth without manipulating your medium. The truth in art is not made up of exact reportage, or of concrete and representational elements alone, but it comes from the artist's own mastery of technique in order to deliver the complexity of his impulse. "Exaggerate in the direction of truth" means to use everything at your fingertips to move closer to that core anxiety.

How much research do you do before you write?

I research things as I write. When I'm working, I'm already immersed in characterization and in the story map, and I sort of know where I'm headed, but I often stop to work on some fact checking, finding the technical word, or identification for something. For instance, today I called the Harvard Map Library to find out the correct name for those raised, three-dimensional maps. They're called "tactile relief maps" with the molded topography.

Other times I might do more complex research that will actually steer my narrative into a new and exciting bend. In my first novel, I contacted the Chrysler Historical Archives to get the specs on the maiden Plymouth Duster. They sent me eight-by-ten glossies and their ad campaign that year; their slogan was "Plymouth Makes It!" I've visited many spots, Coast Guard stations for *Open Water,* a plastic flower warehouse, a motorboat showroom, the Arrow Shirt Company's corporate offices on Madison Avenue, and for the memoir I was in touch with Naval Base Norfolk. I had to find out what ships were in port when my sister lived there. I had to know more about the carrier *Independence,* that she went on, and I researched what was happening in Vietnam at that time. I read about the dishonorable discharge her boyfriend got for "fragging" an officer, and learned why he wasn't convicted for the crime.

In my research about the *Andrea Doria,* it was very compelling to learn more about the two girls who were in the disaster that my sister and I survived. If I hadn't retrieved every tidbit about the actual shipwreck, I couldn't have *felt* all the layers of my reaction to it, that I have now. In this way, research can help direct impulse, but usually it enriches and deepens your levels of information.

How would you define realist fiction?

Of course, I don't really describe my writing that way. It's a given that my work is addressing real human experience. I think "realist fiction" is a description I might have used just to clarify my focus as a teacher of these summer workshops I go to. I think you must have seen this term in the catalog for my fiction workshops at the Fine Arts Work Center or something. Students who are trying to write formula fiction, sci-fi, romances, mystery and intrigue, and all of that, often sign up for these classes. Sometimes they have had no other examples but formulaic novels by Grisham, King, Clancy, Steele, and I want to lead them elsewhere.

Was it true that you had had tickets for that ill-fated crossing on the *Andrea Doria* but instead took an earlier ship, and one of the two girls who were moved into your cabin was killed when it would have been you and your sister?

Yes, there were two other sisters. One was swept away in the collision and lost at sea, but her older sister was plucked from the Italian liner by the prow of the *Stockholm.* She was found two days later in its crumpled bow when the Swedish liner was docked in New York. I learned that the surviving sister, Linda Morgan, is now a nurse. I think about her and her little sister who was swept away. Fate dealt a random blow that touched the four of us, but touched us so differently.

Did you know Willis would be a driver for WASTEC in *Open Water*? How did you come up with that?

I have a real interest in working-class occupations for my characters. I guess because I've had my fair share. I mean I wouldn't know much about Wall Street situations, you know? If you can give some realistic information about the working lives of characters, you are giving them footing in their worlds in a larger context than they might have if you kept them in their kitchens and living rooms. I've worked in banks, in fish-processing plants, as a waitress, as a correction officer; I worked in a factory that makes velveteen boxes for the jewelry industry in Rhode Island. They weren't real velvet, but some kind of stinking resin they sprayed onto these little boxes from high-pressure nozzles. It wasn't good to breathe it.

If you can put your character in some sort of job setting or working conditions a lot can happen. WASTEC was a very low-end and ill-suited occupation for Willis. You wanted him to get out.

One of my favorite work settings in recent fiction is the emergency room in Denis Johnson's brilliant story "Emergency." He has his characters working beyond their job capacities. His main character is lovelorn and doped up and has deeper problems than the hapless patients he attends to, but putting him in that setting, with the hospital routines and familiar details, skewed just right by Johnson's relentless wit and edginess, helps the reader see him as a hero.

You often use the lyric image to reveal character and to instill a deeper resonance in your narrative. For instance, in the story "Rhode Island Fish Company," a teenage girl has a tattoo that's oozing. The narrator, her aunt, recalls seeing statuary in Greece. "I had seen marble limbs discolored, worn concave at the wrist and fingertips, marred by centuries of human touch. Unchecked these habits of adoration can wear away their subjects." Readers feel the narrator's struggle to give the girl space and not smother her with love. How do you arrive at a particular image? How do you then develop the image into a revelatory statement about character?

That's like asking how a poet writes poetry. It's an eruptive and only partly controlled mechanism in its first manifestations. The psychointellectual disturbance that an image creates works to engender a parallel between external and subconscious elements in the narrative. The lyric image evokes an instant recognition, unlike exposition, which accrues differently. Image is *supreme statement*. It's the lightning-bolt instant when perception crosses over from intellectual wisdom to spiritual knowledge. En masse, lyric details are a magic adhesive in fiction; they are the marrow jelly in the skeleton, and without it a narrative would seem staid and anemic. But there's always a risk that the lyric detail will be disruptive or distracting, so it's a constant struggle to find the image that propels the emotional current, but doesn't sweep you off course.

Regarding the image you mention, I have seen ruins and art treasures that have been deformed by tourists' manhandling—and I suppose this goes into the image bank that writers have stockpiled and nurtured throughout our lives. The image surfaces, it *strikes,* but it's not a conscious decision. We recognize the immediate connection it has, and then we try to write it down as well as we can.

You have an uncanny eye for specific physical detail that deepens the narrative and nails it down in place and time. Are these details things you collect in your daily life, or things that simply come to you when writing?

Of course physical description must be impelled by real experience and by real-life sightings of our world around us. But there's another element in writing physical detail that has to do with sensibility, vision, even attitude. Writers have idiosyncratic, even idiopathic ways of *seeing.* The writer John Berger writes, "Seeing comes before words. . . . The relation between what we see and what we know is never settled. . . ."

Recently, I reversed a familiar idiom in conversation. By accident, I said, "I'll see it when I *believe* it." But this reversal makes sense to me. Seeing requires belief. Belief informs our vision. To *see* requires we have unity with our subject. In regards to the actual "things" and "stuff" that I notice and later put into writing, of course I'm always eyeing the curious, threatening, or compelling instants I might witness. These come from both urban life and from the natural world. In my memoir, I describe "burying beetles," insects that climb into a mouse or small animal corpse and make it wriggle and twitch so it looks like its come alive. They're also called "marionette" beetles because they can move a dead animal as if it were on puppet strings.

My new novel has a character who works at a naturalist outpost, and there's a lot of specific wildlife description even in the midst of some lawless, low-end crime activity.

Where do your story ideas come from?

I never use the word "idea" to describe my first attraction to a possible story. My first impulse is less an intellectual germ than a psychological or even an emotional tempest or affliction. No, I don't begin with an idea, but I guess I'm more comfortable calling it an "impulse," or even a "compulsion." I write about issues in human relationships, usually male-female. Sometimes it's a family dynamic that explodes into something sinister or someone becomes vulnerable to a dangerous emotional price. There might be sexual tension, a romantic tether that becomes a monkey on their backs. They're troubled by one another. They *come* from trouble.

My fiction is hitched to real persons and real experience. I've met, worked, or even loved people whose situations marked me somehow. Willis, in *Open Water,* was very like someone I once actually knew in Newport, Rhode Island. His mother, in fact, really was Miss Cuba, and his broken arm, that he breaks more than once in subsequent brawls, was a real detail. He was in a cast the whole time I knew him. Of course, fictional characters are transformed from their first origin, or catalyst, and become a wholly new alchemy. I write about people in peril. I'm interested in seeing how people scramble to get out of a hole.

How does a story come to you?

I start with a character who intrigues me. I want to invent a world around him, but he's somehow demanding it. I didn't pull him out of a hat. He comes from all my demons. He takes over the page. He takes form and becomes his own man, almost, but he's that edgy, relentless anxiety made flesh again.

You say you are working on a new novel?

Yes. One of its main characters works for the Park Service, in the [Cape Cod] National Seashore. Part of her job is to rescue stranded sea turtles and piping plovers, but she's got bigger problems. She has a mystery unfolding the size of Texas. Then there's this man—

My landscape and my cultural community is important in my fiction. I think we often pin down writers to their idiosyncratic locales, right? Much of my previous work takes place in Rhode Island, and this is the first time my setting is Land's End, Massachusetts. I'm trying to evoke the odd juxtaposition of wilderness phenomenon and do-gooders with the edgy disenfranchised subculture in a depressed economic setting in off-season Cape Cod. This is a world of lost souls and washashores, loners who collide. But really, it's a comedic, gothic love story.

How do you know if an idea is going to be a novel, a short story, or even a memoir?

I tell students who ask me if they should start a novel, "Hey, you don't start a novel, a novel starts you." Whether it's a story or a novel, it begins with that gnawing or pecking in your gut. A trouble wants out. The only way out is to get on the page. A novel has a premise and particles that can't be wrapped up soon enough to be a story. Stories let go.

How much did you have to invent for the memoir?

I didn't invent events or characters or the chronology of their actions. These were set, and bigger than life. I made great efforts to conform to its authentic map as much as possible.

To create a narrative about what happened I had to construct scenes, dialogue, and employ all the fictional devices one uses to write a story. My sister didn't carry a dictaphone around when she was working as a prostitute in Norfolk, so I had to re-create that world, make it come alive with voices, faces, with the violence, crimes, and survival tactics that I wasn't witness to in person. These scenes were born from everything my sister had told me and from my *reactions,* and from my empathy and anxiety about these events. I also used police reports, hospital records, newspaper clippings, and other materials relating to my sister's disappearance.

We grew up together in the same household so, of course, I knew first-hand the threats she faced when she was still at home, and I saw the un-happiness or defiance that was bred in us, as we related to our compli-cated parents. We reunited when we had our young babies, and those scenes in the book when we are living under one roof, with the threat of her violent ex finding her, were very difficult to relive. As with my fiction, the memoir has importance as a book, not as a personal trial or personal story. The book is its final meaning.

Having published books of poetry, novels, short stories, and a memoir, do you find it difficult to move from one form into another?

I've been writing fiction expressly for more than a decade. I haven't written a book of poems. Yes, I feel a little guilty, not writing poems, like I'm AWOL from the Union Army or something. But I'm more interested in telling stories, and I think a poem does something else. A poem has im-mediacy, an instant destination that can deliver an incredible wallop, a supreme statement. Reading a poem can destroy me like nothing else. Blake especially. I'm always trying to tame and temper my lyric voice in my fiction because it will take over sometimes, and a novel belongs to its characters' voices.

What precipitated the change from poetry to fiction? I understand that with the memoir the content determined the change in form. Is that true of the switch from poetry to fiction?

I have always written fiction. I published books of poems before my first novel, but I'd been writing stories and publishing them in magazines all along. I had applied to graduate programs in both genres, and a few universities accepted me in fiction. But I was accepted in poetry at the University of Iowa, and my undergraduate teachers were Iowa graduates, and they convinced me it was the place to go. So I studied poetry there, but I was writing and reading fiction all along. I don't think graduate school makes any difference. Writers aren't made from those settings, but

I might have published my first novel sooner if I hadn't been working on poems instead.

Your rendering of your sister Karen's voice in *My Sister Life* **is striking and passionate delivered in the first person. It's a vivid and truthful depiction of a young girl with street smarts, innocence, and an unusual wisdom. In these chapters, one feels the writer's efforts to reclaim her sister and pull her up from those lost years.**

When I wrote in Karen's voice I was trying to let her speak for herself because she'd never had the chance to speak up and explain her torment. She had gone missing. Later, when I talked to her about writing the book, she gave me full license to evoke her grim experiences, her pain, and her eventual triumph over so many obstacles. She was very pleased by the story I wrote. I gave her money from my advance because she needed the money; she's still so disenfranchised. I wanted her to have it, but she didn't ask for it. I had to push it on her. She seemed amazed that what had happened to her had mattered so much to me that I would write a book. The book was a document of that bond that she had never recognized fully, how her experience was embedded in me. Her disappearance had changed my life and had actually precipitated my transformation from silent witness to writer. My remedy was to write, hers was to escape. Of course "sister life" means parallel life.

Do you find it difficult as a fiction writer to stay true to bare facts?

What are bare facts? There are no bare facts. A fact has all kinds of reasons to be. A fact has a lot of strings attached. The psychological weight of an event or problem is a subjective as well as an objective perception. When I worked as a corrections officer, I used to have to fill out reports, using a form called a "SOAP"—the acronym for Subjective, Objective, Assessment, and Plan. We had to write up any squabble between inmates or whatever infraction might have happened. The *subjective* recorded what the inmate had said. The *objective* recorded what had happened. The *analysis* was the officer's perception of what happened. The *plan* presented what punitive measures or changes the system would institute against the perpetrator. They believed in behavior modification, and sometimes an inmate would have to wear a baby hat or a rattle looped around his wrist if he'd been acting out.

Bare facts have a lot of input and participants involved. There isn't a straight road to the truth. Fact is often merely *belief,* and we know that belief is a subjective construct. The most common example: Is God fact? Dostoyevsky writes in *Crime and Punishment,* "I like it when people lie. If you lie—you get to the truth. Lying is what makes me a man. Not one truth has ever been reached without first lying fourteen times or so, maybe a hundred and fourteen. . . ."

I think he means that truth is *evoked* from many teeming human perceptions and emotions.

Your work has an affinity with and compassion for fringe populations, or for people in extreme situations. Of course, after reading your memoir, the reader sees your connection to these characters. Is it painful to write about them?

I'm interested in writing about risks people take to attain something that's out of reach—love, safety, family bonds that have broken. There are a lot of walking wounded out there with long journeys left before them. These are my characters, I think. I'm comfortable with them. Again, as I said earlier, I don't choose who I write about. They just surround me.

The art process itself is the painful thing—the day-to-day struggle to deliver the level of writing I want. In James Lord's *A Giacometti Portrait*, he quotes the artist's recognition about the burden of trying to work at our highest level: "The very measure of our creative drive is that we longingly dream of one day being free of it."

I really understand that. I want to be able to stop when at last I'm satisfied with the work on the page, but the thing is, the art spirit never lets you feel you've done as well as you can do tomorrow.

Conducted: November 2000

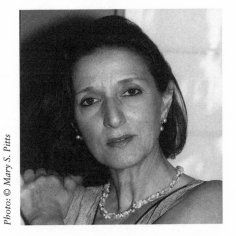

LYNN FREED

Colonizing the Territory of the Fiction

Lynn Freed was born in Durban, South Africa. She came to the United States as a graduate student, receiving a Ph.D. in English literature from Columbia University. She is the author of four novels: *Friends of the Family, Home Ground, The Bungalow*, and *The Mirror*. Her short stories and essays have appeared in *Harper's*, the *New Yorker*, the *Atlantic Monthly*, *Story*, the *New York Times*, and the *Washington Post*, among others. She is a member of the core faculty of the Bennington Writing Seminars and lives in Sonoma, California.*

*Since the time of this interview, Lynn Freed has published *The House of Women*, which was named a "Notable Book of the Year" by the *New York Times Book Review*.

When did you know you wanted to write?

I can't remember ever wanting to write. I just wrote. At first, as a child, and for a number of years into adolescence, I seemed to write partly to show off. I'd write a story or a play—I wrote a lot of plays, mostly awful—and I'd run downstairs to read it to my mother. She was a completely honest critic: harsh and fair. If she came forth with praise, I knew that what I had written wasn't fake.

How did growing up in the theater help shape you as a writer? Did it influence your desire to write?

I didn't grow up in the theater itself, but as the daughter of parents who were in the theater. There is a difference. I could never stand to be onstage, at least not literally. But when you grow up in a family like mine, in which performance, both formal and informal, is prized, you're never quite offstage. As the youngest child, I soon found that the way to attract and keep attention was to perform as myself. Not necessarily the self I was—whatever that was—but the self that I divined they might wish me to be. In this case, it was clown—not an uncommon role for the youngest child in such a family.

How does that sense of drama work in your fiction?

I would consider a "sense of drama" an aspect of timing. Timing is in the ear. To a certain extent, the ear can be trained—reading, writing, performing (on and off the page). But there is also a sort of innate sense of timing that one is born with. My mother had it; my father didn't. He had to be taught by her. Although she was a woman without an apparent sense of humor, her great gift was comic timing. In this, she was faultless. Her dramatic timing was also very good, but the comic timing was brilliant. Anyway, when I would perform, either on or off the page, it was she who would always call me on the timing. "You're off here," she'd say. Or, "Once is enough." Or, "Cut!" Or, occasionally, "Oh, that is good!" One cannot underestimate the value of such a training, and so early. I still feel her voice as I write.

Did your theatrical family support your writing?

There wasn't much to support. Writing was as natural to the life as playing. In addition, we had to write a lot for school, and from a very early age, five or six years old—essays, stories, plays. Every week, there was a story to write for school. My sisters, of course, paid no attention to what I wrote. They were involved in their own tumultuous lives. And my parents worked like mad. When I had a chance, usually before supper, I would take my efforts to my mother.

Is it true that at one time you considered law school?

Yes. I was in the "no future" hell and felt I should secure a means of income so that I could live and write. So I took the LSAT and got into law schools. And then I panicked and withdrew. Sometimes one needs to drive one's self into a situation so horrible that one is forced to make a bold choice. I chose to write, and, more or less, to struggle.

What writers first influenced your work? And whom do you admire now?

I was a sporadic reader as a child. Most of my imaginative time was spent hurling myself out of trees and onto parapets, dancing on the roof, building myself a tree house, racing down steep hills on my bicycle with my feet off the pedals. It is a wonder that I wasn't killed or maimed, but there it is—I wasn't. If I read, I read Enid Blyton, a much maligned, very non-U British children's writer. And I read plays. My parents' study was jammed with plays. I particularly loved Oscar Wilde and Bernard Shaw, read them again and again. And, as I grew a little older, I adored Ibsen, still do. I also became obsessed with their collection of Holocaust books. I looked into that horror, that nightmare, that unthinkable genocide, with real terror. And with fascination too, of course. Could this happen to me? And how? And when? Bear in mind that I was the child of Jewish parents, growing up in South Africa after World War II. Anyway, as I grew more literate—in my teens, really—I memorized huge chunks of Shakespeare. Much of this was required by school, which also required us to memorize chunks of the Bible. I found that I loved having the words by heart, accessible always. If anything got into my blood, it was the wonder of Shakespeare, the wonder of the Psalms. I would prop a book up while I was in the bath and recite a passage in there, over and over, until I had it word perfect. This seemed perfectly normal in a family like mine. No one ever came in to see what the matter was. Or to applaud. God forbid. At about this time, I also fell in love with Jane Austen. I read through all the novels and, thereafter, reread them regularly every few years. What a wonderful training in irony, in timing, in pacing and shaping and characterization! Later still, when I was released from the bondage of academe and was free to read freely again, I found myself falling in love with one book—say, Duras's *The Lover*—and reading it over and over. I fell in love with Alice Munro likewise, with particular stories of hers. Doris Lessing, too—that wonderful intelligence, the brilliant descriptions of Africa, the tie to the land. I have to admit, though, that the Great Gods of Influence—Chekhov, Turgenev, etc.—do not live with me. I have read them; I have admired them; I have put them back on the shelf.

Are there other influences on your work?

I suppose so. But I never think in terms of "influence." If there is a book, or a section of a book, a poem, a line that stays with me, I colonize it, make it my own. Two shelves in my study are filled with such books. When I'm stuck, I reach over and read, to remind myself of what the whole enterprise is supposed to be about.

Reviewers and readers alike comment on your pitch-perfect voice, and this seems to be something that you are especially known for. How did you develop your ability to create such clear voices?

I wrote some very bad, sentimental, predictable short stories while I was a girl. And then a few stories that were better. And then two novels. And only then did I find a voice with which I was comfortable, with which I was at home. This voice came first with a story, "Foreign Student," and then, more strongly, with *Home Ground*. I have no rules for this process of finding one's voice, but I do know that, for me, it took time. Years. A decade or more. In other words, it took a lot of false writing to come upon a voice in which I could tell the truth as I saw and felt it—to know the truth as it was revealed through the writing. This, I suppose, is what authenticity on the page is all about. Again, it is an aspect of ear. So much of training in writing lies in the training of the ear, which is what I emphasize in workshops. What is more difficult to get across in this age of instant gratification is the time it takes, the lifetime it takes, to come to this. If ever.

Let's talk about some of the themes that recur in your work. First, there's the setting in South Africa, your native land. One senses the longing and nostalgia for home, yet the characters so often want to leave South Africa for other lands. Is this aspect of your fiction autobiographical? Can you comment on this?

During my thirty-odd years in America, things have changed. At first, I was so homesick for South Africa that I could not possibly have written about the place. Even after some years, when I was over the worst of it and had begun to write stories placed in South Africa, those stories were sunk by longing and nostalgia. Sentiment and nostalgia are fatal for fiction. One must go into the territory of the imagination with sure feet, not fainting with glorious misery. I had spent my childhood in South Africa both loving the place and, concomitantly, dreaming of getting out. These are not as mutually exclusive as one might imagine. South Africa is an outpost. When I was growing up, it was a quasi-colonial outpost. Anyone who grows up in such a place understands the tremendous need to get out, at least temporarily—to go north to the source, to what is fondly known as the "real world." I have had people from Australia, from Indonesia, from Hawaii, from the

Caribbean, even from the vastness of Alaska—oh, from so many, many places—tell me how they spent their childhoods longing to leave. And then how, in leaving, they put themselves into the bind, so familiar to the expatriate, of belonging nowhere. Of living the life of someone always longing for home and yet not belonging there anymore. It is a bind for which there is no solution. Not only this: it is a bind for which the victim wants no solution. The shuttle itself becomes a form of life. If one is such a person, one needs to leave the place in order to be able to return there. Does this make any sense? One needs to put one's self at a distance. To be perpetually the foreigner. This, it seems to me, is the life of the writer.

Also a theme in your work is the woman striving to define herself amidst a society that wants to place her into a restrictive, traditional role. Your characters are strikingly feminist, frustrated and unhappy with traditional roles, and blazing new ground in their search for fulfillment, adventure, and love. Do you think of your work as feminist?

What is "feminist"? I've never been able to work it out. I never think of things this way, never in the abstract. I write about a character in a situation and take it from there. If there is such a creature as a happy housewife, she would not interest me as a subject of fiction, unless it were being written as satire.

I find the interplay between the races in your South African setting fascinating. These interactions are so different from what you find in the United States. You do not seem to be trying to make a point about racism, or an overt statement against racism. You simply depict it as very real fact of life. Can you comment on this?

This is the writer's job: to write what there is. Making a point about anything will shoot the fiction through the knees. When it comes to South Africa—when it comes to anything, for that matter—I write what I know, what I see, what is there. In the case of *Home Ground* and *The Bungalow*, I was writing about a particular time in South Africa (the fifties through the seventies), from the point of view of white people who, while espousing liberal views, were seldom moved to act upon those views. Which is to say, the vast majority of South African whites, both then and now—although, of course, you'd have a hard time finding any white person in South Africa now who admits to having been anything other than fiercely against apartheid. It's laughable.

The family of which I wrote accepted, as most whites did, the status quo: blacks were the workers, both domestically and industrially. The hierarchy was a given politically, economically, and socially. Whites at the top; blacks at the bottom; Indians and Coloureds in between. Social and economic rigidity is not unique to South Africa—you find this in many countries with large gaps between rich and poor. Many South American countries, for instance. What was unique to South Africa, at least at the time of which I was writing, was codifying this racism into law.

As to Americans, I have seen and heard situations here every bit as casually racist as those I grew up with, every bit as hair-raising as I experienced in South Africa. More so, in fact. I have never understood what Americans have to be so smug about when the great majority have no idea what goes on across the road, across the tracks. And don't care either—proclamations to the contrary notwithstanding.

How do you handle recognizable characters in your fiction, when what you write about them may expose, betray, or hurt them?

When I write, I seem to be subject to the happy delusion that what I am writing will never see its way into print. In other words, I forget completely about the reader. (If I do happen to consider, even vaguely, who might read what I am writing, I shut down and go shopping.) What is more, there is a sort of glee in the exposure of fiction, in getting it right. In a sense, all fiction is revenge, all fiction is betrayal. In some of my novels, it is quite clear that certain characters are based on actual people—my parents, for instance. The odd thing is that one never knows who will be offended. With my parents, even though the portraits seemed to offend some of their friends, both my mother and my father adored seeing themselves in print. They roared with laughter. What is more, they took the fiction literally. In *Home Ground,* for instance, the parents are in the theater, but they also own a physical theater. My own parents did not; they staged their productions in a variety of theaters. Well, some years after it was published, I was in South Africa, visiting. We were having drinks in the study one evening, and my mother, quite mellow on her second scotch, turned to my father and said, "Pity we had to sell the theater, isn't it?" I have endless such stories. If you get the fiction right, people will believe it. The same goes for completely fictional characters. I am always asked on whom this or that character was based. I place this sort of curiosity in the camp of gossip.

What I am saying, I suppose, is that you write as if everyone is dead. Then you face the music. I don't know any other way to keep the teeth sharp and the spirit alive.

You stated once that the real world of your childhood—a large subtropical port on the Indian Ocean, with beaches and bush and sugarcane and steaming heat, a strict Anglican girls' school, massive family gatherings on Friday nights and Jewish holidays, and then your parents' theater

world—did not exist in literature available to you and that you didn't think it should. How did you make the leap from that line of thinking to actually creating fiction that inhabits that world?

I grew up in an ex-British colony, on British literature, with the idea that Britain was the source of all things worthy in the world of letters. By the same token, things South African were considered decidedly second-rate. There were a few exceptions, of course—Laurens van der Post, Olive Schreiner. But, in the main, we looked north for received literature, and it seemed right and good to do so.

When I began to write real stories myself, I ventured tentatively into home territory, but then, as I said before, the work was very poor, very weighed down by the predictable and the worthy. So I struck out and wrote two novels with an American cast—novels about women breaking out of the domestic mold. My first novel was in galleys when, one evening, I was having dinner with Gail Godwin. I was telling her about my family, my background. Then she asked whether I had written about them, and when I said no, she said, "Well, for God's sake!" So home I went and began *Home Ground*. One finds permission to write when one is ready to receive it, I suppose.

This brings us to the issue of authorial invisibility. In writing material that takes place in your hometown, in a family similar to your own, how do you, the author, keep yourself out of the picture?

I don't. I'm in every picture. But I'm in disguise.

How does your writing relate to your sense of home? I'm particularly interested in this because you are a person who writes away from her home of origin, and in fact travels quite a bit to do her writing. Maybe I should start by asking you, Where is home?

Home is an idea, and it is past tense. I am someone who makes a home out of a hotel room. The minute I arrive, I start arranging things to make the place my own. I have felt at home on a dhow on the Nile, and I have not felt at home in a house in which I lived in San Francisco for fourteen years. There is something beyond reason in the places that resonate. I am more likely, for instance, to feel at home with the sound and sight of the sea than in the most idyllic setting inland—which is where I happen to live now. I long for the sea. Why don't I just pack up and move? There is a question I can't seem to answer. Ennui, I suppose.

There is a sense of loneliness, sometimes accompanied by a distance from home, that pervades your characters—loneliness even when surrounded by family.

To my mind, loneliness is at the heart of the human condition. Being at a distance from home is only part of this. There is also the distance from those we love, and from those among whom we live and work. Not to mention the distance from childhood itself, the distance from the places of childhood. Home is an enormous concept. I always think of Carson McCullers saying, "I must go home periodically to renew my sense of horror." I love that.

You've said that travel is part of your writing life, that estrangement is a necessary ingredient to your work because it gives you the perspective of another world from which to examine your own. Can you say more about this?

I am a natural foreigner. I find home all over the place, and not always where I expect to. I suppose travel, for me, is a sort of search for home. And also for romance. And also for hope. When one travels, one has a sense of living in the moment.

For just over a decade, I traveled obsessively, and to wonderfully remote places. Or at least they were then. Now I travel a lot to teach and so forth, and it has become more of a Greyhound experience.

I'm interested to know about your writing process. When you're in the throes of a novel, what is your writing schedule like?

I'm the last one who should be talking of writing habits. I'm haphazard. I write, but I also teach. I have friends I love to see. And I have a passion for travel. All of which is to say that I write in furious surges, and then I take a month or months off. When I'm in the middle of a novel, however, I write all the time. When I'm inching in, starting up, I'm best in the afternoons. Mornings I pretend to write. I write letters and e-mail, I fiddle with what I've written the day before. But the real time for writing, for me, is the late afternoon and evening. This is not the best way to run one's life if there's anyone else in it. But there it is. I have nothing but envy for those who wake up, don't even clean their teeth, and settle into the writing. Not me, not at all. I'm hopeless.

How many revisions will you do for a novel?

It depends. My first two novels were written by hand, with a pencil, and then typed. (The second was never published; *Home Ground* was the third novel I wrote). This limits the possibilities. There are just so many times that one can retype. And it shows. The next two novels were endlessly revised, endlessly. With a computer, there's no counting. But I can only edit on the page, so I would print and edit, put in the corrections, print and edit. And so forth. I am quite obsessional and compulsive, so the process never seems to have a bottom to it. I'll reprint an entire novel if one preposition seems out of place. *The Mirror* was another matter. One rewrite and it was done. I wrote that novel in a trance.

What are the tasks of those final versions?

A final revision is only final because you have a deadline and can take no more time over it. Or because you are so sick of it that any more tampering would produce diminishing returns. There are no rules.

Where do your novel ideas come from? Do you start with a voice, a situation, an image?

I start precisely with those. Where do they come from? I suppose the desire, the need to create the life on the page, the world. And I always have a mad desire to be surprised, and, of course, to laugh. Not that one can intend these things; just that the expectation is there.

When you begin a novel, do you have any idea of the shape or where it's going?

I may have an idea of where I think it will go, but usually in the writing it does not go there. Or it goes beyond. Intention can kill fiction, certainly for me. As soon as I find myself saying, I want this character to accomplish this, to go here, to go there, I know I've lost the piece. I should just shut down and go for a walk.

How about short stories?

They do indeed start from a character in a situation. How to find the way into that situation, how to begin the story—that is the labor. Some emerge from failed beginnings of novels. Some are just written. There are myriad paths to Buddha.

Is the revision process for short stories the same as for novels?

The same and worse. I can go through a ream or two of paper to produce one eight-page story. In a short story, every word must count. Every word.

I recently enjoyed a short short you published in the *Atlantic Monthly* called "The Lovely, Lovely." Could you talk about the form of the short short and what you're trying to achieve in that small space of narrative?

I never start out thinking "short." I just follow the trajectory of the piece and then, suddenly, it ends. It might happen to be short, as in "The Lovely, Lovely," or it might run on and on. Again, this is a matter of ear, and also of something intangible—the right length for the piece at hand, which is, I suppose, the same thing. "The Lovely, Lovely" was written to that last stage of life, when the layers—past, present, future—are fused and confused into a sort of hum. Like words and memories themselves, the piece comes and goes in a few moments. A few pages.

The sense of place—the landscape, the village, the buildings, the social workings—in your novels and stories is remarkable. Are you aware of careful drawing, or do these places rise before you like characters?

When the writing comes properly, the place is there, available to me. If I have to strain to know a place, I'm in the wrong fiction. I'm always saying to students that one must colonize the territory of the fiction. It is the only metaphor that seems to carry with it the presumptuousness of fiction, the sense of making a place one's own. In this case, I mean it literally. One has to make it one's own, so that, in a way, it is more than real; it is assumed.

Richard Ford has said that place is yet another character in your story or novel. Do you agree with this?

No. There is place, and there are characters in the place. Without place, of course, there could be no story, no life, no anything. But place is the ground of the fiction. It is there before the fiction, and after the fiction is over. And it is unchanged. It is the given.

In reading through your novels, starting with *Heart Change [Friends of the Family,]* *Home Ground*, then moving on through *The Bungalow* and *The Mirror,* one can see the development of your craft. You've often referred to *Heart Change* as a "teething novel." How would you describe the others in terms of what you struggled with or sought to develop by way of craft?

I never think of craft. I try not to teach it either. I don't believe that craft creates the writer. Practice does. When I say "teething novel," I mean that there are lapses of ear in there. There are riffs that go on too long. And also quite a bit of what I refer to, thanks to Natalia Ginzburg, as "singing"—prose that takes off into song. With the later novels, I fell more comfortably into my own voice. And my timing was more precise, more crisp. But the real thing that makes a novel live is something far beyond craft—it's something that is not codifiable. It is the life that comes with the novel, as the novel is being written. All the craft in the world cannot hide a novel that doesn't want to be written. I've written both types, and I won't say which is which.

In addition to your novels, short stories, and short shorts, you've pub-

lished essays in newspapers and magazines. **Where do you get your essay ideas?**

Hard to say. Usually either something that gets under my skin—I love being cantankerous—or something that I adore, often a place. The danger of doing too much of such work is that one can find oneself writing to the word constraints—a 1,500 or 2,500 word length, for instance. One begins to feel all work in such lengths, such shapes. It can be dangerous. It can get into the rhythm of the blood.

I know that you spend a lot of time at writers' retreats, such as Yaddo. How do these residencies help you?

There is the blessing of peace in a retreat that happens to suit my fraught nature. I arrive in a heaven like Yaddo, and I sink immediately in a sort of peace from life that I seem to be able to find nowhere else. It has something to do with the way the spirit settles there, away from the noise of my life. But there is also the fact that one is both left alone and taken care of. There are the days in silence, to work, and then the evenings in the company of others who have been working. It is magic. I often write more there in a month than I do otherwise in six months, or more.

What are you working on now?

A novel. Chained by the ankle.

Conducted: June 2000

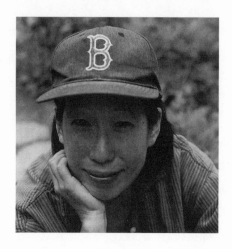

GISH JEN

Writing off into the Darkness

Gish Jen grew up in Scarsdale, New York, and graduated from the Iowa Writers' Workshop. Her work has appeared in the *New Yorker,* the *Atlantic Monthly,* and *The Best American Short Stories of the Century*. The author of two novels, *Typical American* and *Mona in the Promised Land,* as well as a collection of stories, *Who's Irish?* she lives in Massachusetts with her husband and two children and is currently teaching at Harvard.

How did you get started writing?

When I was in college I took a class with Robert Fitzgerald, the translator, in prosody. Today, it seems to me that every English major should have to take this class. Fitzgerald said at the beginning of the semester that there was going to be a weekly exercise; being an English major, I thought that he meant a paper. It turned out that he meant a weekly exercise in verse. I thought I'd try the class and, if I didn't like it, I'd drop it. But I wrote my first poem in Catullan hendecasyllables, and immediately I loved it. I remember saying to a friend that if I could do this every day for the rest of my life, I would.

But I am the child of immigrants; it never occurred to me that I could try to be a poet. I didn't know any poets. Also, my parents had come from China, where they'd seen a lot of upheaval. First their country was invaded by the Japanese, then there was a world war. They ended up in America quite by accident. I had internalized all of their desire for security.

I was a premed student when Fitzgerald pulled me aside at the end of a class and asked me why I was premed. I can't imagine what I said, given that there was no reasonable explanation, and I had just gotten a C in chemistry. He said that I should think about being a writer, and that if I wasn't going to be a writer, I should go into publishing. Sure enough, when I graduated, he did get me my first job, which was in publishing at Doubleday. He called up Pike Johnson, the managing editor at the time, and that was that.

Once I was in publishing, I did, at Doubleday's expense, take a course in writing at the New School. And later I went to business school for a year at Stanford, because I knew they had a good writing program. You may gather from this how confused I was at the time. I immediately realized when I got to Stanford that I had no interest in business, that I was only interested in writing. I spent the entire year taking writing classes. I also read over a hundred novels. Who knows how I managed to pass business school? Anyway, I didn't go back for my second year. Instead, I went to China, and when I came back I went to the Iowa Writers' Workshop.

How do your novel and story ideas come to you?

They come in many different ways. Often, I identify what I like to think of as a nerve in myself—a nerve that I've developed as a result of my contact with the world—and I try to follow that nerve. The work is not autobiographical, exactly. The things that happen have not happened to me, but the nerve, or the nature of the conflict, is often something with which I am familiar. I write this way partly because I was very conflicted for a long time about being engaged in an activity that seemed to me so selfish. I found this a way of producing work that was both personally compelling and relevant to other people.

How do you know when an idea is worth pursuing?
My friend Martha Collins used to say that she'd write about the forbidden. When you can hear the bells going off, you're on the right track.

What is your process like for working on a novel?
I write my novels much in the same way that I write my short stories, which is to say intuitively. With both, I write off into the darkness and don't know where I'm going until I get to my end. I know a lot of people don't write novels that way. When I was writing my first novel, it seemed that about once a month I'd go to a reading, and there would be some famous writer up there who would say that with a novel, it's a good idea to have some sort of a plan. I'd think, *Oh my god, I don't have a plan!* In fact, it's a very nerve-wracking way to write. I swore after I finished *Typical American* that I'd never do it again, but then I wrote *Mona in the Promised Land* in the same way, and now I'm writing a third novel in the same way.

That said, there is a fair amount of analytical thinking that goes on. I write off into the darkness, but then I spend time reading over what I've written and trying to understand it. I try to understand why I wrote it, and where it might be going, and whether in fact I'm writing more than one story, and whether that's okay.

What writers have influenced your work, and who do you admire now?
I admire more writers than I can name. Certainly Grace Paley has been an enormous influence on me, I think because I struggled so much with the question of what writing has to do with the world. Her humor, her humanity, her interest in society were very big influences on me. Her honesty and directness, too. But there have been a lot of other people. I've read a lot of Alice Munro. I've looked to Jamaica Kincaid for inspiration. She's very, very "bad." Whenever I hesitate to be bad, I think of Jamaica and I go ahead.

There is a lot of humor in your work, even in the face of tragedy. Where does your comic outlook come from?
I have to say that I think that it's genetic. I say that because my father has a tremendous sense of humor, and I see now that my children do, too. My daughter started with the humor really early. Even when she was eighteen months she would stick her bum right in my face when I was trying to change her diaper and say, "Ta da!" and start laughing.

You were at the Iowa Writers' Workshop before multiculturalism became a trend in American literature. Were you concerned at that time about how your work would be received?

It was commonly understood at the time that people like me, i.e., Chinese-American people, would never be published in mainstream publications. People now say that it was obvious that multiculturalism was right around the corner. But it wasn't, and that was okay. Most people were not going to be in the *New Yorker*. It wasn't what we were doing. It's not like I carried it around like this big wound. At the same time, multiculturalism was a gift.

What were your early attempts at publication like? When did you start to break through?

I was very lucky from very early on. My first publication was a piece I'd written for the Raymond Carver Write Alike contest in Barry Hannah's class my first year at Iowa. He had this contest, and we were all supposed to write something in the manner of Raymond Carver. All the women in the class were sure that a woman would never win, so we signed our stories Raymond Carver. I still remember the shock I felt when Barry held up these pages and asked, "Now who wrote this?" There were a full three seconds before I realized that I was going to have to raise my hand. That story became my first published piece. The *Iowa Review* took it.

You are such a quintessentially American writer in that you turn what it means to be American on its head and redefine it altogether. You first did this in *Typical American,* where you depict the Chang family pursuing the American dream and struggling with homesickness, assimilation, racism, and greed. When you're writing, are you aware of making these points, or do they rise out of character?

They rise out of character, and I bring it up a little bit. That would be the analytical part. I try to stay ahead of the critics, and see what I wrote myself. That said, no novel can be written by sitting down and saying, "Now I'm going to turn ideas about the American dream on their head." You better have a lot of cappuccino before you start that one. I write about these nerves, and some of these nerves have to do with how American I am. The whole question of whether an Asian-American is an American or a foreigner has been with me my whole life, even after *Who's Irish?* came out.

Does it make you angry?

I have to say that I mostly think it's ridiculous. It's so ridiculous that it's hard to be angry. It'd be like being angry at a child. The level of ignorance can be so unbelievable, but I see it as a kind of amiable irritant. When *Who's Irish?* came out, the first line of one of my reviews referred to the collection as a series of stories about America as seen by foreigners. I thought, this is 1999! What can you do but laugh? If I didn't feel the weight of the culture and educated people behind me, I'm sure I'd be furious, but that's not the case.

When I wrote *Typical American,* I was aware that to call a book about Chinese-Americans *Typical American* was provocative, and that felt good. I don't know if that's anger, or what that is. It's a desire to set something straight at some level, sure, and there's a measure of defiance in it. The world is full of nonsense; if you can use it more than it uses you, for a writer, it's a gift.

Typical American is told in the third-person personal point of view looking over the shoulder of Ralph Chang. How did you decide on this point of view?

I think that because people were so convinced that I must be writing immigrant autobiography, I instinctively shied away from first person.

Do you find it more or less difficult to inhabit characters of the opposite sex? Are there inherent challenges in this?

I don't find it difficult.

Ralph's assimilation begins with his renaming from Y. Fang Chang to the American Ralph Chang by a secretary at the Foreign Student Affairs Office. While this is a common experience for many immigrants, it's ironic that upon entrance into America, where people hope to find a new freedom, they must first give away an essential part of themselves—their name!

There are many ironies in this book, and that certainly is one of them. I have to say that Ralph finds, ironically, a kind of freedom in his new name. For many people the new name might not be freeing, but in Ralph's case it is. One of the many things that, in hindsight, I was trying to do was to complicate the immigrant story. There isn't one story; there are millions of stories. Some people come and find restriction here, and some people come and find liberty. Sometimes that liberty is what we think it is, and sometimes it's a totally different kind of liberty. For Ralph, it's liberty from his family. "Goodbye, Dad!" That was probably 90 percent of it for him.

You describe that point in the immigration experience at which Ralph is no longer Chinese, and not yet an American. Ralph ". . . refused to be

made an American citizen. He thumbed his nose at the relief act meant to help him, as though to claim his home was China was to make China indeed his home. And wasn't it still? Even if his place in it was fading like a picture hung too long in a barbershop—even if he didn't know where his family was anymore?" There seems to be resistance to claim a home in either China or America.

That's pretty common, don't you think? We often imagine that everybody comes here and is dying to become American. I actually think that most people are not dying to become American, even the ones who are not unhappy to be partaking of the American feast, and that's not everyone either. We don't read that much about the people who go home, and that's a lot of people. As for the ones who stay here, a lot of them are quite ambivalent for a long time, if not forever.

In *Typical American*, the Changs eventually adopt the culture and values that they originally despised. Do you think this is an inevitable result of assimilation?

One irony of *Typical American* is that "typical American" is something they call other people, but by the end of the novel, they are the kind of people that others might call "typical American." It's not like they've whole-hog adopted every facet of American culture. They've simply availed themselves of the freedom here in a way that makes them think hard about who they are now; they spend much more time thinking about their identities than they would have if they'd stayed in China.

Typical American begins, "It's an American story: . . ." And yet, many critics labeled you as an Asian-American writer, which seems to me reductive. In fact, your work seeks to redefine what it means to be American. Was *Mona in the Promised Land* written in any way as a response to those early classifications?

I suppose I wanted to complicate people's ideas about ethnicity in general, and how better to do that than to write about the invention of ethnicity?

I do struggle with the Asian-American thing. I don't mind it being used as a description of me, but I do mind it being used as a definition of me. Frank McCourt is an Irish-American writer who writes about Irish things. And yet sometimes he's "Irish-American writer Frank McCourt," and sometimes he's simply "writer Frank McCourt," or more often "bestselling writer Frank McCourt." The term "Irish-American" is somehow detachable from "writer" in a way that "Asian-American" is not.

That said, I'm happy to report that in many places now I am seen as someone who writes about the American dream.

In this novel you expand your territory from the Chinese immigrant experience in *Typical American* to explore a larger canvas of characters with a variety of backgrounds including WASP, Jewish, African-American, and Chinese immigrants. How do you discover and define your territory as a writer?

I write about whatever I'm interested in. I didn't for a minute wonder if I had the right to write about other groups, but I did think I needed to do my homework if I was going to. I knew that if I got one thing wrong, I would get called on it. But that's as it should be. I think anyone writing about anything should get it all right.

As *Mona in the Promised Land* progresses, each character becomes less fixed in her or his cultural identity. Mona even converts to Judaism, and her friends call her Changowitz. What interests you about the fluidity of ethnic or cultural identity?

It is a kind of reclaiming of a reality that threatens to be lost. There is a way in which someone like me is always in danger of being frozen into an ethnic mold. I think the fact that people find the book so funny is proof that it is a challenge to ideas that are held right now in our culture. Is an Irish-American turning Jewish funny? But for a Chinese-American to turn Jewish, now that's funny!

You also capture a range of voices and inflections from New York Jewish to African-American to Chinese-American with apparent ease. Are there any pitfalls to watch for in rendering these voices?

You try to listen to the way that people really talk. If you do, it's not that complicated. I have no advice to the young writer, other than to *pay attention.*

The title story of *Who's Irish?* is narrated in pidgin English by a Chinese grandmother. Did you have any concerns about writing a story in this voice?

People have suggested that the way to gain freedom as a writer is to use a pseudonym, but for the ethnic writer, freedom actually comes with having a name and creating your own context. If I had written that story twenty years ago and sent it to the The New Yorker, I guarantee that I would've gotten a little slip back saying "please try again when your English is better." I don't think they would've assumed the voice was artifice. Today they get the story and it says Gish Jen on it, and they know I speak English.

I've seen this again and again. If I didn't have a name of some sort, I wouldn't have been able to publish a book called *Who's Irish?* with no subtitle. As it was, nobody at my publishing house said we have to subtitle this "Stories about Asian-Americans."

One of my greatest satisfactions as a writer has been earning myself a context different than the one supplied to me by our culture.

You depict this grandmother's racism with clarity, humor, and sensitivity. For example, "Even the black people doing better these days, some of them live so fancy, you'd be surprised. Why the Shea family have so much trouble? They are white people, they speak English. When I come to this country, I have no money and do not speak English. But my husband and I own our restaurant before he die. Free and clear, no mortgage. Of course, I understand I am just lucky, come from a country where the food is popular all over the world. I understand it is not the Shea family's fault they come from a country where everything is boiled." This seems a fine line to walk for any writer, yet you do it beautifully and without offense.

This is related to that desire to write about things that are hard. I don't know why it is that I seem to be able to keep my balance through difficult terrain. I don't know exactly why it is either that I'm attracted to this terrain. But there it is. I am attracted to it, and I haven't totally screwed up yet.

In this short-story collection, you continue to explore the friction of assimilation through a variety of characters of Irish and Chinese backgrounds. In the title story, you explore the difficulties between generations, as well as cultures, and in the end, the two grandmothers who share the same generation and immigrant experience wind up together in spite of their different backgrounds, rather than the grandmother winding up with her daughter. Comment?

I think it is one of the great gifts of America that a lot of the old attitudes are remade. That happens in *Mona in the Promised Land,* too. The mother begins being very anti-Japanese, but once a Japanese woman actually drives up on her lawn, a lot of the prejudice falls away. She doesn't have the heart to actually start yelling at the lady in person. Immigrants bring their ethnic grudges with them, but a lot of that stuff tends to lose its force.

You have two more stories about the Changs narrated this time by Callie. Can readers expect to encounter the Changs again in future works?

Never say never, but I'm not writing about them now. I've completely forgotten about them. I don't know why.

What are you working on now?

A new novel, not about the Chang family.

Conducted: October 2001

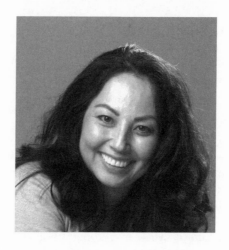

NORA OKJA KELLER

Trying to Inhabit a Soul

Nora Okja Keller was born in Seoul, Korea, and grew up in Hawaii, where she attended the University of Hawaii. In 1995 she received the Pushcart Prize for a short story, "Mother Tongue," which later became a part of *Comfort Woman,* her first novel and winner of a 1998 American Book Award. *Fox Girl* is her recently published second novel.

How did you get started writing fiction?
I had always been writing since I was in elementary school, doing little poems or stories that I would illustrate myself! I've been writing for as long as I can remember, but I never thought that I would do it for a career, or that I would become an author and write for a living. That wasn't a part of my family life. No one in my community was writing; no one that I knew personally was doing any sort of writing.

How did you come to writing professionally?
Even though I'd written as a hobby over the years, it was only after I wrote *Comfort Woman* that I realized writing could be my profession. I started writing *Comfort Woman* in 1993 after I heard a talk given by a former comfort woman at a human rights symposium. Up until then I'd only written short stories. I told a writer friend of mine that the comfort woman issue was a really important topic that the whole nation, the whole world, should be aware of. I told her that she should write the story. I tried to push it off, but she turned it back on me and said that I was Korean and this story was part of my history, and that I should write it. I resisted because I didn't think I was up to the task of writing something so big in scope and emotion. That talk was the first time I'd ever heard about comfort women and the history of it, and I felt that if I couldn't even express how I felt after hearing about their experience, how would I write about it? But the story stayed with me and haunted me. A few months later, I got up one night and started making notes and sketching out a story. I wrote a story called "Mother Tongue," which eventually turned into chapter 2 of the novel. Still, I didn't think of doing anything more. I didn't think of my project as a novel. If I'd thought of it as a novel, I wouldn't have been able to do it. I would have been paralyzed.

The title of your book, *Comfort Woman*, holds a sad irony, that the Japanese soldiers could turn "comfort" into something ugly and destructive.
I really struggled with even using the term "comfort women," because it was a term given by the Japanese soldiers to these women. As you said, it's so horribly ironic to us, but to the soldiers it wasn't. I was concerned that if I used the term, I'd be validating the term given to them, but I wanted to underscore the irony and expand the idea of comfort beyond the time of the war to the relationship between the mother and the daughter.

So how did you approach it?
I approached it like I was writing short stories. I wrote all these stories from Akiko's point of view. I had about seven short stories, and I thought maybe there was a possibility of doing a collection of stories, something

larger, but I still would not use the word "novel." At the point where I wanted to expand it, I realized that I needed another access point. Everything from Akiko's point of view was emotionally heavy, and also set in that one particular time. I thought of bringing in the daughter to give an emotional time-out to the reader, and to myself in writing it. Beccah brings the story more up to date and gives an American, present-day viewpoint that helps readers access her mother's story. I wrote short stories in Beccah's voice, and when I had an equal number of stories in both voices, I had started looking at how to put it together. I took all of Akiko's stories in one row, and put Beccah's stories in a row right below. I started piecing the chapters together like a puzzle, shuffling and putting it together. So it's not chronological in terms of how I wrote it, but I made a different sort of pattern by weaving the voices.

Once you put it together, did you have to splice and bridge the pieces in places to make it flow?

Yes. Once I put it together I could see an arc that went through the whole story, but there were gaps that I had to fill in to make it work. I did this very visually, with papers and chapters on the floor so that the gaps were actually visual. I'd type notes on a blank piece of paper to fill the gap, and then later write the missing pieces. I can look at my chapters now and see that the earlier chapters have the form of a story—they're self-contained and stand on their own. Then I can look at the other bridge chapters and see how they were written to link things together. Those chapters are more open-ended.

What did you do, and what do you continue to do, to develop and deepen your craft?

I read. I don't read while I write, but otherwise I read a lot. I consider reading the best way to learn how to write, reading with awareness and consciousness of the choices an author makes to bring a character to life or to brighten dialogue. I don't think you can be a good writer without being an avid reader. I've had students say that they want to write, but they're not really interested in reading, which is just bizarre to me.

Who are some of the writers who've influenced you, and who do you admire now?

I always say Maxine Hong Kingston because she was the first Asian-American writer who I read. I had a strong background in American literature, but to me, up until that point, American literature meant Steinbeck, Hemingway, and Faulkner, these great men. I admired them and enjoyed them, but never felt a personal connection. I think that's another reason that I never considered writing as a profession: the models I had up until that point didn't fit my life or my style at all. It wasn't until I read *Woman Warrior* by Maxine Hong Kingston that a little light went on. Here was someone with a similar experience growing up, and she was writing about it from a very ethnic perspective. It was amazing that people were writing about this experience, and also that people were reading it! Once I read her work, I became very hungry to read other works by Asian-Americans.

What did you find?

At that time, I took an Asian-American literature course, which at that time meant Japanese-American or Chinese-American. We read Maxine Hong Kingston, Frank Chin, Joy Kogawa, Lawson Inada, but there were still no Korean-American authors. I remember asking my professor if there were any Korean-American writers, and she just said no. Then she remembered a writer who was half Korean and half Chinese, and I was so excited. I was trying to find literary mothers and fathers whom I could draw on for my own work. Now there are so many people reclaiming and studying Asian-American writing over the past hundred years, it seems a given that there was a whole legacy, generations of Asian-Americans— not just Chinese- and Japanese- but Filipino- and Korean-Americans too—writing as soon as they set foot in this country, but back then it was a real struggle to find those role models.

Where did you conduct research about the war and the recreation camps?

I tried to do as much research as I could for both novels. For *Comfort Woman* there was very little written material. It was just in the early nineties that women started speaking out about their experience. Forty years later they started feeling that they were at the end of their lives and needed to bear witness for all of the women who didn't survive the war, to speak out before it was too late. Even hearing that was powerfully moving to me.

Once I realized that I was going to write a book—even though I didn't use that term—I tried to look things up and found that there was hardly anything written in English. I contacted one of the professors at the University of Hawaii who helped to organize the human rights symposium where I heard Kim Ju Hwang speak. She gave me some documents that she had translated from Korean into English. These documents verified that there were in fact comfort camps, and included a letter from former comfort women to the Japanese government demanding reparation. There was nothing that provided details as to what life was like in the camps themselves.

At a certain point, I had some materials from which I could build a framework based on history and research. Then came the scary part: I had to make that imaginative leap and try to put myself in this framework and imagine what life was like for these women on a daily basis. That was scary because there was so little material from which to build that foundation. I remember right before *Comfort Woman* was released, George Hicks's book *Comfort Women* was published. This is a collection of about a hundred oral testimonials from comfort women primarily from Korea but also from the Philippines, Indonesia, even some Dutch women who were taken into these camps. I was so nervous when that book came out because I kept thinking, What if I imagined everything in my book wrong? I ran down to the bookstore and pulled George Hicks's book off the shelf, and I was flipping and reading through it with amazement and relief, thinking, This is what happened to Akiko. It really validates the strength of the imagination and empathy, and also how when you write you connect to something so much larger than yourself.

Were there challenges you encountered writing from two narrators' perspectives?
Not really, because I wrote all of Akiko's chapters first. Also, I thought of the book as a dialogue between the mother and daughter, but the mother's voice comes first. Beccah's life and her reaction is a response to her mother. Even though she doesn't know the secrets of her mother's past, she's responding to how her mother raises her because of that past. It was important for me to get Akiko's experience down first. Beccah came later, with a very Americanized viewpoint. I saw them as very, very different people. Also, Akiko's chapters are more dreamlike, while Beccah is much more grounded in the physical world.

In addition to shifting between the two women's voices, you frequently move back and forth in time, not only between chapters, but also within each chapter. Beccah lives in contemporary America but recalls her childhood with her mother, while Akiko recalls her life as a "comfort woman" and dreams back even further to recall the lives of her ancestors. Was it difficult to make these transitions work for the reader and to manage it all within the context of the novel?
No. I trust the reader will be smart enough to go with the time shifts because really, that's how we all think. Everything is layered upon our daily life. We live in the present, but also part of us lives in the past as well. Naturally, there's always that time shift going on with everyone. What *was* difficult for me was when I didn't trust the reader. In an earlier draft I thought of putting in the dates, which became incredibly confus-

ing and intrusive. Especially with Akiko, where the narrative is more dreamlike and she's flowing in and out of time, in and out of the spiritual and physical world, I couldn't have these markers on every page stating the date.

There is something seamless about how you're able to pull it off. The reader knows that the time is changing without being told, which is beautiful because it does replicate how we have our own memories.
     Thank you. I did try to replicate how memory works, and especially in Akiko's chapters, I was very conscious of how memories are evoked.

"The baby I could keep came when I was already dead. I was twelve when I was murdered, fourteen when I looked into the Yalu River and, finding no face looking back at me, knew that I was dead." Akiko, in order to save herself, kills herself, or suffers what would now be called a disassociative reaction, killing off Induk to become Akiko, the comfort girl working in the camp. Only by leaving Induk behind, by casting her into the world of spirits, can she survive. How did you come to this?
     It's not like I went to a psychology book and looked up posttraumatic stress syndrome, although some psychologists who read the book wrote to me and said that the story mirrored exactly a typical posttraumatic reaction. The choice was intuitive for me. When I reflect back on it, I can look at two specific things. One is how many people who've experienced trauma talk about how they felt separated from themselves, their body and their consciousness split. So, I knew that was part of what happened in very traumatic situations, but I didn't think about it as I was writing. Second, years before I was working on *Comfort Woman,* I had been interested in the tradition of shamanism in Korea, which is a very woman-centered tradition. In it, to become a shaman, one of the things that a woman must go through is a split between body and spirit. I did think about this in the writing, because later, as Akiko becomes a shaman, I wanted those chapters after she left the camp to mirror the experience of the traditional Korean shaman, and often there is that split between body and self or consciousness.
     Ultimately, I can say that this was part of the background, and these are some of the things that I see reflected in the work now. But in the writing of it, I'm in the imaginative world. I'm not planning the psychology. I'm trying to inhabit her soul.

It's interesting that psychologists told you that Akiko's response was psychologically accurate given her experience. Your ability to empathize and enter into the character and capture her humanity and be truly

present is reflected in your accuracy. It's as though you lived through her experience and had the same reaction that any person in that experience would have.

My main goal with both novels was not to give a political message or to depict the history, which are both important, and I realize that, but each time I went into a story it was to get into the character's heart and her spirit and to write directly from her voice.

Your narrators, especially Akiko, drift between dreams and reality, between memory and awareness, between insanity and sanity, between the spirit world and the mortal world. These transitions are so deftly woven into the fabric of the narrative that I'm wondering if you had any difficulties working them in or in keeping the narrative grounded?

These states flowed in much the same way that time and memory flowed through the novel with her chapters. It's almost a dream state, where the boundaries between time are shifted or not so marked. The same holds true with the spirit or the physical world. One thing that helped was that Beccah gave another way to see her mother and her mother's story. Some readers have said that they only wanted to hear Akiko's story, but I think Beccah is critical in helping the reader gain some perspective on Akiko. Otherwise, it would be easier to get lost in Akiko's mind and to lose track of what was going on. After the Akiko chapters, we have Beccah giving some reflection. Whether or not we agree with her interpretation, it gives us the perspective of an outside mind looking at Akiko. Akiko's chapters are so internal readers could get lost in there. Also, that's what daughters do; they mirror the mother's experience.

Did you have to research the spirit names and stories, or the rituals that Akiko carries out throughout Beccah-san's childhood?

The spirits that Akiko invokes—like the birth grandmother that Akiko later fuses with Induk from the camp—are traditional figures from Korean shamanism. I did research those spirits and their personalities, as well as the rituals involved. But shamanism is something that I've long been interested in. The women who become shamans are outrageous and bold in ways that women in Korea are not usually allowed to be. I've heard that even today the president of Korea will consult shamans, and for the most sought-after shaman, you have to make an appointment a year and a half in advance. But at the same time that they have this power, they're considered outcasts. It's very odd. They hold a very important place in society, but no mother would want her daughter to become a shaman.

The role of story is very important in the lives of Akiko and Beccah. Story is a way to pass down experience and knowledge, superstition and tradition, as well as a way to cover up painful truths about the past, or a way to assuage fear and anger and grief, or a way to understand one's life. What did you want to show about the importance of telling stories?

Well, that's exactly it. Stories are to teach and to warn, not just enjoyment. They impart important cultural values as well. Storytelling was such an important part of my growing up. My mother and older sister and brother always told stories about Korea as well as folktales and fables. I grew up loving them. All of these interests, in shamanism, stories, and history, come through when I sit down to write.

Are the stories that you include actual Korean folktales?

They're based on real stories, yes. In *Comfort Woman,* the frogs and toads represent particular things in stories, like rebirth and fertility, just as they do in Korean myths. Then, of course, in *Fox Girl* the story of the fox runs throughout the novel. I enjoy playing with the different versions of stories, and the different perspectives of stories, and how a story can twist with just a change in perspective. With *Fox Girl,* I did a little bit more tweaking with the traditional Korean fox story. One version I made up, wondering what would happen if the story ended differently, or if it was told by the fox.

It underlines what you were saying about the role of story and how it can be used in different ways by people in different situations.

Right. A story's not just a story, but there's some kind of underlying reason for why it's told at a particular time. Also, I wanted to say that the frog story in *Comfort Woman,* where the mother frog warns the child frog about disobedience, is a story that is always told. Almost every Korean person I know has been told that story by a parent wanting to teach their child a lesson.

Akiko narrates her impressions on visiting her first American city: "That's what all of America was like to me. When you see it for the first time, it glitters, beautiful, like a dream. But then, the longer you walk through it, the more you realize that the dream is empty, false, sterile. You realize that you have no face and no place in this country." This disappointment in the reality versus the dream of America crops up throughout your work. Comment?

I think it's a common experience with many immigrants coming to this country, which is represented in terms of Disneyland and gold in the streets and a McDonald's on every corner. America's a very mythic place outside this country, and to get here and realize that there are homeless people on the street, there are hungry people, there are shantytowns in every city, "America Towns" in every city, can come as a shock to anyone coming here for the first time.

Here you also bring up the theme of facelessness among the Americans, and that theme comes up again in *Fox Girl*. What interests you about this idea? I'm thinking of the scene in *Fox Girl* when the mother is painting the girls' faces and describing how Americans don't really see them.

This comes from a lot of Asian-American history and fiction, that so many Asian-Americans have felt invisible throughout history and under-represented or misrepresented.

Your Asian-American literature class is a perfect example.

That's true. The professor was an expert in her field at that time, and she told me that there were no Korean writers. And beyond that class, throughout all the American literature that I had to study, there were no Asian-American characters or authors in the American literature cannon. Even on TV, I don't see Asian-Americans represented in a strong way.

***Fox Girl* seems a very natural progression from *Comfort Woman*. How did you come up with this story?**

I did want to link the books in terms of theme and history. *Comfort Woman* takes place during World War II, and in *Fox Girl* the children are born during the Korean War. There's a natural progression in terms of history, and also, literally. Some of the comfort women who felt that they couldn't return to their families because they'd been shamed—they felt that the girl they'd been no longer existed—migrated down to the camp towns that sprung up around the American military bases after World War II. They continued as prostitutes but for soldiers of a different country. As those camp towns grew, the women and the children of those women stayed on. Now some of the prostitutes in these camp towns are fourth-generation descendants from comfort women. The children now are only a quarter or an eighth Korean, but they identify themselves as Korean; they speak Korean, they're culturally Korean, but racially they're not more than a quarter Korean. Because of their mixed race, there's no way that they can leave and integrate with the rest of the homogenous Korean society. These towns are incredibly desolate. These women and children don't belong anywhere. They live in this no-man's-land where they are not accepted by Korea and not accepted by America.

Was this a difficult novel to research? How did you learn about the post-war culture and America Town and all the details of how the prostitutes

lived and worked, from their visits to VD Road, to their working cards, to the Monkey House, to the fish tanks where Duk Hee winds up?

Yes, those are all real. It's strange. There is a silence surrounding these camp towns in the same way that there was once a silence surrounding the comfort women's history. The difference is that while the silence of the comfort women was due to the fact that the women themselves didn't speak out—they held that silence out of shame or pain—the silence surrounding the camp towns is one that arises out of people feeling that it's distasteful to talk about it. Many people know about it, but no one wants to talk about it for fear of making a social offense. So the Koreans don't acknowledge or discuss it in any way, and the Americans don't want to discuss it either. And the camp towns aren't only in Korea but also in Okinawa, the Philippines, or Germany—wherever they have American military bases there are these camp towns around them.

Because of this silence, I had experienced difficulty in finding research for *Comfort Woman,* so I had expected the same difficulty in finding information about these camp towns. In reality, there was so much material that it was shocking, because, as I said, nobody talks about these places and what goes on there. There's so much written about the American military presence in Asia, American-Korean relations, oral histories of American GIs during the Korean War. All of this material discusses the camp towns, but the more I read, the more I realized that the material didn't treat the women in the towns like humans but more like props, in the same way that Japanese documents during World War II showed comfort women as military supplies. The women were there, but I got no sense of who the women were or their pain or their histories—they were part of the background setting. Some great documentaries came out later by a couple of great Korean-American women. One is *Camp Arirang,* and another is *The Women Outside.* Both are fairly recent documentaries that get at the woman's experience of living in these camps. Just as I was finishing *Fox Girl,* Kathy Moon came out with *Sex among Allies,* which is an excellent political analysis of the camp towns. But academic. The more I researched, the more I was pulled to try to get at the heart of the story and the heart of the characters through fiction.

Was it difficult to write about disenfranchised children suffering the harsh realities of postwar Korea?

Yes, especially since I have two girls of my own, and one of them is about the age that Hyun Jin and Sookie are when they get pulled into prostitution. It makes you realize how precarious life is for so many children around the world. It made me want to protect my daughter more.

How do you know how far to go with a scene like the one in which Hyun Jin has sex with three men during her first prostitution experience? The scene is very horrifying and graphic, and it goes from bad to worse. With a scene like that, how do you know how far to go?

I actually didn't know how far to go. That was one of the last and most difficult scenes that I wrote. Someone asked me if it was as bad in the camps as I write in my book, and really the answer is that it's worse. I pulled back in certain scenes, and pulled back on some of the things that would've happened to these girls. I felt that it would be difficult to write about and maybe more difficult to read about. Some places I decided to imply but not tell, and other places I pulled back entirely from how bad it could get.

It seems important that you have that one brutal scene because it lets readers know the reality of what goes on. You don't have to have innumerable scenes like that, but the one scene says, "This is what it is."

I didn't want to turn away from that. It's ugly, and it's brutal and it's graphic and it's violent. I didn't want to ignore that those kind of things do go on. While writing, I tried to walk the fine line between dwelling in it, not wanting to dwell in it, not wanting to exploit it, and yet not wanting to deny it either.

I guess it comes down to honoring the character's experience.

That's always what I came back to: trying to get in touch with the viewpoint of the character, empathize with her and feel her emotions and her spirit and her voice. But it was hard. As an author, I went into *Fox Girl* knowing that it was a novel. I couldn't trick myself the way I did with *Comfort Woman,* and I was very conscious of the choices I could make as an author. I wanted to challenge myself. I didn't want to take the easy way out. I wanted to let the characters do their own unpredictable things and not try to guide them along a preconceived plot. At one point, it got very difficult, and the girls had made so many bad life choices. About two-thirds of the way in I got stuck. I'd come to a dead end, where I didn't know how to get the girls out. I didn't have the energy, and I was emotionally and intellectually stuck. I showed up at my monthly writing group empty-handed, ready to quit. I told them I didn't know how it was going to end, and they all said that they'd been reading for months and they wanted an ending. They wouldn't let me quit. For four or five months I was determined that I was done with it, that I wouldn't go back. It was very difficult to go back, because some of the characters' cynicism was working its way into my life. After a few months—I realize now that I probably needed those months to gain some perspective and have some breathing space—I thought that not only was I obligated to my writing group but to my characters as well. I owed it to them to get them out of this horrible mess. I went through from the very beginning and looked for places to interject some hope so that when they reach that dead end, it wasn't a dead end. There was a little window of light open at the top that they could escape through. But really, I almost had to quit.

You open *Fox Girl* with a description about how ugly the girls are, Sookie "bulbous eyes and dark skinned," and Hyun Jin's cheek covered with a birthmark. Why was it important for them to be ugly?

Part of that has to do with the idea of transformation that runs through and the myth of the fox girl and taking on different skin. Part of it also had to do with the whole confrontation that takes place in America Town between the Korean ways of seeing and the American viewpoint, so that you have this clash. The girls, once seen as ugly, are redefined, revisioned later, when skinny and dark is considered exotic and desirable by the Americans. It emphasizes the difference in viewpoint and in values and the constant clash between these two cultural perspectives. The birthmark also represents race and how race is viewed, how skin is marked.

Is the story of the fox girl that gets passed down to Hyun Jin an actual Korean story?

Yes. There are many myths about the fox spirit. It's usually a demonic spirit who comes in and devours the livers or hearts of humans, young men.

Did you have the fox girl image in the beginning, or did you come up with it through the writing?

It's hard to say now. I was aware of it from the beginning and drawn to it in the way that the fox spirit is always a woman. She represents both danger and power.

Both novels capture a particular dialect and rhythm of speaking that stays with readers long after putting the books down. How did you develop the language, and did you face any challenges in establishing the dialects?

For both novels I tried to be aware of language in the sense that there are so many different languages and dialects being spoken—you have English, Hawaiian pidgin, Korean, and variations of camp town pidgin—so I was always trying to be aware of the differences as they came up. I wanted it to come off without the Korean sounding very stilted. I wanted to avoid that accenty, stilted language that signified that this was true Korean. So that was a challenge. At one point I was so concerned with it that every time someone spoke, I was overanalyzing and running it by my writing group. But they assured me that the reader would be caught up enough in the story and the characters were speaking in strong enough voices that I didn't need to question it so much.

Both *Comfort Woman* and *Fox Girl* are based on historical truths. With each novel, how much did you rely on historical fact, and how much did you rely on the imaginative gifts of fiction? To what point do you feel obligated to be historically accurate?

I try to be as historically accurate as possible throughout. I consider that the foundation. I build the framework with that history. With *Fox Girl*, I tried to give historical markers to set the time period, but there were a couple of times where I stepped outside the accuracy of history. For instance, there was a well-documented case in the papers about a GI murdering a girl by inserting an umbrella into her vagina. That was an actual case in the early nineties, and I allude to it in the text, so it's outside the time frame of the novel, yet I included it because that sort of thing was happening at the time *Fox Girl* is set as well. I'm sure it wasn't an isolated event that occurred only once. These murders and abuses have been going on for decades. So, I'll say that I base the foundation on history, and if I have to make an emotional leap, I do.

So much of your themes have to do with the mother-daughter relationship. What draws you to this complicated and unruly terrain?

In part, it's the life that I'm living now. I'm raising two young daughters. It's so much of my emotional life so that it naturally filters down into the work that I'm doing. I also told my mom that *Comfort Woman* is an apology to her for all of my rebellion against her and rejecting her culture, her traditional identity. I think of the novel as my coming home and addressing the relationship from another viewpoint.

Both novels end on a redemptive note. In *Comfort Woman,* Beccah cements and honors her bond to her mother through seeing to the details of her preparation and burial, while in *Fox Girl* Hyun Jin finds joy and solace in her daughter, who she realizes embodies the best of the people most important to her. Redemption is experienced through one's ability to love and connect with a misunderstood past, to take something good forward into the future. Comment?

Well, you said it all right there. The redemption is critical to me. It's a way to survive and move on. If you look at the differences in how Sookie and Hyun Jin survive, you'll see that Sookie has to kill all of that emotional contact with the world and try to repress any connection between her and another human being. For Hyun Jin, her way to survive was to build on that love. That was her redemption—it was the way that she survived America Town. I think it was an important way to end, but I struggled with that ending in Fox Girl. Originally it had a much darker ending where characters were emotionally or literally killed off, but it became too dark and too painful, and my work became about trying to interject some light. Neither novel ends with a traditional happy ending neatly tied in a bow. But each does end with hope for the future.

What do you look for in an ending?

In an ending, I want the characters to come to some sense of peace or realization, and also an ending should offer hope for a new beginning. Coming to the end of both *Comfort Woman* and *Fox Girl*, I do think that there was hope for the new beginning, so much so in *Fox Girl* that I'm going to write a sequel.

What's the next book?

Not to talk too much about it, because it's still formulating in my head, but it will be a sequel to *Fox Girl*.

So you have a trilogy.

Yes, a loosely based trilogy. It definitely connects themewise, and in time. It's a sense of history from World War II to the Korean War, and the aftermath of the Korean War to the eighties. I'll take some of the same characters and some of the same themes from *Fox Girl* into the new book, but I need to find a new twist, a new perspective that offers its own version of events.

Comfort Woman **was very successful, winning an American Book Award and enjoying wide sales and excellent reviews. That must've been very exciting.**

It was much more successful than I had ever dreamed. After I finished writing *Comfort Woman*, I expected that it would be published with a local press in Hawaii, maybe a thousand copies, and I was fine with that. I hadn't told people that I was writing a novel, partly because I was trying to trick myself into writing it and partly because I was afraid of failing and worried that if it didn't get published I'd have to deal with people's expectations, and that was too much to think about on top of the writing, which is hard enough in itself. When Viking decided to publish it, I couldn't believe it. People came up to me and wanted to know why I'd never told them I was a writer. Then I was worried about how people would view my mother, because already people were asking me if my mother was a comfort woman. I was so worried about how my mother would handle this.

And how did she?

Well, I called her up and told that I'd written this book and that Viking was going to publish it, and I explained what the book was about and let her know that people were going to ask her if she'd been a comfort woman and that people would assume that it was in some way autobiographical. I assured her that I would make it clear that the book was fiction and that she was never a comfort woman. She said, "If it sells more books, tell them I was a comfort woman!" She was great!

How long was there between *Fox Girl* and *Comfort Woman*?

There were five years, and part of that was spent writing what I thought would be my second novel—which was not *Fox Girl*—but I got distracted by the research I did, and the more references I read about America Town and the camp towns around these bases, the more I was drawn to that story. Also, tying into what we said about letting the characters develop as you write it, part of the trouble with that second novel was that I told so many people what I was going to write. I told the whole story, what the characters were like, what was going to happen, and so I lost that vital sense of discovery, which is one of the joys of writing.

How did you decide in *Fox Girl* to write about the kids instead of the adults like in *Comfort Woman*?

Well, with Hyun Jin we experience her loss of innocence and her realizing what life really is in America Town. Her vulnerability is very important in showing how desolate the life is there, and the fact that she is a child underscores her vulnerability as she's worrying about how to feed herself and find shelter and survive.

I found the humor in light of the desperate circumstances surprising and interesting. It makes the story more realistic, and it shows how resilient kids really are.

Yes, and it also plays into this whole thing about transformation. All children are constantly in a state of transformation, and we don't know how they're going to turn out.

I like what you said earlier too about letting your characters surprise you

and be spontaneous and not being married to some idea of what you think they're going to do.

That's so important. When you first start out, you don't know your characters well enough to know what they're going to do. The fun of writing is the discovery of who your characters are and what's going to happen to them. When you start with an outline and a preconceived idea, I think you kill something off. It deadens your characters.

What would you say to writers working on their first stories or novel?

I would say to not worry so much about the end product, or if it's going to get published, or what your message is. Start from your characters, and let your characters tell the story. Let the story develop on its own from your characters' viewpoint, and be as honest as possible to that. Then all the rest will come. If you keep trying to get to the emotional heart or truth of the characters, the story will come from that. I've read so many things that say to plot out your book, and I feel that that puts even more pressure on the writing. I tried it once and found my story going off in different directions and had to go back and erase my outline and rewrite it to make it conform with how the story was developing. Now that's backwards.

Do you think you'll write any more short stories?

At this point I'm really drawn to the larger work, and part of that has to do with this idea of discovery, of getting to know my characters. With short stories, I feel like you have to know the punch ahead of time. Now, I'm drawn to these situations and characters, and I don't know what the story is or the punch is or the climax is. I need the time and space to develop it that a novel provides.

Conducted: May 2002

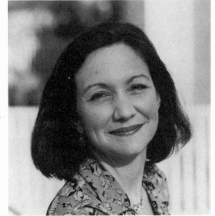

JILL MCCORKLE

Always Looking for the Bite

Jill McCorkle is the author of five novels—*The Cheer Leader, July 7th, Tending to Virginia, Ferris Beach, Carolina Moon*—and two collections of short stories—*Crash Diet* and *Final Vinyl Days*. She's taught writing at the University of North Carolina, Bennington College, Tufts University, and Harvard University.*

*Since this interview, Jill McCorkle has published *Creatures of Habit*, a collection of stories.

Readers and reviewers agree: you are a natural-born storyteller. How do you come by this?

There's a really strong southern tradition of storytelling that I did grow up with. I always like to tell people that I did not come from a long line of literary people, but definitely a long line of creative ones, and this desire not just to tell stories but to fill in all the blanks was constant. I grew up in the town where my parents grew up and my grandparents before them, and so every story was prefaced with "well you know, it used to be this way. . . . " For me, growing up in that town was like I had these layers of visions to know what the town looked like when my parents were children and beyond that when my grandmother was a child. Through those stories I also got a strong sense of history both of my family and of the place. People just told stories—it was a form of entertainment.

Did you really sell your first story when you were seven?

To my mother for a quarter, which I'm sure I spent on bubble gum or Squirrel Nut Zippers or whatever.

What made you want to write that story down at such a young age?

I loved to write. I watch my son now, who's seven—I was seven then—and he will go off with a stack of paper and just draw and draw and draw. You watch him, and you see from his expressions he's in another world, on that stage in his mind. He's acting out things that no one can see or hear. I think for me that's what writing was. It really was my imaginary friend.

Was it hard to translate your storytelling ability into fiction?

Well, yeah. I think the biggest difference, and it's one that's still a plus when I write a book, is I usually write far more than I need in that first draft. Because like my relatives, I have that need to wander off and fill in all the blanks whether I'm going to need it or not. I'm a big believer in editing. I know that I always have to be editing, yet I don't think I would get where I wanted to go if I didn't completely pull out all the stops in that first draft.

Did you ever want to be anything other than a writer?

Yes, I wanted to be a dancer. I took ballet from the time I was eight on into college. I was actually still dancing—I was way too tall to be a ballerina—and I had gotten to the point where it was something that I could do, and I was probably above average, but I had this moment when I realized that I was not prima ballerina material, that I was just never going to get there, as much I loved it and no matter how hard I worked. That realization coincided with starting to take the formal writing classes.

When was that?

I was a sophomore in college. But I had always thought that I would probably be a women's coach. I was actually a phys ed major, dancing, thinking that I was going to be teaching dance and swimming. I took my first creative writing class thinking that it sounded like a slide, because I was a very lax student and it was spring and everyone was working on their suntan. I thought, That sounds easy because I always write late at night anyway, so what's the big deal? So I signed up for this class, and I immediately fell in love with the professor and everything. I was hooked. That's what constituted the change from a PE major to an English major. If I was an English major it all took place in the same building, and before that I was running back and forth with wet hair. The trade-off is my thighs have never been the same. I guess in retrospect it was worth the trade.

Was there any crossover in the expressiveness of dancing and writing?

Absolutely. I keep thinking of those old Mary Tyler Moore reruns where she pulls out her old toe shoes to make sure she can still go up. For me, I loved the bar, because it was that kind of experience when your body is doing something but really, in your mind, you disappear. The same thing happens to me when I garden. And it happens to me when I write. Your mind is free to roam. I loved that about dance. As a high school student in the middle of these active weeks, except for the music in these classes it was silent, and I really loved that.

Are you ever surprised writing, when you let your mind go, at where you wind up?

Very much, and at what comes out. I mean that's when I can always tell a good day. A good day is when I can read back over and find at least a sentence or two that I have no recall of constructing. That's where you loose track of all time.

You're in the zone.

Yes. That's the kind of meditation that I'm always striving to find, that place where you momentarily disappear.

Was your family supportive of your choice to be a writer?

Yes, they were. I think there were a lot of those natural worries. "What are you going to do?" My parents would say things like, "Shouldn't you get that teacher's certificate so that you have something to fall back on?"

The way the courses were set up, it would've been hard to take all the education courses necessary to get a teacher's certificate as well as the writing classes. So I did not do it. It was really one of those big leaps of faith where I thought, If it doesn't work, I'll deal with it later.

Well, it certainly worked out.

But I really did have to reassure my parents, many, many times, that I would find something to do.

How have you managed to write and publish seven books in only fourteen years?

I think that aside from caring for my children, it's the one area of my life that I'm obsessive about. Not obsessive in that I have a rigid schedule. I don't. I don't work that way. But obsessive in that I don't feel good about myself unless I'm doing it.

Do you carve out time between teaching and taking care of your family? How do you do it?

I do. I think one of the greatest realizations I had was when my children were real little—you know, when your eyes and ears are always attuned for something—I realized that if I only waited for huge blocks of time, and that if I only counted those huge blocks of time as my work, I would be an incredibly frustrated, bitter woman. I would never get there. And it occurred to me that much of my best work is done away from the keyboard.

So you work a lot of it out ahead of time?

I work out almost all of it ahead of time. I keep lots of notes and lots of notebooks and save up and trade off until I have a big block of time where I then just begin typing up everything. As a student I began working longhand, then quickly moved to the typewriter. That Smith Corona put in a lot of miles. It's only in the past eight years that I've gone back to writing longhand, and I like it. I don't do that actual writing so much as that I sit and make notes so that when I get that time, I'm ready to go.

When you have all this material and you sit down to do the first draft, do you get something that's further along than a typical first draft?

Yes. Now, a lot happens in the air that used to happen on the page and get tossed.

How does your teaching life affect your reading and writing life. Or does it?

It does. I'm someone who needs some kind of schedule. There's nothing more unproductive to me than open-ended time. I become very lazy quickly. I'm definitely a deadline person, or I'll put it off and put it off. So the schedule of teaching helps me.

It gives you some structure.
Yes.

What are you reading these days?
Richard Buach's new stories, and Chris Tillman's stories, and I just bought Michael Cunningham's book *The Hours,* which I'm looking forward to.

How does your reading inform your writing life?
There are all these different compartments to how I read. There's how I read my student work, as a teacher. For a while, my reading was so slowed down by my teaching because anything I read, I read in teacher mode. And now I don't; now I can sit down and read a story and enjoy it and find it relaxing. I also read a lot of nonfiction when I'm working. I usually read about subjects I'm interested in that some way or another begin to tie into the work. For example, when I was writing *Carolina Moon,* I had this one character, and I gave him my whole interest in the ocean and Atlantis and all these old pirate stories and ghost stories. Very little made it to the actual page, but the whole time I was reading everything from Rachel Carson to *The Ghost of the Carolinas* just to get back in touch with the whole coastal scene and history. I love reading folktales and ghost stories and mythology, and forensics.

Oh no. Forensics?
I know, I love reading forensics, all these things like the Egyptian tombs and the bog bodies. I just recently read this wonderful book called *Women Who Kill.*

Do you think you would ever write anything dark like that?
I think I could. I think I'm more interested, as a writer, in the awareness of what's out there and the awareness of the possibilities. In my novels, I have had murders, but they haven't been the primary focus. I think my work is much more about the characters involved. I grew up in an area that's really quite violent. There were always murders. You read the accounts in the newspaper, and it was just mind-boggling that it was

going on right there. Perfect example: I was talking to my mama on the phone and she called me with what I call the cancer update, you know who's been diagnosed.

. . . the dead and the dying, the size of their melanoma. . . .
Right, the dead and the dying, who's having therapy, who's had a visitation. So she called me one day with all this, and I said, "Don't you have any good news?" She paused for a minute, and then she said, "Well yes, they finally found that body they been dragging the river for. It was an Indian man who'd been shot in the head." I went, "Oh, thank you, that's good news!" That's the kind of quirky crazy detail that laced the conversation I grew up with.

You consider yourself a southern writer?
Yeah, I do.

I've been reading a lot of southern writers. I just read *The Heart Is a Lonely Hunter*. I was struck by how, when McCuller's was so young, she could have such a deep understanding spiritually and emotionally of these characters who are so different from her.
I think a lot of it is growing up with the stories, and I think it's also not limited to the South, but something a lot of southern writers share is that kind of extended family.

Within a town?
Yes. And you find it in other groups. I've always thought there are a lot of similarities between the Jewish oral tradition and the southern. Maybe it comes from people who for whatever reason were prevented from writing things down, so there's a real necessity in the memory and in passing on the memory. I grew up with a lot of old relatives who I was very close to. So a lot of things kids these days are spared or sheltered from, like going to spend Sunday in the old folks' home, were part of my week.

So you hear the same stories from different perspectives?
You do, and you see that the able-bodied adults treat the extremely old the same way they treat you. As a child I was very much aware of the ends of the line sort of bending into a circle. I have all these old relatives who got reprimanded in the same way I did, for saying bad words or eating something they weren't supposed to. So there is a kind of compassion that you have as a very young child.

There's that feeling in a lot of stories that the town is like a family.
Sure. One thing I've noticed, teaching, is that more and more the biggest difference rather than North and South is urban and rural. Teaching at Harvard, I had a lot of students who'd grown up in small towns in Maine. Different accent, but it could just as easily have been the South.

What's the "New South"?
A few years ago when I was asked that question, I said, "What really marks the New South is that we have finally put the war behind us." And of course no sooner did I say that than Charles Frazier came out with *Cold Mountain* and Kaye Gibbons had her novel about the Civil War, and then I thought, Well maybe not. I think what really marks the New South is the whole surge in the media and the growth of chains and all that's served to homogenize our country. When I was growing up, there were no chains. I was in junior high when Howard Johnson's and Holiday Inn came in. And then of course the McDonald's and everything we see on the highway that make every town look the same—those things did not exist. The South was still very much isolated. You didn't have cable TV, you didn't rent videos. If the movie didn't come to your town, you never saw it. Well, in a town like mine, there were a lot of movies that passed us by. It's like the communication lines were cut off in a certain way. Especially if you lived off a main thoroughfare. I-95 was constructed during my childhood. I've always seen it as a symbol of growth and connection. I use it often in my work because I see it as this artery to the rest of the world.

Is your town near I-95?
It's right on it. You had old 301, which for years was the road people took to Florida.

Is that the road in your story "Gold Mine"?
Yeah, and it really is like that. You can drive 301, it's like a ghost town. Being on I-95, a lot came to my town that other small towns in the area did not get.

Were all those things good things?
No. You got Pizza Hut and McDonald's, but I think, and rightly so, a lot of people attribute drug traffic to that freeway, because it's an easy shot to the coast. Michael Jordan's dad was killed at an intersection of one of the coastal highways and I-95. The same way that a highway like that provides flight, it also enables outside things to come in, things that are not always desirable. That's something I'm often writing about, too,

and that's the trade-off. When I was growing up, I remember thinking of big cities and being terrified because the only person I ever heard of going to Chicago was this friend of my great Aunt Claudia who went to Chicago and got murdered. So my childhood stories—I would hear "Chicago" and I would think, Oh no, Chicago, that's a terrible place. And yet right here in this county there were shoot-outs that were commonplace. People were fearful of the rest of the world.

What other writers influence your work?

Those old faithful southern writers. Eudora Welty and Katherine Anne Porter in a major way, Capote, Harper Lee's *To Kill a Mockingbird* is a favorite and always will be, Carson McCullers's *The Heart Is a Lonely Hunter*.

Did you read all those books as a kid?

Just *To Kill a Mockingbird,* and I knew some Capote stories. I got hooked on "A Christmas Memory" thanks to that wonderful Geraldine Page special that I happened to see as a very young child and always remembered. I didn't even know who'd written the story, and then I discovered it. I read Eudora Welty for the first time in college.

Where do your novel ideas come from? How do you know if what you start with is a novel or a short story?

I don't always know, but I find that more and more I do when it happens. Often I have a character who I think should be a story, and never get it to go full circle. Those characters will sometimes get folded into a novel. The most recent example of that is the character Denny in *Carolina Moon,* because I had this monologue I kept thinking was going into a story and never got it there. Oftentimes, the idea for a novel is something bigger, and I'll have an idea where it's going, but then I don't reach that ultimate goal. It becomes much more about the characters along the way.

Does it come in an image or a voice?

The ones I've done in first person are pretty easy because it's a person telling of an experience of a particular time. *The Cheer Leader* and *Ferris Beach*—they both were somewhat coming-of-age novels, and so it was easy because I felt limited. In a novel like *Tending to Virginia,* which deals with three generations of women within a family, the main idea for me was that I was interested in collecting these characters' memories of the big topics—love, marriage, birth, death—and then to see how they all fit together, how they blend into each other.

So you were exploring something in writing that novel?

Yes, to see how this person's memory is colored in a different light by the memory of the generation before her. At one point when I finished that novel, which is probably the most challenging one I wrote, at the end of my rough draft I had all these little packets of character information color-coded with paper clips. It really didn't have a present plot. That had to be forced like an overlay to pull it all together. For me, writing it, it was one of those novels that heavily zeroed in on the voice. And it was a book that I was very pleased with the critical response, and it did get what I had anticipated, which was that it was one of those novels where you had to read the first third to know everybody and get into it. I kept thinking of it like an orchestra piece where you introduce each instrument, each one has a little solo, and then you begin to pull them all together and let it build. A similar situation in writing *Carolina Moon,* because again I wanted to have all these different characters and in the process of writing to discover how they connect, to know that two lives can bump up against each other and cause results that you're unaware of at the time. A lot of these characters—sometimes the connections were very slight, but having placed them in a small town it was credible that you could find something.

Did *Tending to Virginia* have to do with your family?

Yes, definitely. That would be the closest to my own world. The facts are not based on truth and embellished often and vividly, but the voices of the grandmother and the great-aunt Lena are very much the voices of my grandmother and my great-aunt Claudia, who I was very close to. Actually, my grandmother was still alive when the book came out, and Claudia died during the final stages of me writing it. Really the whole inspiration for writing it was to capture those voices.

Did your grandmother like it?

She didn't read it; she saw it. She was excited about it, but she was quite out there at that point. I was just so fascinated watching her going through that process because you could go see her some days, and some days I was me, and some days my mother, and some days her mother. You never knew even what century you'd be in, and elaborate things would have happened or she would've just been somewhere. I was always curious if these were real memories or her imagination.

In her review of *Tending to Virginia,* Alice McDermott said, "It is as if Ms. McCorkle, finding herself with this cast of marvelously rich, garrulous, complex women whose lives span a century, sought to contain them in a conventional tale of a young woman's coming of age. When they

would not be contained, she simply threw up her hands and let them keep talking. It was a wise decision." Is this true? Did you throw up your hands and let them keep talking?

Yes, totally, and there too is an example of what I was talking about earlier, just letting the work take over, the idea being that you deal with those problems when editing. Yeah, it became a very different book. I think what I was most pleased with, with that novel, is that ultimately it was as much about what was never said as what is. I think it's very hard to write about that kind of silence, or secrets, you know, what people choose not to reveal.

What they choose not to reveal, or what they collude in not discussing or never mentioning.

Yes, exactly. There were all these family stories that would get told, and as a kid I remember listening and hearing the disagreement among the grown-ups as to what really happened. "Oh no, so-and-so wasn't there, so-and-so was there." It's sort of like, "In the beginning God created the heavens and the earth." When do you just step up and just take this blind leap of faith? All of us have these histories, and there are these big places where you accept with a kind of blind faith because it makes sense of other parts of your life. So that's what it was really about.

I'm interested in the germination process. You talked about how you process the material ahead of time, then sit down to do your draft. From that draft to the final book, what goes on?

A lot goes on. Revision varies from book to book. The novel *July 7th*, except for some cutting, required very little revision.

You said once that book was a gift.

Yes, and I had helped myself. It's a limited amount of time. It takes place in a day, so the whole time you're working on it this clock is ticking as a way to keep it contained. It was also my first time experimenting with a cast of voices. When I look at it, I see it as a clunkier prelude to *Carolina Moon*, because there I wanted the voices to be more subtle, and I think in *July 7th* you really feel the gears shifting. But that also enabled it to move at a faster pace.

When you start to write, do you know more about the characters than gets on the page? How do you get to know them?

I feel like I know a lot more about them than gets on the page. Oftentimes they grow along the way, so that revision is going back to where you first meet them and getting that personality in there.

What do you do to get to know them ahead of time?
For me it's important to get a sense of the voice, to really hear that person. The times that I've had a character that I could not get up and running, I would have that character write a letter. I did that with the character of Madge in *Tending to Virginia*. I just could not get this woman's voice, and then I had her write a confessional letter, and I ended up keeping the letter in the book because she was someone you weren't really going to get much of her from her voice. She was someone with secrets. Oftentimes I like to think about that person's history or childhood.

It's interesting that you bring up how to show things about a character that a character cannot reveal themselves by having them write a letter. Are there other ways you can achieve that?
Mainly in other people's reactions to them, but also using the physical world to simulate or reflect what's going on emotionally.

How did you get the idea to use the photographs in *The Cheer Leader*?
That was actually an exercise that I gave myself as a way to get to know the character, and I was having a lot of fun with it. I've actually assigned that as an exercise since, because it's a way of containing little parts. I think a lot of times when you're working on a novel, not just a first novel, there's always the question, Where do I begin this chapter, where do I end this chapter? This was a way of setting up very natural beginnings and endings. So I learned a lot.

It worked for me, because I remember being a kid and sitting on the living room floor with all the pictures spread out on the floor in front of me. The decision to switch to third-person narrative works well as the girl starts to disintegrate, because it not only shows her dissociation, but it brings the reader right up against how she's feeling. How did you arrive at that?
It made perfect sense to me. It was interesting because it just felt right as I was writing it. Then I did my homework and realized that it would be a psychological result. I can remember one time being in the grocery store and surprising myself—you know how you just get in the grocery store and space out—and it surprised me when I realized that I was narrating my walk through the vegetable aisle. "She is getting lettuce now." It was a little ominous when I realized that I was narrating my trip. This was around the same time that I was writing the book, and it occurred to me that it was that kind of detachment we sometimes feel. And we do have those times when we feel like an observer of our own lives, where there's

this moment of detachment as if you'd pulled back. Often people describe it. You're at a dinner party and maybe you feel uncomfortable, like you're not fitting in, and that is the feeling. You can take advantage of it. When you feel removed or off center, it gives you a look at the picture or the scene that you don't get when you're actively involved. In many ways that's why the South is always very sharp and clear for me in a way, living up here, that I don't know it would be if I were there. Here I'm able to rely totally on memory. In my mind, when I write, my hometown looks very much like it did in my adolescence, or it's very easy to get what I knew from stories about my parents' adolescence or my grandmother's. It's not as easy when you're actually seeing the place. To be slightly removed can clarify.

What, in your mind, makes a story?

I really hold to that old definition, an event or series of events that lead to an emotional change. As a reader and a writer, I'm always looking for the emotional impact, because that's what stands to tie us all together. That's what enables me to read anybody's story about any world and come away feeling personal in some way. That's why I'm often bothered by stories where I don't experience the emotion, or I don't feel something.

How do you know when a story is done?

You know what? I want to say you just do. There's the instinct usually to overshoot it. That's what I see most often in students' work.

You mean write beyond the end?

Yes. I always picture it like a sprinter out on the track, because they run that lap to warm up, and you don't need that. Then there's the race; then they keep running to cool down. That happens very often with stories. People warm up, then the story happens, then they walk that lap that you just don't need. So, it becomes completely subjective, a word or two. I don't like endings that feel like they've got a great big bow or a THE END sign. What I really like in an ending is to feel satisfied that there's been a completion within, and yet in some way it's still open.

What do you think constitutes a "collection" of stories?

It depends. A lot of times writers who regularly write stories and publish them, you often have a collection that's just that—a collection of stories that have been published. Other times stories do start to have a common thread. I know that when I was getting ready to publish C D [*Crash Diet*] I had a couple of stories that were narrated by men, one of them the story "Final Vinyl Days," and my editor, Shannon Ravenel, thinking that this poor man was so overwhelmed by the women. So I took him out and I saved him.

Poor guy.

I know. He was living in the drawer for years. He's all moldy. What's funny is that ended up being the title of the collection, because I'd sort of given up, you know. I'd published it elsewhere, and then I thought, well. What was interesting is you start looking at stories and seeing the common variables, and in all those stories there was this kind of nostalgia. All the characters were at the crossroads of some kind of major life change. The same was true of the women, but it was more of a sink-or-swim kind of desperation point. Oftentimes I start to see common variables in stories when those stories are coming together all at the same time, and I tend to write stories that way, not unlike the way I write a novel. I think at heart I'm a novelist, because I like to sit on all these stories. Right now I have ten stories sketched out, and when I get that big block of time, I will go in and complete them, and I know what I want to do. I think by working that way, like in *Final Vinyl Days,* you are more aware of possible links between the different stories.

You do a book almost every two years.

Well, every three years, if I'm lucky.

When you're writing, are you aware of technical aspects of storytelling like structure, voice, plot?

I try not to be. I go for the "zone" first. All technical aspects I deal with in revision. I can't stress enough how much emphasis I do place on revision. That first draft is wonderful and exciting; that's when you fall in love. The revision is more like the marriage. It's like taking what you love and facing the practical, domestic life with it in reality. For me, the revision is when you really sink the roots and take what's sometimes pure, raw emotion and figure out how it works—how does it fit?

Your work is so full of humor, and at the same time compassionate and tender. Are you aware of that working? Are you in command of it?

I feel that I am in command of it. Often my humor will go too far to left field, and I've even gotten comments back from Shannon, [my editor]. She'll write in the margin, "You've gone a little too far here." Like with anything, I can get a little slaphappy and silly with it. But I'm always looking for the bite, in the same way I would expect a poet is looking for the turn, or what I'm looking for when I'm reading a poet. So I'm aware, when I'm having a lot of fun, I'm also always looking for the shot. And I love the blend of the two. I don't know if that's particularly southern. I know it's very common in the South to find the two blended. It definitely was in my family. People had a good sense of humor. We laughed at funerals. Things are still sad in ways that are funny in the most somber situations. If somebody uses incorrect English, she's not going to go to the funeral home and suddenly sound like the queen. So maybe you have this very sad situation, but you have someone using English that blows you away and you laugh, you smile, when you hear it. That's what I'm always looking for. It's not so much the situation that I'm finding funny, because oftentimes those situations do turn into slapstick. For me it's more about the person's reaction or words at the height of what is a serious situation. Like what my mother said on the phone. That was funny.

You use a lot of details from popular culture. This always comes up in workshops because people do not handle it well. What are the issues that arise for you in choosing and considering those details? When do they work?

I know. I always get upset when people are so ready to say never do it, because you strip somebody's work of the details and references. James Joyce did it. But because it's Irish and old we think that's okay, even though you have to pull out a book and look it up and find out what it means. I think it works if what you're doing is using it to paint the picture and supply the right color. I think if you're relying on it to deliver the whole picture, then it's a problem. That's where the whole business about Kmart fiction came into being. People were using cliché and stereotype to tell a story. When you're trying to capture a certain time, especially when you're dealing with an adolescent character, I don't see how you can realistically paint the world without references to the music, and the movies, and the television. For my whole generation, there's that wonderful link between—probably for every generation—between reality and what was represented there, a child's fantasy life as tied to what's being portrayed in popular culture. What's funny is there's this whole turning back to all those old programs. My children love *The Brady Bunch*. It's so funny that they're able to watch *The Brady Bunch*.

What three things would you tell a beginning writer to be aware of?

The first thing, the overwhelming thing, would be to pay attention to what story you really want to tell. It's very easy to feel pressured by ideas of the kind of story I should tell as opposed to the kind of story you naturally *can* tell. For me that was a big issue, to learn to let go of the reins. I'm sure there are people who would say that was a bad choice, but for me the real pleasure was in throwing that in and getting rid of that self-consciousness that makes you want to sound smarter, or cultured, or whatever. The most important thing is to strip down and throw everything that doesn't belong to you away. If it feels artificial to you, it will to your reader. If it bores you, it will sure as hell bore your reader. You want to be true to the story you can tell. Sometimes that means putting down a story that you really want to write, because you're not ready yet. I've done that many, many times. There's the story you want to tell and the story you're able to tell, and when the two come together, that's perfect magic. That's what, as a writer, you're always striving for. Sometimes you have to wait. I would say, rely on your instincts. I would say zip up the second layer of skin to fend off the critical darts, but certainly to learn from them. If you don't learn to take criticism and learn to use it in a positive way, I don't see how you can continue. I certainly couldn't have. It's why I'm not one of those poison dart-teachers, because I know that if I'd ever gotten one early on, I would've just headed for the woods and not resurfaced. I could've easily been scared off. I'd be teaching PE. It wouldn't be an unhappy life, just a different life. So, I think, like Eudora Welty said, go out as far on the limb as you can without snapping. Be true to your natural impulses to tell the story; you take the criticism and use of it what you can, and you push the limits. You can't stop pushing the limits. As soon as you do, you become stagnant and stinky. I'm thinking of the little water garden I have now that's stagnant and stinky. We need rain! We need movement! Ultimately, I feel that life is too short to invite suffering and torture. If you don't love writing, and if you wouldn't be doing it anyway, there are a lot of things you can do. I feel that more strongly than anything. I remember being at this conference with all these women writers in California one time. I was sitting at the table with all these strangers, and people were talking philosophically about writing, and I remember saying that if I had the choice between a happy life and being a writer, I would. . . . And this woman reached across the table and said to me, "You'd be a writer." And I said, "No, never." Life is just too short.

Conducted: July 1999

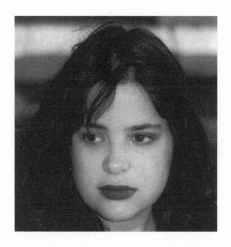

ELIZABETH MCCRACKEN

You Must Be Prepared to Break Your Own Heart

Elizabeth McCracken is the author of *The Giant's House* and the short-story collection *Here's Your Hat What's Your Hurry*. She's the recipient of the Harold Vursell Award from the American Academy of Arts and Letters and has received grants from the Guggenheim Foundation, the Michener Foundation, the Fine Arts Work Center in Provincetown, Massachusetts, and the National Endowment for the Arts.*

*Since this interview, Elizabeth McCracken has published the novel *Niagara Falls All over Again*.

Did you start writing in college?

I was one of those kids who always wrote, but most of what I wrote was poetry—rhymed and metered verse. Not deep poetry. It was flip. I always went for the easy joke. Then I went to Boston University and started writing fiction more seriously. I'm sure I wrote a finished story in high school, but I have no memory of it, whereas I can remember writing poems and a play.

What made you decide to stick with fiction writing, as opposed to poetry and playwriting?

This is such bad motivation, but I applied to three graduate programs in both poetry and fiction. I knew that I didn't want to become a playwright. My lack of talent had already revealed itself to me. I took three and a half years of playwriting classes. I wrote a one-act play to get into the class, and that was the best play that I ever wrote. I went firmly downhill after that. I was rejected from one school in both poetry and fiction, and accepted by one program in both, but didn't receive any financial aid. Iowa accepted me in fiction and not in poetry. In some ways that is the reason I hardly ever wrote a poem again. I wasn't a very good poet, and even when I was at the height of my poetry output, I wrote only ten poems a year.

It makes sense to hear that you wrote poetry. Your fiction has a poetic quality.

Both playwriting and poetry were good for my fiction. If I'm giving myself a break on why I stopped writing those and turned to fiction, I can see that it was a natural progression, that I figured out what I was interested in writing and realized that I could still do the things I enjoyed in poetry and in fiction. It didn't have to be one or the other.

How did playwriting feed into your fiction?

I still have to remind myself of what I learned in playwriting. Playwriting requires practicality, which is good for me, especially when I am making early drafts. I'm a self-indulgent writer. Sometimes I write long lists of things, people saying "Well, you know what I think," et cetera, with no action or no dialogue for pages and pages. Playwriting made me think about action and economy. There is no budget in fiction, while in playwriting you have to think about how many actors each scene requires, and depending on your budget, you may have to limit the number of characters. I have a habit of writing too many characters into scenes, and when I'm revising—this is happening to me in my writing now—I always have to winnow characters out. When I do, I always think of it in terms of playwriting. You can reassign dialogue and make a piece more dramatic by having fewer characters. That isn't true for all plays, but in my drafts, I tend to spread the emotion between too many characters.

Where do your short-story ideas come from?

I wish I knew. I haven't written any for a long time. I've written one story in the past six years.

Do you consider yourself more of a novelist?

I feel the same way about fiction writing as I do about playwriting and poetry. It's hard to go back to a specific genre when I am very aware of my deficiencies. One of the reasons I haven't written any short stories recently is that I'm aware of how little I know about the form. I think I would write very different stories now. I want to concentrate on what the form itself can accomplish, rather than trying to pack as much as I can into twenty-five pages. The one short story that I wrote in the past six years was different than my other stories. I don't think it was better, just different.

How did you come to realize these deficiencies? From reading stories, or from your maturation as a novelist?

Both. Certainly reading a lot of short stories. Also, having stretched my brain out to novel size, it's flabby now, so when I try to go back and fit a story into twenty-five pages I think, How could anybody ever do this? I'm aware of how hard it is to write something twenty-five pages long with real emotional weight and resonance. In a novel, twenty-five pages is just the beginning. Hopefully, your novel is under way at that point, but you're still on the upward part of the novel's arc. I didn't realize that when I was writing short stories. When I was in graduate school, I wrote a short story that some said could have become a novel.

Was that "Some Have Entertained Angels, Unaware?"

Yes. I incorrectly believed my critics for a while. I wrote the first chapter of that story as a novel; then I realized I'd already written the version I meant to write. Novels that come out of successful short stories are frequently bad books. That's been my experience. They were conceived of as short stories: a short story is not just a shorter novel. You do character development differently. The characters are not conceived of as novel characters. I've read too many bad novels published by good writers, based on really good short stories. I don't think it's a universal truth, but I think it is a frequent truth.

What draws you to such quirky characters?

They don't seem quirky to me. Some relatives of mine lived in Des Moines, and while I was in graduate school, a friend of mine gave me a ride to visit them. She met my grandmother and cousin Elizabeth. She came back and said to our friends, "You may think Elizabeth doesn't write realistic fiction. I've met her family. She writes very realistic fiction." I come from a family of unbelievable eccentrics on both sides, who are very quirky characters themselves. Not always as physically quirky as they are in my fiction, but certainly in terms of personality. My cousin Elizabeth, my uncle David, my aunt Edna—I hear many stories about her. My grandmother had eleven brothers and sisters, and they were all wonderfully bizarre.

How many revisions of a story do you usually go through, and what happens during each revision?

I have to make myself write chronologically, first page to last page. I try to do that but don't always succeed when writing a novel. I'll take notes for later scenes but won't look at them until after I've already written the scene. I'll try to write without looking at the notes, then incorporate the notes at a later date. I have to forbid myself from doing the fun parts first, partially because I'm worried that I'll lose interest in the project after I've done all the parts that I wanted to write. Also, I can't think about writing unless I'm actually writing.

Ann Patchett, my great friend and first reader, is somebody who spends time thinking about the work. She conceives of it and understands it and turns it around in her head, and then sits down to write. She wrote her first two books in a relatively short period of time. She wrote *The Patron Saint of Liars* when she was a fellow at the Fine Arts Work Center, a five-hundred-page book in six months. She spent the last month revising, then sold it three weeks later. She's a real legend at the Work Center. People say the strict rules of fiction writing require that you revise often, yet she scarcely revised at all on the page. In many ways she'd been revising in her head for a year, before she even began.

I, on the other hand, can't do that. I can sit and think and write paragraphs in my head, but as far as any useful work about writing—I can't do it. The minute I start to write, it changes. I could come up with a whole novel in my head and turn it around, and the minute I tried to put it into words, it would be totally different. It's amazing how much my work changes from conception to finish, and it changes rapidly, especially when I'm first working on a project. That's the reason I have to write from beginning to end. Otherwise, the concept is going to be off. I won't have thought enough about the big scenes unless I've written right up to them.

I revise endlessly. Drafts don't mean anything in this computer age. Sometimes I retype sections, but I have never retyped an entire book from beginning to end. I have a typewriter that I write on because it seems different from my computer, but once I'm rolling, I switch to the computer. I use the typewriter when I'm stuck on something because it makes me type the words over and over again. I'm probably on my fourth or fifth major draft on my new novel, but there have been zillions of revisions and rearrangment within that. What usually happens is, in the beginning, I'm very indulgent. I only show my work to people who will tell me it's wonderful. I don't show it to anyone who will give me any kind of serious criticism, because it will break my heart. My friends know not to say too much. I want them to tell me if it's awful or misguided, but if they think it's on the right track, I don't want to hear any more criticism. If they suggest something, I always say, "No, I don't want to do that!" But as I go on, I become more and more hard-hearted. On Wednesday I cut the first fifty pages of the book I'm working on, and it was no problem. It was a section I'd been holding onto desperately, for ages. I called up Ann and said, "I have to lose the scenes in Iowa," and she said, "You knew that." And I couldn't say, "Why didn't you tell me this before?" because she probably had and I'd forgotten.

Eventually I begin to loathe what I'm working on. That's when I know it's done. When I really hate it.

Are you just sick of looking at it at that point?

Yes, sick of looking at it, and I know some of the passages too well, by heart. I realize again that I have not written the great American novel and that beautiful idea I had four or five years ago—well, the actual thing is not living up to my hopes and dreams.

Did you feel that way about *The Giant's House*?

I despised *The Giant's House*. I feel better about it now, but when I finished the novel, I was so convinced about how bad it was that friends who hadn't read the book said, "Sorry you wrote such a bad book." I was despondent.

Why did you decide to go to librarians' school?

I'd always worked in libraries. I worked in the Newton Free Library in Newton Corner from the time I was fifteen until I was twenty-two. It was the only job I ever had. I wanted to have a skill. I'd promised myself that I would never count on my writing as a way to make money. I was allowed to do anything I wanted with the money I made from writing, but I didn't want to feel like I was finishing something in a hurry for the money. Even though I had a book contract when I graduated from Iowa, I never could have found a good teaching job. I also had an inkling that I wouldn't finish much work when I taught, though I enjoy teaching. I knew that I didn't want a permanent teaching job. My parents were academics, and I wanted to leave the family business. I'm not saying that if someone had offered me a great teaching job I would've turned it down, but no one offered me a teaching job, and I wasn't qualified to do anything. I loved libraries. I'm extremely pragmatic, so I decided that I would go to librarian school. I would have a portable skill. I could live anywhere and get a job.

The sad truth is, when teaching goes badly, you go home and you can't write. When teaching goes well, you go home and you can't write. I'm not sure if teaching plays with the same part of the brain, but it certainly plays with the same part of the soul that feeds your writing. I wanted a job that I could leave at the office. Library work is like that. People kept saying to me, "You probably write when you're at the library," and I'd say "No, I have to work. That's why I'm there." I didn't write when I was working, but when I returned home, I could do it. People would ask me questions during the day, but by the end of the day they were all answered. Writing is such solitary work, but it is also good to go out into the world and serve people. I don't mean that in some sort of "Mother Teresa washing the feet of the lepers" way. It is good to stand behind a desk and have people ask you to do things, and you do them. And you deal with colleagues. The thing that I didn't and still don't like about teaching is the lack of colleagues. Even if there are people in your department, you don't go to work with them. I love that about library work. I love hanging around the staff lounge and complaining and gossiping about people. That social interaction with co-workers and patrons is important to me. I still think about going back to library work because of that. After *The Giant's House* came out, I still worked part-time at the library.

Your library work is probably where you formed the idea for Peggy in *The Giant's House*. Where did you find the idea for the giant?
    I remember finding the idea for the giant in my special libraries class at Drexel University in Philadelphia. I had a teacher who I adored. I didn't adore many of my teachers, but she was a real librarian, a "librarian's librarian." Nevertheless, I spent a certain amount of time daydreaming in her class. I remember thinking in the special collections class, "I want to write a book about a librarian in the nineties who is the archivist at a museum housed in the house of the world's tallest man." That was the initial idea for *The Giant's House*. You can see the difference between the initial concept and the final book.

Why a museum in the house of the world's tallest man?

I always loved the *Guinness Book of World Records*, and I'm fascinated with the human extremes: the oldest mother, the youngest mother, the longest fingernails, and the longest mustache with two women holding each end out. There was Mrs. Ethel Granger, who had a thirteen-inch waist. I always thought that was her natural waist. It was reduced from twenty-two inches over the course of several years, and I thought that meant dieting. Much later on, I discovered that Mr. and Mrs. Granger were famous fetishists, and she was a corseter. She'd corseted herself down to thirteen inches. If you go back to that picture you'll see this very 1950s-looking housewife touching her hair, but her ear is pierced all the way around. Someday, I want to write something about Mrs. Ethel Granger. I love the idea of her. There she is, standing so innocently in the *Guinness Book of World Records*, but still, there's the danger of her ear.

I always liked house museums. The Maxfield Parrish house in New Hampshire, for instance, looked like he just stepped out of it, as if they never changed anything. It was dirty and homey and sweet. I like bad museums—well, not necessarily bad museums. I visited a museum in Niagara Falls, the Houdini Museum, this unbelievably cheesy, horrible museum. I always thought I'd write something about a museum like that, a two-bit museum where the people who came in were always disappointed by what they found. I thought if the museum housed the world's tallest man, it would be physically interesting. I wanted a house that belonged to someone you had never heard of, but was still intriguing enough to enter.

How did you travel from that initial idea to the characters of Peggy and James?

This is an example of why it doesn't do me any good to think about things beforehand. I had that idea four or five months before I started writing the novel. I was finishing library science school, and I decided to wait to start writing, which is not unusual for me—I don't write every day. I went to the Work Center, sat down for my first day of work—I thought the book was going to be narrated by James's cousin, Alice. I wrote an opening, a third-person opening, and I thought the book was going to be third person. This opening included the line "Everybody said the librarian was in love with him." I thought maybe this librarian could be an important character, because she'll be the person who establishes the museum and then leaves it to Alice, and Alice always feels the shadow of this great librarian looking over her shoulder. Peggy Cort was scarcely going to be in the book. She was dead before the book began, but I decided to write a little bit in her voice, to get a handle on her, find out what she was like. Well, she just wouldn't stop talking.

Did you always have the opening line, "I do not love mankind?"

When Peggy was going to narrate the book, that was always the first line. The only immortality I ask is that fifty years from now, in the back of literary magazines when they have quizzes where you match the first line of the book up with the book title—I want to be in those quizzes. I don't understand books that begin, "It was June." I don't understand why you would start your book that way. I don't object to the sentence when I am further into the book, but when I read books, I want to know something about the writer and the book from the first sentence.

How much research did you have to do about giants in order to write accurately about James?

I did a lot. I love research. I have to be careful, because I sometimes use research as a way of procrastinating. I did most of the research after I'd written the book. This was something that was useful about writing the book in Provincetown—I couldn't do much research. I didn't have a car. I couldn't find the nearest library on the Outer Cape. I hadn't done that research in advance, because I didn't know I was going to need it—James was going to be dead. I made a lot of it up, and when I returned to Boston, I did the research. I looked at medical journals. I looked up an actual world's tallest man's appearances and read a book by a family friend of his. I did research specifically on him and on giantism and put that into the book afterwards. But on the first draft, I just concentrated on the characters without trying to bend them to the facts.

How do you think James's outstanding physical stature shapes him emotionally?

One of my basic theories of life is both that who we are physically defines who we are as people, and the exact opposite—that who we are physically has no bearing on who we are as people. The assumptions people make based on how you look can't help but shape who you are. I was the shortest kid growing up, and I loved it. I didn't think about this before I started working on *The Giant's House,* but then I thought about it. How much of my personality is shaped by the fact that I'm only about five feet tall? And there are significant parts of my personality that are shaped by that, so I think I just chose a character at the opposite extreme.

What's an example of how being five feet tall has shaped your personality?

I don't like parties. I can't see across the room. It's very claustrophobic to be short at a party where everyone stands. I don't like crowds for that same reason. It's not that I don't like people. I simply never have the experience of being able to look over a crowd. There are places I don't go, because of my height. I never go to outdoor concerts. I would almost never go anywhere without assigned seating. I also remember loving, when I was a kid, that in class pictures I always knew where I belonged: front and center. In gym lineups, I knew where I belonged. In cars I always sat on the hump, and I still do that. Whenever I travel in a car with three people, or I'm picked up by strangers at an airport and someone politely, because I'm the visitor, goes toward the back seat, I say, "Don't be crazy." It doesn't make sense for someone of normal height to ride in the back seat, and people understand this. They thank me and take the front seat. It often gives me a sense of false modesty.

You were at the Provincetown Fine Arts Work Center when you were writing *The Giant's House*. What impact did that experience have on *The Giant's House* and on you as a writer?

I can never say enough good things about the Fine Arts Work Center. The first time I received a fellowship I was in my last year of graduate school. I'd never worked for a living, and I don't think I truly understood what a gift I'd received. I figured I'd keep on riding the art gravy train as long as I could. But when I received a second-year fellowship, I was rescued from library science school, which was horrible, and Philadelphia, which I also believe is horrible. I was so profoundly grateful and realized what a wonderful thing it was. I mean, seven months, and they give you your own apartment. The first time they called, I asked, "How many people do I have to share an apartment with?" She said, "Oh no, you get your own apartment." It meant so much to me, like a punch in the arm and someone saying "You're all right, kid." It also meant a great deal to me in terms of time. During both residencies, I was able to put the seven months to work, and I met people who are still my best friends.

Why did you set *The Giant's House* on Cape Cod?

Because I have a very small imagination, and I was living on the Cape. I could write, "It was February and it was ——— out," and stick my head out the window. I remembered from when I lived there the first time that Provincetown held a kind of private joke for me. People left as the winter became deeper; those people would return in the spring, and I had this sense that only the people who were there in February understood the place. I remember walking along the streets on April weekends and running into tourists who were walking slowly. I was unaccustomed to seeing people on the street! A resort town in the off-season has a sort of snowglobe feeling that nothing can penetrate. It's an enclosed world. Provincetown is especially like that because it's nearly an island. I wanted that feeling of the outside world not affecting the world of the novel, which I'm sure was partial laziness. I was figuring out how to write the world of the novel, and it was easier to write one in which the outside world rarely intrudes on the lives of the characters. Practically no historical event has any bearing on the novel. It takes place in the fifties, and there's a single reference to Elvis. That's about it.

Why did you set the story in a fictional town rather than a real town?

Everyone thinks the novel is set in Brewster, but I wanted Brewsterville to be a cross between Brewster and Osterville. It's not Brewster. The closest I can say is that it's somewhere along the Cape. The reason I set it in a fictional town is that I didn't want to be beholden to the geography and the particularities of a specific town. Again, this is the snowglobe effect, and I didn't want to have to be historically accurate. The book has a vaguely fairy-tale feeling to it, and because of that, I wanted it set in an imaginary place.

You said in an interview: "I believe that most people are extraordinary . . . to me that is one of the pleasures of writing fiction, getting to know characters in a complex way, in a way that you sometimes don't get to know mere acquaintances." How do you get to know your characters?

As I said, largely through the writing, and through extra writing assignments. When I was first working on the book I'm working on now, the narrative was third-person multiple point of view, and now it's a first-person book. I feel like the key to writing a first-person book is to train yourself to think like the narrator; everything else takes care of itself. The deeper you delve into the book, the easier you slip into it when you sit down to write because you've probably been living in it for hours anyhow. It's not a matter of saying, "What would Peggy do now?" You're thinking like Peggy, so accessing her brain is easy. That's how it felt when I was writing *The Giant's House,* and that's how it feels on this new book, too. When I was working on *The Giant's House,* I thought it was a tremendously autobiographical book. Then when I read it, I realized that it was in no way at all autobiographical. The narrator and I have certain characteristics in common, but she's a completely different person. I guess I had to believe that it was autobiographical in order to write the book, because I was thinking like her. When it's working well, it feels like channeling. You have your characters say all kinds of unbelievable things. They're better people than you are, and they're worse people than you are. Their strengths are not your strengths, and their weaknesses are not your weaknesses, but you may not even have thought about your own strengths and weaknesses until you began to write this character.

One of the reasons I wrote things in the voices of other characters outside of the text was that it was hard for me to shape the characters with Peggy narrating, partially because of her personality. If I have one major dissatisfaction with *The Giant's House* as it is now, that's it. Peggy obscures the other characters, which makes some logical sense, since that's intrinsic to her character. But the next level of characters, like James, Caroline, and Oscar, are not as vivid as Peggy. Part of that is just Peggy; her general clumsiness with other human beings means that she couldn't quite fathom them. That's something that I'm working on in the new book. Once I am able to think like the narrator, then I can develop the other characters beyond them. Plus, I have to write down biographical details so that I know them before I sit down to work on the book.

Who is the narrator of the new book?

A man named Mose Sharp. He's a straight man in a comedy team. He goes into vaudeville after the death of his favorite sister, and he teams up with a comic named Rocky Carter. They're the comedy team of Carter and Sharp, and they become quite successful in vaudeville and movies for a short period of time. The book follows their career.

Did you conduct a lot of research about vaudeville before you could write the novel, or did you wait until you'd already written the draft, like with *The Giant's House*?

I did more research before I wrote. There was a real temptation to stay in the basement at the Boston Public Library and read back issues of *Variety* for days on end. I love that kind of research, but in the end I wind up tossing much of it aside. Frequently I do research to get an idea of what I'm writing about; then I try to forget it all and write. In the beginning, though, historical accuracy is essential. I can only mention vaudeville theaters that really existed. If there isn't an Orpheum in St. Paul, I can't put one there. Then, after a while, I don't care. Surely I'll receive a letter from a vaudeville aficionado saying that there was never an Orpheum in St. Paul, and in the beginning, that would've been the worst thing that could've happened, but at this point in the writing, I don't care.

How has being named one of the twenty best young American novelists by *Granta* affected you, if at all?

Of the people selected, I think I'm probably the person it did the most good for. They wrote articles about the list when it was published, and there were many mean articles about who deserved to be on the list and who didn't deserve to be on the list. There were the people who were expected to be on the list, and the people on the list that no one had ever heard of. I was always one of those novelists, always, and in that way I could pleasantly surprise people. No one was going to say, "She was over-rated," because I wasn't rated at all. The publication date of the *Granta* issue was the same as the publication date of *The Giant's House*. It was perfectly timed. I did a few interviews with local papers and magazines, and the interviewers would tell me that they were interviewing me be-cause they'd heard of me because of the *Granta* issue. So I think I received a little more attention when the book came out because of *Granta*. As a result of that list, I was able to meet some lovely people. I met Katharine Weber, now a dear friend of mine, and Stewart O'Nan and Sherman Alexie.

You said in an interview after *The Giant's House:* "I think our lives are constantly transformed by love. Not just by what we think of as romantic love, you know, love with the person you sleep with. But that our daily lives are constantly shaped by the people we love, our friends, our families." Can you talk about how that belief influences your fiction?

Although I failed to do this, one of the things that I intended to do with *The Giant's House* was write about nonromantic love. *The Giant's House* was not a romance in the early versions, at least not consciously. My readers said, "You've got to face up to this. She loves the guy." I wrote *The Giant's House* in eight months, then revised it for two and a half years, and a lot of the revision was developing that romance in a nat-ural way. I'd start at the beginning and work my way through the book, bringing it a little closer every time.

What's your schedule like when you're writing?

I'm so bad. When I write, I write hard, frequently in Provincetown. It's a point of superstition that a huge percentage of all three of my books have been written in 6 Fishbourne Upper at the Work Center. That's the apartment I had both years when I was a fellow, and I've rented that apartment for a total of five months over the last few years. I've written much of this [new] book in that apartment. I certainly do plenty of work away from Provincetown. It's not like I write two months out of the year, but I don't write every day. I don't write even close to every day. When I do, I write awful stuff. I know it's important for some people, but for me it's not a useful exercise at all. Which isn't to say that I don't have to make myself write. I really do. I vow I'm going to be good, then I turn on the TV and waste time, and I hate doing that. If I'm reading a book, I'm much more likely to write. I write the best at night. My concentration is better then. I sometimes write in the afternoon. The only time I write in the mornings is when I'm in Provincetown and I'm really in writing mode. I go to sleep and I wake up in the morning and go right to work.

You teach at different universities and workshops around the country. How does the travel and moving around, not to mention the actual teaching, affect your writing schedule?

It has a directly negative affect. No, that's not true. At Iowa, I was teaching a class that I invented, a class in novel writing. This came about because when I was teaching at Eugene I had a workshop with seven people, two of whom were working on novels, and their classmates had read their novels over previous semesters. This is the best situation you can be in if you're writing a novel in a workshop. They brought in their twenty pages, and still it was unsatisfactory. The people in the program were smart, respectful, and acute critics, but even though they'd read the other work, it was still like peeking in through a keyhole. Any criticism of the work becomes bogged down in things that aren't important in the early drafts. We learned that novels in their tender stages need a different kind of attention than short stories do. Prescriptive advice is a term I hadn't heard before Iowa, and it's not recommended; it's when you tell the author what should happen rather than what's wrong and leave the solution to the writer. Personally, I love prescriptive advice. I'll reject it if it's wrong. Novels can benefit from this kind of advice. So my idea was to teach a class in which we read a different student's novel each week, fifty to a hundred pages. We didn't line edit. We gave a whole-project critique. The first half of the class we talked about the work, and the second half I spoke about novel writing with some specific reference to the work at hand. I hadn't known how the novel-writing class would turn out, but it went really well. With that class, more than usual, I would say something, then go home and say, "You fool, you've been talking to yourself." So I was articulating things that had been a concern for me in a way that I wouldn't have without teaching. Other than that, I don't get very much work done when I'm teaching, because I'm away from home, and I also tend to travel to see friends in the area who I haven't seen for a long time.

What would you say to someone working on a first novel?

If you think: Is this a novel? How do I know that I'm writing a novel? How do I know it's not just one damn page after another?—that's how it is. Most of my advice has to do with preparing yourself for depression and heartbreak in the actual writing of the book. You must be prepared to break your own heart.

Conducted: January 2002

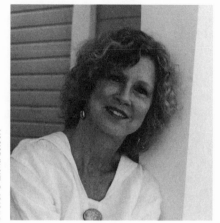

SUE MILLER

The Hot Dramas of the Domestic Scene

Sue Miller is the best-selling author of *The Good Mother, Inventing the Abbots, Family Pictures, For Love, The Distinguished Guest,* and *While I Was Gone.* She lives in Boston.*

*Since this interview, Sue Miller has published the novel *The World Below.*

You haven't written short stories since *Inventing the Abbots*? Do you think you'll write short stories again?

I wrote one about two years ago, but it has some problems. It's a very long short story for one thing. I think that I've gotten used to working in the longer, more expansive form of the novel. Certainly, it's true that most of the ideas that I have tend to be ones that I want to explore in greater depth than a short story. And once I get going, most of the situations or embodiments of my ideas tend to be very fleshed out and with a lot of complications, too. So, I'm not sure. I'd like to, because I like the short story. It's an elegant form. I think I did a good job at it when I was writing more of them. I just haven't thought that way in a while. It may partly be because when I'm finished with a novel, I'm trying to think of another novel—that's my desperation, to launch myself into another book. If I don't have a book-length idea afloat, I feel worried. That's always been true. Even when I was writing a lot of short stories I was thinking about and working on a novel.

How do your novel and story ideas come to you?

Usually they come as a vague notion, an idea of what I want to be talking about. Then I begin to imagine situations which would convey that idea or contain it, and then I begin to people the situations with characters. It starts abstractly for me, but it happens closely together. I'm not pondering an abstraction for a long time. One comes on the heels of another, but it's the idea that interests me first.

In a novel such as *Family Pictures*, which has a large cast of family members, how do you draw each character enough so that the reader doesn't lose track of who's who?

Partly by eliminating some of the characters as "round" characters. This means there were at least several characters whom I didn't take too much into account. They're there, but I account for them with a comment or two. Mary, or Liddie, for instance. Quickly done, quickly dismissed. In the scenes in which all the characters are present, usually there's more focus on one or the other. Also, most of those scenes occur late in the book, by which time they've all defined themselves or been defined by how their lives have spun out, essentially. People's understanding of what's going on in the characters' lives is part of the ongoing conversation that everyone has.

I did feel sometimes when I was writing certain events in *Family Pictures,* particularly when the children were young, that it was hard to keep track of them all—as it is in life. There was a prolonged Christmas scene, for instance, in which there's a family meal, everyone at the table. There's a baby in the house who's just been born, and Mack at some point in the day steps on an ornament and has to be taken to the emergency room to have his foot stitched up. In some of that chapter it did feel that there were a lot of people to take care of. But even there, the only people who were important as *developed characters* were David and Lainey and Mack. Even Nina, who's important elsewhere, was little enough at this stage not to count that much. Even so, I needed to know how Mary and Nina would talk at this young age, so I had to think about her a little.

There are some exchanges between Liddie and Mack, but my job was easier because of this issue of the round and the flat characters. By focusing on one character's perspective at a time, and seeing the other characters through that character's set of eyes, I used the family repeatedly nearly as a sociogram. But all the characters were very clear to me as personalities. I knew what was going to happen to each of them in a rough sense even before I began writing. Even as children, their natures were clear to me—one would be sunny and easy, and one would be more defiant.

You have four different points of view in *Family Pictures*. You use third-person personal with David, Lainey, and Mack, and the first person with Nina. How did you decide whose point of view to use to narrate different parts of the story?

Each time I started a new chapter, I spent a lot of time looking at what I had and then trying to decide with whom I should *be* for this chapter. It seemed a matter of balance in each case: now I needed to move over here so that we'd have a sense of how this character was growing and changing and feeling. There was also the matter of dynamism. With whom were changes occurring at this point in time? Who was being most affected at this point in time by the family's situation, and therefore whom I should be tracing? Whose reactions were important—whose life was in flux in responding to what was going on in the family most at any given time? I sought in each case to imagine the character very deeply.

Is that something you do on the page?

With *Family Pictures,* I made an enormous number of notes on all the characters before I started. Often they focused on points of conflict, bits of dialogue that might occur which would encapsulate each one's perspective and personality. "He says this, she says this back." I wouldn't know where these things would go in the novel exactly, but they helped me know what their personalities were like. I started the book initially writing about David and Lainey before they were married, when they were both single people. Their first meeting, their courtship. I got about two hundred pages done of that, but I didn't use it because Doug [Bauer] and my literary agent looked at it and didn't think it was very good. But my notes rescued me then. I think if I hadn't done the huge amount of work ahead of time—taking notes, thinking about it, asking myself questions about what I wanted to get out of this book, what I was doing with it—if I hadn't been so enormously committed to it, if they'd said what they'd said without that background, I don't know that I would've gone back to it. I might have thought it wasn't meant to be. Instead, I felt so committed that I tried to figure out where else I could begin or where I could cut into this material. I *was* in misery. I *wanted* to give up in some ways, but I was able to come back to it because I knew the characters so well. I cared about them, and I knew what I wanted to get out of the story.

So the work you do ahead of time is taking notes, and thinking about the interactions and personalities of the characters?

Yes. Sometimes they're very specific—dialogue, let's say—because it expresses the crux of a situation, and at other times they're more general description. But they don't cover everything—for instance, the scene in which Mack and Nina destroy Randall's room. Mack essentially seduces her into this as a way of mourning Randall, but also in this scene, Nina's taking sides against her parents and stepping over toward Mack's vision of what's going on in the family. I had notes that took me that far, but the chapter is long, and much more happens around that event than I'd planned out. I knew that scene was coming up, but I didn't know how it would happen, only that they would peel the wallpaper and that it would be a defining moment in Nina's life, in her allegiance with Mack.

Did you ever choose the wrong point of view or narrator and have to reconsider?

I made a lot of wrong choices with that book, and there was a lot that I cut. It was a hard book to write because of all the characters and because of the way the narration moved. I don't think that I've ever had as much trouble. I've never written from as many characters' perspectives as I did in that book. Also, it's such a plotless book. There was never a *necessary* event that had to happen. In any chapter, anything could've happened, and there were so few things that *had* to happen that it became very arbitrary. Because of that, I made a lot of false starts. But also, I was learning a lot while working on that book. I *hope* that I learned a lot. It was very difficult to write structurally, and it was very messed up structurally when I first wrote it. Figuring out how to pull it together was a tremendous learning experience for me.

In *While I Was Gone,* you return to using the first-person point of view, as you did in *The Good Mother.* Why did you decide to return to the first person? What did you gain from it in the telling of this particular story?
I've always felt that the first person is more propulsive, and more immediately seductive to a reader, so that was part of it. I was also interested in and wanted to play with the notion of unreliability in that particular narrator. That wasn't the focus for me in *The Good Mother.* In that book there was no real question about what the narrator saw or didn't see or didn't understand. She had blindnesses, but they were not problems in her personality that caused her to be blind to certain things. That's not true for Jo in *While I Was Gone.* Jo is trying very hard to explain to you, the reader, at all times what was truly going on, but she's not fully conscious of all that's going on. I hoped the reader would see things in spite of the fact that Jo didn't sometimes. That was the pleasure of the book, playing with that only partially unconscious narrator, but still a narrator trying hard to *be* conscious and take everything into account.

When a story idea comes to you, how do you decide what point of view to use?
Sometimes I've fretted, moved back and forth—tried passages in the first person, then in the third person. For instance, the whole of *For Love* is very close to Lottie's point of view, almost a first-person narration, but not quite, and that's partly because I also tried it in the first person. But I ended up feeling that I liked the third-person ability to step back and say what she was thinking, even things she might not have been entirely aware that she was thinking: to note slightly subconscious responses that she was having to things. I also think that the first person is very confining, finally. It was wonderful to work with it in *Family Pictures,* where I combined it with the third person, because I got away with a lot, but more typically you only have one person's perspective, and only one person's experience of the story. You don't have the possibility of looking at the way the person she's interacting with felt about the same events. Unless there's a compelling reason for a story to be in the first person, I wouldn't choose it. You can lose a lot more than you gain. It seems easier, and in many ways it is easier, but you slowly become aware of what you cannot do as you work through a first-person novel. You may want to give the history or the feelings of someone else, and you can only do it as the first person perceives it or doesn't perceive it. It's a complicated decision, and one I've not always been certain of when I undertook a book at the start. More of my books are in the third person. I love the third person because you can use it in so many ways. You can move in so close to a character, and then pull way back and be very godlike and comment on

the whole thing. That's great freedom, and I really enjoy that. It can be hard to work it well, but I love it.

In *While I Was Gone*, you have a good understanding not only of the life of a veterinarian but also of the police procedure and lingo surrounding a homicide investigation, and also the inner workings of the life of a minister. Do you have to do research in order to create authentic details for the lives of your characters?

I did do research for that book, but not for the minister's life, because that was something very familiar to me from my family background. But I leaned on others for different kinds of information. My brother, for instance, is a vet, and he was enormously helpful to me. We had a prolonged correspondence about certain episodes in the book, which was really enjoyable. He's my youngest brother, and I didn't know a lot about his work or his feelings about it. It was great to have him be able to help me and tell me what he knew. He told me what it *felt* like to be a vet. He could talk openly about things like euthanasia in a way that I think someone who didn't know me might not have been able to.

The police were wonderful too. I went down to the Cambridge Police Station, in part because I wanted to see it—I have a few little scenes set in it. Three detectives sat down and talked to me. I asked them about my hypothetical situation, and they were very concrete in telling me what would happen. They were willing to discuss differences, too, between police procedures when the crime in my book happened, and what they are like now. I also asked about what the procedures would be around an unresolved case which got opened up again, about how much evidence is left around, and that sort of thing. They were tremendously helpful to me.

There's always been some level of research in every book that I've done. For *The Good Mother*, I did a lot of research about contested divorce cases, which I didn't know anything about, and the way that civil institutions deal with custody issues. I read a lot of trial transcripts, and went and sat in on some civil cases—you can't sit in on custody cases—just to get a sense of the courtroom. There are usually things that I have to learn. It gets me out into the world, asking questions about characters' lives.

I've heard readers comment that they think Daniel is too good, which I don't agree with. I see him as more involved in his work than his marriage at times, and unrealistic about what actually happened between Eli and Jo. Do you think that Daniel is too good? How do you avoid the pitfall of creating characters who are too good, or on the other hand, too bad?

I thought his "goodness" was a problem within the novel, a part of what *itched* between Daniel and Jo. Jo says early on that she doesn't tell him something, because he'll see it as a problem that he can solve. He'll want to work on it with her. (This is the feeling of unease she has in the boat.) He's not able to dwell in ambiguity, to let things go. He's always coming back at her with an answer. I see him as a very good person but also as someone whose work dominates his life. And his approach to his work means that he is a certain way with his family too, which is a liability for her because she is by nature a little secretive. Difficult. So they have some problems with each other, ways in which their personalities conflict with each other. Jo is a person who wants a lot of privacy and needs a lot of privacy, and he's a person who can't allow that in some ways, while also being a person who's terribly busy. When he turns his attention to you there will be this complete sympathy, yes, but some of the time he will just not be there. I think that's hard, and Jo talks about it as being hard—that when she needs him he's not always there. In the novel, a terribly important thing has happened to her, and he's not concerned with it because he genuinely has other things that seem of more vital concern to him. That's the way it is.

I don't find him too good either. And in general, I don't think I've had the problem of creating characters who are too good, so it's not something I think about avoiding.

The sermon in *While I Was Gone* is so authentic and beautiful. It surprises Jo because she realizes that Daniel has been paying attention to her suffering, and it makes her fall in love with him all over again. That's powerful stuff. How were you able to create such an utterly credible sermon and weave in the aspects that would make it work within the narrative?

I know sermons really well because I went to church all my life, and because my father was an ordained minister. He never had a church, but he preached frequently, as did all our family friends. We were big-time church attenders. It's in my blood. Both my grandfathers were ministers, too. My parents talked a lot about sermons at home. Weighed them, evaluated them. It was the form of writing I understood first in my life, though I didn't take it in as a form of writing. I took it in as a spoken form. But I really began to recognize the way sermons move, even as a child. When I sit down in church now, I know in my bones what six steps are coming.

As far as incorporating the sermon into this fiction goes, I had it much easier than a preacher. I was able to summarize the parts that would be tedious to write out. I had very much in mind as I thought about it ahead of time, that it was coming up around Halloween and All Saints' Day. Daniel was writing the sermon in response to these events in the calendar but also to his having just presided very painfully over the funeral of a parishioner that he'd been fond of. Initially, I thought I would just have Jo respond to the beauty of the form. He would be so good at it that she would feel the way that we do when we see someone whom we deeply love, even if we're angry with them, do something beautifully. She would be exalted. But then I began to think as I wrote it that it could contain a reference to Dana, possibly something that Daniel put in spontaneously as a way of coming closer to Jo when she arrived unexpectedly in church. So my original impulse was to have Jo be very moved just by the sermon, but then, as often happens when you start to write, something else comes up, another fictional opportunity reveals itself.

By making Daniel a minister, you give yourself the room to discuss issues of faith that are important to the narrative, but why did you decide to make Jo a veterinarian?
I wanted to write about animals in people's lives because I think they're so important. I wanted the animals in the story to be characters themselves, in effect, and to have them be very important to the human characters. And of course, every character you write about needs work, so it seemed like a wonderful job to give Jo. I was interested in it; I was interested in learning more about it; I was interested in communicating with my brother about it. In all those ways it really worked.

Then I became interested in the notion of animals as animals, as creatures who remain innocent even though they do quite terrible things. There's a remembered scene in which one of Jo's dogs is dreaming of killing something, and for me that was further reflection on the notions that are running under the book: guilt and innocence, when we are redeemed, how we get redeemed, and whether we need forgiveness. I wanted to have this sense of another kind of life altogether, the animal life, in which these things are not issues at all, contrasting with the way these things are playing out in the novel. To have that life be comforting to Jo, to have it rescue her at a certain time in her life, says something about her as a character: that she yearns for something simpler. She might be happier living in a less complicated universe than the one she's landed in, because she doesn't like to deal with humans. She must, of course, and she does, and it changes her that she does in the course of this book, but it's symptomatic of something in her that she doesn't very much want to.

In *For Love*, the first passage is of Lottie imagining the accident that is at the core of the novel. From there, you go back and describe the events in

both the recent and not-so-recent past leading up to the accident. By placing the horror of the accident scene first, the scenes leading up to it are cast in a different light than if the story had been told chronologically. There is more weight to every exchange and innuendo and event that keeps readers engaged more deeply. Is the order of these scenes something that you work on, or does the story simply come out this way?

I work on it. Very much so. I knew I didn't want to have the story occur chronologically, because then the motion of the book would build toward the accident. The accident would seem to be the climax of the book. That's more the way that *While I Was Gone* works. But I didn't want that to be the case in this book, because for me that wasn't the issue at all here. The concern I had in this book had to do with Lottie, with her thinking about her ability to love. I felt that putting the accident at the beginning would get it *out of the way*, essentially, as a plot element. We would all know from the start what was going to happen, so there wouldn't be this sense of focus on that when it did. I recognize that in a way it makes the focus on it more intense, but I think it also signals that this is not going to be a novel about this sweet, drunken baby-sitter who gets killed.

The structure doesn't necessarily focus the novel on the accident, but on all the issues leading up to the accident and why the accident happened.

And how it happened, and so forth. I concede that it may point to the accident more *dramatically*. But my reasoning was to get it out of the body of the story. I wasn't thinking of the other possibilities at the time. It does give an added weight to everything. But that's useful, too, in that it's a slow story getting off its feet. Starting with the accident plunges the reader right in there. I knew in some ways that the story would be slow, that I wanted to have a lot of *speculation about* love on Lottie's part, that she'd be doing all this reading about love. So I thought, let's have this crazy *love* thing happen right at the start: someone actually dies for love, this sad bystander of a baby-sitter.

Similarly, in *Family Pictures*, after the account of this family's loss and sadness, you leave readers with a young Lainey and David about to make love, until Lainey's water breaks, and she is on the verge of giving birth to Randall. Reminding us of "reckless courage . . . the great loving carelessness" that started this family in the first place makes readers wonder if Lainey and David had it to do all over again, they would. It contrasts their naive love with the harsh realities of life. Again, was the placement of this scene something that you had to struggle for?

I knew that I wanted to end somehow with Nina forgiving her parents, seeing them as young and hopeful and loving. I had that particular scene written for an earlier chapter, but I was about halfway through when it occurred to me that it belonged at the very end. I felt from the moment that I made that decision that I knew where I was going. I had to get Nina to the point where she'd be capable of thinking of them this way, because, of course, it's what she imagines for them. But I knew that's what I wanted to end with, a time before they knew all the things that were going to change them, when they thought their lives were going to be like other people's lives, when they still have the privilege of proceeding spontaneously. They want to enlarge their marriage by having children without, at this point, recognizing that part of that is an embrace of potential calamity. To me this moment seemed perfect for the ending because of precisely where Nina has gotten to in her life. She is recovered from the way she's grown up; she's miscarried a damaged child in her failed marriage; she's ready to undertake the step of risking having a child in her new marriage. But I didn't want to be blindly positive about all this. This family was profoundly changed and in some ways damaged because of its experience. A character like Mack reflects that aspect of the situation. Mack is the sad character, the negative side of all this. He's been injured permanently by his growing up. That's not the way he would've ended the story.

You've described sex as a sacred act through a couple of characters. In *Family Pictures,* **for instance: "She [Lainey] told him later that sex with him felt nearly holy to her now, that she thought of it in words that came to her with doubled potency from religion, words like** *riven, cleft.* **She said that even in church she was sometimes swept with desire; she had to lower her head when they read aloud the words of Scripture: flesh, blood." What do you think is the connection between sexuality and spirituality?**

I think Lainey is a little off the charts in terms of that. I mean in general it's very clear that for someone who is a deep believer, sexuality, married sexuality in particular for people who believe that marriage is a kind of sacrament, can be an expression of deep faith in some ways, and is enriched and made more complicated by that. For Lainey it works the other way, too. Her faith is enriched by her notion of sexuality as being all-pervasive. I saw it as an idiosyncratic thing in her, that she would feel this so intensely. She even goes to the minister and talks to him about it because she wonders if there's something not right about her experience. He, of course, says that it's all okay, it's human. That's the voice of a minister I would be very sympathetic with, someone who would say: "This is good. How you come to God is not important. That you come to God is important. There's nothing obscene about this." But I'm sure there are many people who would think it was the height of obscenity.

You also use a character's sexuality to deepen character or demonstrate psychology. What do you think a character's sexuality can show?

Sex is a very intense act between people who are usually quite literally stripped bare, but also very exposed emotionally. Of course I recognize there's always the possibility of sexuality without that, but I'm usually more interested in using it to expose a character's deepest needs. For instance, Nina's feelings about Phillip: she just has to *have* somebody at that stage of her life. Her desperation is very clear throughout that prolonged sexual episode. Sexuality can do that for a character—expose her at her most vulnerable. It can also expose other things—for instance, with Lottie in *For Love,* for whom sex is so much more exciting when she's in an illicit relationship than it is after she gets married. She doesn't know if she can ever make this adjustment. There were other complications, too, such as her husband's sorrow over his previous wife's incapacity and death, but even his sorrow was more tolerable to her when they were meeting in hotels. All this is central in revealing Lottie's incapacity to commit herself deeply to another person, which is her struggle in this book.

You can use sexuality to expose the least conscious elements of a character's personality—because we don't ponder that much about our sexual responses. They're just what we have, what we own, and we don't feel that we can teach ourselves, as with other things in life, to feel differently about them. We feel about sex the way that we feel about sex. It's a less controlled, a less conscious aspect of the personality. Or it can be.

Many of your female characters struggle between their need for stability and security, their sense of duty, and their desire for passion and excitement in their relationships with men. Anna in *The Good Mother* actually pays a large price for her need for passion, as does Jo in *While I Was Gone,* and she didn't even act on her desire. In *For Love,* the accident dramatizes the conflict between passion and domestic life. What draws you to this duplicity? Do you think there is always a price to pay for seeking passion outside the traditional boundaries of marriage?

No, I don't think that at all. I think lots and lots of people are very successful at it. But I think the conflict is charged and can be used dramatically very effectively. Hmmm . . . maybe I should write a novel in which someone successfully commits adultery. Of course, there's a certain way in which David in *Family Pictures* does. He has an adulterous relationship, and then he ends up happily married to that woman later on. The affair is very damaging to his marriage, but it doesn't end it. He and his wife get back together. It's only much later they decide, for entirely different reasons, that they can't stay together. They have to deal with what has happened between them, rather than what he's done outside of the marriage, and it's that which makes it impossible for them to go on together. And Lottie has had a prolonged adulterous relationship that turns into a marriage. So, I don't think I've necessarily made this equation.

You're more drawn to the dramatic tensions in this struggle then.

Yes. And there are enormous dramatic tensions. Even successful adultery wouldn't be a very interesting topic without tensions. Look, sometimes I wish I *could* write a lighter book, a book that seems less fraught, but I don't seem to be able to. I think it's because I'm drawn to the trouble and conflict that that kind of an event leads to. Also, I tend to work on the domestic scene, and that's certainly one of the possible hot dramas in the domestic scene.

In a *New York Times* book review, Jane Smiley called *Family Pictures* "an important example of a new American tradition that explores what it means, not to light out for the territories but to make a home, live at home and learn what home is." Do you agree with this statement? Do you see yourself as part of this tradition?

I do. There's been a lot of writing about this, so what I have to say may not be particularly fresh. The novel in English has a long tradition of being about the home. This "lighting out for the territories" was a new wrinkle at a certain point in American fiction, but became the American novel, more or less. The novel as it developed in other parts of the world didn't experience that *On the Road,* let's-throw-domesticity-away kind of thing. Read Lesley Fiedler, *Love and Death.* It was especially true of the period I grew up in, when I was reading people like Roth, and Mailer, and Bellow. But you can write about an awful lot using the home, using elements that are very domestic. They are equally as rich; they demonstrate the human condition fully as much as books which represent fleeing or rejecting domesticity. In either case, the point is to have a character struggle against himself. Where you put him, what you give him to struggle against, is whimsical and entirely up to you—what you know and what you're most interested in. Whether you have him run off to Mexico, or whether you have him stay at home and make a decision about what to do with his autistic child, what you're trying to do is expose what makes him how he is, and how he thinks about fate as opposed to freedom.

I do think that Smiley is right about me as a writer. There's no question as to where I've placed myself. I think we don't have much choice about this. I remember reading as passage in Cheever's journals—he'd just finished reading a new Bellow book, and his great sorrow was that all he could write about were small domestic things. I think we have what we have to work with. I can't imagine starting now to try to write a novel about war. I see myself as someone like Ian McEwan, who *is* domestic, but then the world impinges enormously in his books, and often very violently. I think there are similarities in our concerns—his discussions of faith and belief, what man can control and what he can't control—these seem parallel to some of what I'm doing. Also the intrusion of violence is like what happens in a lot of my work.

He stays in the kitchen a lot less, though; I'll admit it.

I know that readers often ask what aspects of a story are autobiographical, and which are invented, and this never ceases to frustrate writers. But it does raise an important question. What is the role of autobiography in fiction?

Well, of course, people have what they have to work with because of who they are. I suppose there are people who invent whole national histories, personal histories, which are purely imagined, but most people use their lives in one way or another. They work closer to the bone, or in some cases a little further away from it. For instance, I have trouble imagining writing directly about someone that I know, and I don't believe I ever have. It would be very confining not to be able to invent a character. I'm working now on a memoir about my father's illness in which I have to write about him. Normally, I think of the act of writing as being fundamentally very playful, and I don't feel that way at all about this memoir. It's hard. I write on it, turn away and write a novel, then work on it again. I've been working on it for years and years, in part because it feels so different and uncomfortable to me to confine myself that tightly to what's real. When I'm writing fiction, my sense is very much of letting myself invent anything, while also using things that I know from my own life, or things that I've lived through. But I feel that at their cores my stories are completely invented in every case.

I remember when my son was little: I'd listen to him playing with his friends, actually preparing to play. They'd say, "I'm going to come in, and I'm going to say da-da-da-da, and you'll say. . . ." That is, in effect, what the writer is doing a lot of the time, thinking about what her characters will say or do. And it *feels* very playful. And open, as though you can do whatever you want with it. I *do* feel that I can do what I want with my work. In that sense it's not autobiographical at all. Nothing I write is dictated by anything that's ever happened to me, and nothing is dictated by my needing to reproduce any character I've known in my life. Certainly I've used traits or ways of speaking lifted from people that I've known or from myself, but the moment that kind of thing starts to confine me, I have to break the mold.

We all know how isolating a writer's life can be. What are some of the things that you do to interact with a larger community and engage in public literature?

Well, I'm the chair of PEN/New England right now. PEN is very active in the Boston area—literacy programs, readings, panels for writers. I'm the person who oversees a lot of decisions and responsibilities. I enjoy it. Before I was chair, I was the clerk, and before that I was the treasurer, and before that I did volunteer work, and I did more teaching. When my chairperson role is up, I'll be looking for something that will keep me in the world in something like those ways. I'm really pleased with this role, though, especially with the Diversity Committee, which I've been very involved in developing, and I'm hoping that it will be a big success. We're taking a look at all of the things that we do, and all of the events, and trying to make sure that they are more inclusive and offer more a sense of how rich our writing community is.

You mentioned that when you wrote the beginning to *Family Pictures* that Doug Bauer and your agent gave you some feedback, and you changed your plans with the novel. How much are your agent and editor involved in your work?

My agent is a wonderful reader, and she does fine editing. She doesn't do as much line editing as my editors, but she does as much in terms of saying something like, "Do you really want us to feel that this character is sappy? Because here he does this sappy thing, and he does it again here and here." And I'll realize she's right; I've made him a sap. Then I correct six small things, and it's better. I've also gotten better at being my own editor, at turning in work where there aren't so many differences between what I intend and what I end up with. But my agent is great, and Doug is great, and they've both been my teachers in that regard. I've sort of jumped around between editors, but my first editor and the one that I have now have both been very attentive.

Do they help you with simple editing, or do they also help you deepen the narrative or more fully achieve your intention?

The latter happened most with *Family Pictures*. Ted Solatarof, who was my editor for that, asked a question that made me write a short scene between Lainey and Nina at the end of the book. He said that he felt that the narrative didn't *come around* enough at the end, that the conflicts in the book hadn't quite crystallized. In response, I wrote a scene in which Nina accuses her mother of loving Randall more than she loved her "normal" children. Her mother says to her that she wished she could have loved him exactly the way that she loved the other children, but she had to love him the way she did, because he *was* damaged. It all gets laid out at that point. I'd come very close to making this clear, but Nina hadn't said that to her before. It hadn't come around to this moment where the meaning of Randall in her life got articulated, and the feeling about her parents got spoken. I think that scene helped the book enormously. It was only about an extra five pages. For the most part, though, Ted used to say things like, "A question will linger in the reader's mind about. . . ." Then it would be up to me to decide whether or not I *wanted* that question to linger in the reader's mind, or whether I wanted to answer it, and if so, where. Ted was very good at articulating anything that troubled him, but he never offered prescriptive advice. He never said, "Take this out, put this in." He never did that.

What would you say to someone working on their first novel?

You're talking to someone who wrote two novels she never published before writing her "first novel," so my experience, and therefore my advice, is probably different from that of someone who was more instantly successful. I think it would be to be patient with yourself. To allow yourself to fail, as most of us probably do with our first, and perhaps even our second, short story. To think of yourself as learning, and as open to learning, as you work on a novel. And to wait to try to publish until you have something that seems to you to be as strong and powerful as the work you love best to read is.

Conducted: November 2000

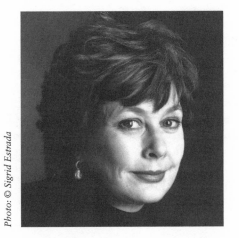

Photo: © Sigrid Estrada

SENA JETER NASLUND

To Be Human Is to Be
Artistically Creative

Sena Jeter Naslund grew up in Birmingham, Alabama. She received M.A. and Ph.D. degrees from the University of Iowa Writers' Workshop. She is the author of the novels *Ahab's Wife* and *Sherlock in Love* and the collection of stories *The Disobedience of Water*. The author is Distinguished Teaching Professor at the University of Louisville and Program Director of the brief-residency M.F.A. in writing at Spalding University, Louisville. She is the editor of the *Louisville Review* and Fleur-de-Lis Press, housed at Spalding University. Sena has received grants from the National Endowment for the Arts, the Kentucky Foundation for Women, and the Kentucky Arts Council.

Can you describe your development as a writer?

When I was young, I knew at a certain point that I wanted to write because I loved to read so much. Reading and writing were two sides of the same coin for me. I've had to struggle with all the main elements of fiction writing: plot, character, theme, and voice. I wanted to write but I didn't know any plots, so I was in trouble as a fiction writer. I didn't have any sense of how to manufacture a plot. Eventually I read something that Virginia Woolf wrote saying that we don't believe in plots anymore. That was a very liberating idea to me: I couldn't invent a plot because I was of the wrong sensibility to think in those terms. It gave me permission to write stories of sensibility, with very little action. But of course, those are not very exciting stories to read, though I did get practice with beginnings, middles, and ends.

How did you move past this struggle with plot?

Well, I decided to be playful with it. I read Nicholas Myer's novel *The Seven-Percent Solution,* which was a Sherlock Holmes expansion, not because I was interested in Holmes, but because I was interested in Freud, and I wanted to see what a fictive portrait of Freud would be like. I was very entertained by the book. I thought: This is good entertainment for smart people. I can do this. Writing my own Holmes mystery gave me the chance to work with plot while entertaining both myself and my readers. I learned to manage plot by writing *Sherlock in Love.* Although it came out with Godine in 1993, it was written more than ten years before, and it came out only after a great deal of revising.

What about the other aspects of writing you mentioned, such as theme?

Once I was liberated from struggling with plot, I was faced with theme. Finally I could make something happen. Then I had to ask, "What does it mean?" I was mostly dealing with these questions as an undergraduate student and as a graduate student at the Iowa Writers' Workshop. While I was still grappling with the question about how writers get meaning into their stories, Kennedy was assassinated. The day he was assassinated, I had to travel across the city of Birmingham, and I saw that many people were very happy that Kennedy had been killed. They felt that he had forced integration on the South. It was a horrifying spectacle to me. That Friday evening I worked at my job as a switchboard operator and I looked out over the people in the store, many of whom I knew; I felt this great alienation. Even as I was having this experience, I realized that this was thematic material, when you get alienated from people you consider your people, thoroughly disapprove of them and hate their thoughts and feelings, yet you still love them—they're still yours. I set about to write a short story with that theme, but I never got to the death of Kennedy, though I wrote a pretty good story. Now, many years later, I'm writing about that situation in a new novel titled *Four Spirits*.

Were there other influences on your development as a writer?

In 1980, I had a daughter, and my whole attitude toward my writing changed. I thought that I should be writing something that I would really like for my daughter to know. I wanted to write about what had been of sustaining value in difficult times. Not that I thought my daughter would find the same things sustaining, but that she would know that there were things that could sustain you. Many of the stories in my first collection, *Ice Skating at the North Pole,* are about surviving a painful situation and finding some sustaining value. Often for me that value came from classical music. My mother was a musician, and as I grew up I heard her playing for several hours every day.

I also had to struggle with the question of character, with how to get depth and complexity and realism in the characters. I had a breakthrough story when I was at Iowa called "The Death of Julius Gesseler," which is in *The Disobedience of Water.* That collection has stories that span many decades of my writing. The title story was the last thing that I wrote before *Ahab's Wife* and was a kind of preliminary study for that novel. With "The Death of Julius Gesseler" I was building on an anecdote my mother had told me about a famous violinist who used to like to dress up as a bum and play music in the park. I was intrigued because I thought it was a pure and adventuresome thing to do. What kind of a person would *want* to do that? Her tale became the nucleus for creating a complex character. At that stage in my career, I needed to deal with characters with whom I had something in common, yet who were very different from me. I couldn't adjust my distance from the characters. Either I was writing autobiographical characters and they were flat because I couldn't get what was in my head onto the page, or I was writing about people I didn't have enough in common with. With Julius Gesseler, who was an older man, hence different from myself, I shared a love for music. I also looked at how other writers drew characters. D. H. Lawrence helped me because he was able to put hate and love so close together in his characters and to show how very ambivalent we are about so much. Also Woolf helped me with how a sense of the self can disappear and reappear: character is not fixed and stable.

What is your writing process like when you're working on a novel? For instance, what goes on through each draft or revision?

With *Ahab's Wife,* the idea for the novel came to me with the first

line—"Captain Ahab was neither my first husband nor my last"—out of
the blue. When the idea came to me in that voice, I trusted the voice in
that sentence. One writes each novel from a different place, and that
novel is definitely a voice book. I didn't know who the first husband was
going to be, and I didn't know who the last husband was going to be, but
I knew I had to trust the voice to get me there. This was the voice of an independent woman with a life of her own.

That sentence gave me a structure because it suggested three romances, and I could embroider other things around that. But I'd written a
great deal of this book and felt that I still wasn't reaching the heart of it.
This part of the process is like a diving expedition, during which I dive
deeper and deeper into what's really the power and the engine and the
pulse of the material. The material closer to the surface tends to come
first. I have to train myself to go deeper.

I was visiting a friend's pool house, and she'd made a tablecloth on
which she'd written quotations about the stars. Cinda had quoted part of
a poem by a mutual friend of ours, Maureen Morehead: "One must take
off her fear like clothing. / One must travel by night. / This is the seeking
after God." When I read those lines, I thought that this was the heart of
my novel. I wanted to write about a woman's quest for a spiritual or
philosophical stance.

I thought about the fact that in the American novel, this subject has
not been dealt with well. The model is Elmer Gantry, where the writer
spotlights a character who is religious, exposes the hypocrisy of the
church, and satirizes everybody's foolishness, and the novel is done. The
American novel doesn't often take on exploring what is for many people
a very important part of their lives—their spiritual questioning.

When you're working on deepening your novel, everything you see is
trying to answer your questions about your novel for you. It's all potential material or a spark for something new. So seeing those words on the
tablecloth became an organizing factor that came back to the origin of
my idea for that book.

How did you get the idea for *Ahab's Wife?*
I was driving a rented car after the publication of *Sherlock in Love* in
Boston, and I was feeling happy and confident about myself as a writer.
Suddenly, I had a vision and heard a voice. The vision was of a woman on
a widow's walk at night, looking out to sea, waiting for her husband's
whaling ship to come home. As she was looking she realized he wasn't
going to come home, and her gaze shifted into the night sky. She began to
ask, "Who am I in the face of all of this glory of the stars? What's my
place in the cosmos?" With that she began her spiritual quest, rather than

waiting for someone to come home and define her. As I had this vision, a voice said, "Captain Ahab was neither my first husband nor my last."

What was your background that led to *Moby-Dick* and the wife of Captain Ahab?
The most recent event in my history with *Moby-Dick* before that vision happened was with my daughter in the summer of 1993. As we traveled a lot in the car, we listened to abridged versions of classic novels on tape to make the miles go. My daughter loved *Moby-Dick* the most out of all the tapes, and she effortlessly memorized Ahab's speeches. When the tape was off, she'd start reciting the speeches. Of course, I was pleased that she had such a good ear. It began to make me sad that there wasn't any great woman character in the book with whom she might identify and whose speeches she could recite. By this time I'd already invaded male territory with *Sherlock in Love*. The world of Sherlock Holmes is a very masculine world. Women are quite peripheral for the most part. I had wanted to create a woman who was as smart as Holmes, who had just as much integrity and courage as Holmes. That, of course, was in the background of my response to my daughter reciting Ahab's speeches.

I thought about how *Huckleberry Finn* and *Moby-Dick* are often described as the great American novel, so I asked myself what these books have in common. They're both quest stories, quests over water, in fact. Both deal with friendships between men of different races. These *are* great subjects. But neither book had any important women characters in it. This made me suspicious of the canon. It implied that if you're going to write the great American novel, you're going to have to leave out women, an unsettling idea.

In "creating" history to fit an existing story, what challenges did you face in weaving the two together?
For *Sherlock in Love*, the first challenge was finding a specific time to write about. Critics of Sherlock Holmes have said that 1886 was a missing year. People don't know what he was doing then—they always treat him as if he were real. When I started rummaging around in 1886, I discovered that that was the year in which Ludwig II of Bavaria had died. He was a great patron of music and the arts. I had wanted to root myself into the reality of that time by reading the general history of the time, but then the character of Ludwig just worked its way into the novel. Like Holmes (and me), Ludwig II loved music.

Now, with the historical period for *Ahab's Wife*, I already knew about Margaret Fuller. Una [Ahab's wife] lived at about the same time as

Margaret Fuller, and I could easily make her acquainted with Margaret Fuller. Fuller interested me because she was a great intellect and friend of great intellects, mostly men, who found such a brainy female threatening. I tell a little story in *Ahab's Wife*, of Fuller's visiting Emerson, and even though she was in his house they wrote letters back and forth, with his little son serving as a postman. All of that was true. Sometimes, Fuller wrote, she felt like bursting through the wall, and you can imagine Emerson shaking in his boots. So Margaret had this great intellect that was met, but she had a passionate nature that wasn't met. She left the U.S. to be the first foreign correspondent, male or female, for an American newspaper. Eventually she went to Italy and was involved in nursing, where she fell in love with a soldier who could barely read. She got pregnant, and they eventually married and then set sail for the U.S.—very concerned about how her intellectual friends, especially Emerson, would receive her and her husband. Her death by drowning was something of a suicide. The witnesses say that she didn't try to save herself, but I don't let Una believe that. I saw Margaret Fuller's story as a kind of shadow version of Una's story. But Una was going to get it all together. She was going to have what she needed, that is, the response by an individual male to all aspects of herself, not fragmenting her and accepting some parts while rejecting others. I pulled Margaret Fuller's story in because I wanted it to be better known, and also to show that there were strong, smart, independent women back then. For the same reason, I pulled in Maria Mitchell, who was an astronomer on Nantucket. I envisioned them like Wonder Woman's bracelets, one on each of Una's wrists. A great woman of science and a great woman of letters, both feminists, both very courageous and intelligent and historically real. These historical women helped me meet credibility issues that might arise about Una.

One of the things that Melville didn't do in *Moby-Dick* was deal with the slavery issue. I thought that if I was going to write an epic novel of this historic period, I couldn't not deal with the issue of slavery. Melville was an abolitionist. His heart was in the right place, but slavery wasn't an important issue in *Moby-Dick*. I wanted to include the slavery issue, which led me to Frederick Douglass. The opening scene in *Ahab's Wife*, where the runaway slave Susan hides in Una's bed, is meant to say right off that I'm going to deal with the issue of slavery, but it's also an allusion to one of the important scenes which opens *Moby-Dick*, in which Ishmael and Queequeg share a bed. (Back then travelers didn't always rent a whole hotel room or a whole bed; they shared a bed.) I put my dark and light characters in bed together, too, but doing something quintessentially female, having a baby.

Some historical characters, like Frederick Douglass, came from my desire to treat the themes that Melville had not treated, and others were meant to validate the reality of my character. Emerson has a very tiny part, then Hawthorne. I included him because I was angry with his failure to support Melville. *Moby-Dick* is dedicated to Hawthorne, but he didn't really recognize the genius of it. *Moby-Dick* was attacked by critics. Melville continued to write, but he was greatly damaged by the critical reception to his book. I wanted to let Una poke at Hawthorne a little bit, so again, I was mixing up the real and the imaginary. I've always felt that memory, or history, and imagination are very close together.

Both *Sherlock in Love* and *Ahab's Wife* required extensive research about history and place. What techniques do you use to conduct your research?

First I read about the period in a general way. When my story brings me to certain points where I need to know more, then I do more focused research. I find things that I get interested in, and they take me to different and unexpected paths. As I said, I started my research for *Ahab's Wife* by rereading *Moby-Dick,* the Norton critical edition, which has excerpts from Melville's sources. I found out that Melville's source for his plotline had been an incident narrated in *The Narrative of the Shipwreck of the Whale Ship Essex from Nantucket.* I was in the Nantucket Historical Society doing research, and I decided to read all about that so that I'd know what Melville knew. The narrative was published in 1821, and *Moby-Dick* was in 1851. The *Essex* story was very well known at Melville's time. Eventually, Melville interviewed the captain, who survived and lived on Nantucket. Melville only used the first half of that historic story, that of the whale ship being stove by a sperm whale and sinking, which is the end of *Moby-Dick.* But what happened next was that people escaped with provisions in several small whaling boats. When they ran out of food and water, they drew lots, and whoever lost was killed and eaten. I was fascinated by this aspect of the narrative and fascinated that Melville chose not to include it. I wanted to go where Melville hadn't gone.

The research led me into an episode that I had a need for. What I mean is this: If I was going to make Una a true wife of Ahab, an equal, I needed to send her through some sort of darkening process, and I needed her to acknowledge the shadow part of herself, a darkness within. This idea of cannibalism was such a grisly thing. If I could send her through that, she would be ready to meet Ahab.

Were you daunted by the enormity of your task at any point in the writing?

I accepted that it had to be big: you don't send a minnow out after *Moby-Dick.* You have to create another big fish to swim in those waters.

People do ask me, "Weren't you intimidated by following after Melville?" To answer truthfully, I have to say no. I was inspired by what he had accomplished. I continued to reread *Moby-Dick* the whole time I was writing my book. Sometimes people open the Bible at random and put a finger down and read the sentence and say that's their lesson for the day. I did that with *Moby-Dick,* and it always was my lesson for the day, whether it was about how to write a sentence, or what to do psychologically, or what kinds of scenes could be evoked. He was endlessly instructive, and at the same time, inspiring. There are a lot things that are very playful in *Moby-Dick.* Even though it's a tragedy, there's a lot of wit and flexibility in the text.

The last chapter in *Ahab's Wife* has Una and Ishmael talking on the roof walk. Una asks Ishmael if he minds that they're writing the same book. The language he responds with is taken from *Moby-Dick.* He says, "Think of the mighty Cathedral of Cologne, left with the crane still standing upon the top of the uncompleted tower." Then I made up the next part. "Think of the Cathedral of Chartres. Think of its two towers. They do not match at all. Built perhaps a century apart, or more; but without both spires, our Chartres would not be Chartres." The next part is from Melville: "Small erections may be finished by their first architects; grand ones, true ones, ever leave the finishing to posterity." I thought, Aha! Permission granted!

It was a lot of fun to weave some of *Moby-Dick* into my book, but from Una's perspective.

In *Sherlock in Love* and *Ahab's Wife,* your stories are set in other times and places, yet they're so convincing. How do you create a realistic sense of a historical setting that draws readers in without distracting them about what's accurate and what is not?

The challenge for a person who does research is to inhale so that it doesn't seem musty when you exhale. One of the ways that I did this in *Ahab's Wife* was by going to Nantucket and using my own body as a research instrument to see how the light fell there, what colors were there, what was the force of the wind. I went in all different seasons. I've also experienced many of the buildings that my historical characters would have seen, because the structures are still there in Nantucket.

Besides the library research, I try to use my senses. Reality in fiction is always conveyed by using language that appeals to the senses—imagery, we call it—that not only relates to sight but to sound, taste, touch, and smell. This is a basic technique that all good fiction writers need, and so I just apply it to the historical setting as if I were there, and take myself there physically inasmuch as that is possible.

In *Ahab's Wife,* Una says of her writing: "... adherence to fact is slavery. Think how Shakespeare distorted, compressed, rearranged historical events in his history plays. Such license would be mine, if I wrote." Where do you draw the line between historical accuracy and fictive license, and what are your guiding principles?

I try to be accurate as possible, though I might shift things slightly in time. For example, in *Ahab's Wife,* I needed the Sankaty lighthouse, which is close to 'Sconset on the eastmost edge of Nantucket Island. In the novel, I had it built three or four years before it was actually built. I give myself license, in that small slippage of the time, but I didn't consider it a serious violation. With *Sherlock in Love,* even the weather is accurate on that June day in 1886 when Ludwig died. And Albert Einstein, as a child, did take violin lessons in Munich.

The theme of the power of writing and of story as a means of examining one's life recurs throughout your work. What do you see as the importance of writing as a tool through which people can understand or reimagine their experience?

I love this question, but I don't know if I can answer it adequately. Let me try. I've always loved and been inspired by the cave drawings at Lascaux and other caves. What they say to me is that to be human is to be artistically creative. Their stories, what they might have said to each other, are lost, but those pictures are there saying, "We're human beings." It's a very deep human impulse that separates us from animals: to create art.

When my daughter was very little, whenever her feet were on a new surface, to know that surface, she would begin to dance. I saw this as a basic human impulse: to know by creating something artistic. We know ourselves by creating something out of what we've experienced, whether with writing or painting or whatever it is. The stimulation of the imagination is something that makes us moral in an indirect way. Simply, it lets us inside the skins of other people to feel how they feel, to identify. It keeps us from evil impulses.

The book that speaks to your question so well is not one that I wrote. It's a book by Ernest J. Gaines, *A Lesson before Dying.* The end of it includes Jefferson's diaries. It's through writing that Jefferson becomes a fuller human being. When he becomes aware of his own senses by using the language of the senses to describe his environment, and when he writes about his inner feelings and the way he feels when the children come to visit him, he discovers his humanness. While that book is of course about racial injustice, the subtext is about redemption through the act of writing. Gaines's novel speaks so well as to how the act of creation helps us realize our potential for being alive as human beings.

A student at the Spalding M.F.A. in writing program who teaches poetry to boys who are incarcerated told me this story: This student had to miss some of her writing classes with the incarcerated boys. When she came back, one of the boys was in the classroom waiting for her. He told her that he missed her, and he confided, "When I'm in here, in this writing room, then I feel like a real boy." Doesn't that just break your heart? Writing made him real. Whether you're incarcerated, or just locked into your own self, it's a liberating thing to have language to express yourself and to make it into some artistic shape.

I know that you started the M.F.A. program at Spalding University. How important do you think it is that new writers attend an M.F.A. program?

Instruction in writing was crucial to my own development, not only for actual advice that was given by people who were more experienced, but also because it legitimized the act of writing and provided a home for it. Some people don't need either side of that to become writers, but to me it's a very supportive framework. I've heard many people say that by studying at one school or another, they learned more quickly what they would've learned eventually on their own. I don't know if that's true or not. It took me so long to learn anything.

I've certainly seen people develop enormously because of their instruction. It's fashionable to say that creative writing can't be taught, but I don't agree with that. I think that an enormous amount can be taught. I've taught in a number of M.F.A. programs at University of Montana, at Indiana University, and at the brief-residency M.F.A. program at Vermont College. I wanted to start this new program drawing on my experiences and doing some things a little differently. In the Spalding M.F.A. in writing program, I wanted to have a program that encouraged writers in any particular area of concentration to know something about the other areas of concentration, so we do a cross-genre exercise every time. We also read a book in common before we come to the brief residency. The first night we discuss the book we've all read, so that we start off with ourselves as readers in a community. Each time we read from a different genre. Having been a student of poetry as an undergraduate greatly enriched my fiction writing, and I wanted to open the possibility of cross-genre fertilization up to students.

Another thing at Spalding that we do differently is that not only do we write in other genres but also in relationship to the sister arts. We go to concerts and plays and talk about aesthetic issues in those arts and how they translate into our own writing. How is *form* achieved in any art? We also do the standard workshops focused on the craft of writing in each core area of concentration, but my philosophy is that you become a better expert by putting things in contexts, then in still larger contexts.

Between getting your first book published and your most recent book published, what have you learned about the publishing industry? Is there anything that newer writers should be aware to look out for?

I've had experience with three different kinds of publishing. My first two books were published by the small press Ampersand, which is now out of business. Then my next two books were published by David R. Godine, which is a very prestigious, small publisher in Boston. *Ahab's Wife* was with Morrow-HarperCollins. I found they all have a lot in common. The people with whom I worked have been very nurturing to me, whether in New York or in smaller places. I found them intelligent, talented, and committed to excellence.

One piece of advice I would have to writers is to remember that you're dealing with real human beings who have their own tastes and hopes and fears. I've heard of editors having to work with writers who are so full of themselves that they can't get anything done. The editor for *Ahab's Wife,* Paul Bresnick, was immensely helpful to me in cutting the novel but also in suggesting scenes which should be in the novel.

Did his suggestions resonate with you?

At first I didn't know how I'd ever do what he'd asked me to do. I had to live with some suggestions for a while, and mull them over, and be patient. In the end, his suggestions made *Ahab's Wife* a better book. A lot of writers take a defensive posture toward the publishing industry, and I think that's very counterproductive.

As a teacher, what are some of the common problems you see in the work of new writers?

In the work of new writers I see a tendency toward abstraction where the language should be concrete. I see the necessity for learning to write dialogue that is fragmentary and natural-sounding instead of speechifying. I see the tendency sometimes for writers to manufacture bigger events than a story needs. I see a neglect of character for the sake of action. I don't think that I'm unique in seeing these things. Any experienced reader or writer would see similar problems in the work of new writers. As I've said, I had to struggle with all major elements of fiction writing.

Do you have any techniques you use when you find that a section isn't working or simply isn't as good as it should or could be?

I try to reimagine the scene as vividly as I can. Then I try to find the words that more truly capture those moments.

What would you say to new writers working on their first stories or novels?

Be ready to abandon your original intention. When characters or scenes come to you for whom you have not planned, embrace them. That's the real creative spirit.

Conducted: July 2002

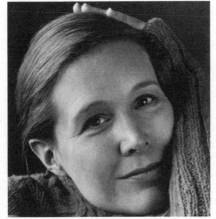

ANN PATCHETT

Constantly Plagiarizing Myself

Ann Patchett is the author most recently of *Bel Canto*, winner of the PEN/Faulk-
ner Award and the Orange Prize for Fiction, and finalist for a National Book Critics Circle award. Her other novels include *The Magician's Assistant*, which
earned her a Guggenheim Fellowship in 1994, and *Taft*, which won the Janet Hei-
dinger Kafka Prize. Patchett wrote her first novel, *The Patron Saint of Liars*, while
a fellow at the Fine Arts Work Center in Provincetown, Massachusetts. This
novel was awarded the James A. Michener/Copernicus Award for a book in progress and was a *New York Times* "Notable Book of the Year." Patchett has written
for many publications, including the *New York Times Magazine*, the *Chicago
Tribune*, the *Village Voice*, *GQ*, *Elle*, *Gourmet*, and *Vogue*.

Let's talk about your development as a writer. How did you get started writing fiction?

I don't have any other skills. I was one of those kids. When somebody said, "What do you want to be when you grow up?" when I was five, I said that I wanted to be a writer. I don't know where that came from, but it came very young and it never seemed to stop.

What did you do to develop your craft?

It depends at what point at which you're speaking. I came home from school and wrote a lot of stories. I read copiously. I spent an enormous amount of time alone. I've always been a real loner. I have the exact disposition for the job. I have no attention deficit disorder. I can sit in a straight-backed chair for eight hours and read Proust. I might have a hard time sitting in a straight-backed chair for eight hours when I'm trying to write, but even then, when I'm on a roll, when I'm really into a project, I can do it.

How does a novel idea come to you?

The novel idea for *Bel Canto* came to me because I was reading the newspapers. But many times, my novels are inspired by my novels. There will be something that's small in one book that will nag at me a little or interest me more, and I want to go back and develop it in another book. Or there will be something that I didn't do in one book that I want to do in another book. For example, in *The Patron Saint of Liars*, there's no sense of time. There's no sense of society, news, responsibility to the world. Everything takes place outside of time. So, in *Taft*, I wanted to write a book that took place in a real city, with city problems, but also a book that takes place on a clock. That book covers ten days. In *Taft*, with the people from East Tennessee, Carl and Fay, I was interested in the idea of coming from another place, a stranger in a strange land. This is present in *The Patron Saint of Liars* as well. But it's really central to *The Magician's Assistant*—the idea of coming to a place where you don't know the rules and you don't know how to behave, which is what that whole book is about. That theme goes on even farther in *Bel Canto*. I'm constantly plagiarizing myself.

Your novels all have brilliant openings. My favorite being the opening sentence for *Taft*, "A girl walked into the bar." Can you talk about how and at what point in the writing of the novel that that sentence, or any opening sentence, comes to you?

I plagiarized that from Elizabeth McCracken. She has a line "a dog ran into a bar," and I loved that. Usually the first line comes to me a long time before I start the novel. This is true of *The Magician's Assistant.* I had the first line for a year before I started writing it. I think this is true of each novel, that I had the first line before I had anything else

What do you think makes a great opening?
It's one of those things; you know it when you see it.

Like hitting the right note.
Or a good piece of jewelry. Whatever's got flash.

Elizabeth McCracken told me that you often conceive of a novel, turn it around in your head and consider your idea from all angles for months and months, then sit down and simply write the book. Is that true?
Yes, except take the word "simply" out of that sentence. I just wrote one of those "Writers on Writing" columns for the *New York Times,* and I'm writing about the fact that I have this beautiful book in my head for such a long time, and I'm so happy dreaming about it, and I get all settled, and it's so lovely. Then comes the moment when I have to take it out of the air and put it onto paper, which is the process of killing it, beating all of the life and the beauty out of it. It's incredibly depressing for me to start writing a novel, because it's going from this fantastic realm of imagination to the reality of words. It's as if you had a pen pal that you were in love with, and then one day you had to get married and start living together. From everything being your perfect and beautiful dream, to having to go through the physical aspects of the day with somebody. It's very hard. Not as hard as having a real job, of course.

I know that your friendship with Elizabeth is very much a part of your writing life. Can you talk about the role of your friendship in your work?
Elizabeth is pretty much the only person who reads anything that I'm doing while I'm doing it. With *Bel Canto,* there were a couple of things that I showed to Manette Ansay, but it's all very, very much about Elizabeth. The funny thing about Elizabeth, and I think that this is true for her as well—we've gotten to the point where we know each other so well, and we know what the other one is going to say, that in a way we've rendered each other useless. I know what she's going to say, so it becomes this game for me to fix the things that she would criticize or have problems with before she sees it. When we started off, I would show her what I did every day. I'd show her every chapter as I had written it. That's not true anymore. Now we'll get a hundred pages together before we show it. We nag at each other to send the pages, and say, "Why haven't you sent me those pages? You're going out of town. All you have to do is put them

in the mail before you go." She had forty-two pages and didn't want to send them until she had fifty pages. We're like an old married couple, and more than anything, we spur each other on to work. We keep each other going. People often ask if we're competitive. We're not competitive in terms of who sells more copies or who gets better reviews, but we're very competitive in terms of, "What page are you on? Did you work today?" She'd been working on her new book for a couple of months before I started mine, and it was driving me insane. Now that I've started mine—and quite lamely started it, I might add—she keeps saying, "God, I just know you're going to shoot out in front of me." She's moving and has all this stuff going on and it's making her crazy, but it's the kind of crazy that will make her get up in the middle of the night and work for a couple of hours. And the thought of her getting up in the middle of the night to work while she's moving makes me want to get back to work.

For so long it really was about line editing, and hands-on fine-tuning, and now it's much more about work. It gets harder and harder to work as you get older, because there's so much other great stuff that comes along. Today, I have to write the front section for the *New York Times Magazine,* and it's due tomorrow, and I have no topic for it. I can't come up with anything. If you come up with anything, there'll be twenty bucks in it for you. And I'm finishing up this "Writers on Writing" piece, and next week I'm going to Oregon to give a reading with a symphony. There are all sorts of opportunities now, 95 percent of which I pass up so that I can keep my life simple and quiet, so I can sit in front of my computer and write. Or I do phone interviews, or answer e-mails from a newspaper in Australia asking me to answer ten questions for an article they're writing.

Your life suddenly gets whittled away into nothing because you're doing things that have varying degrees of silliness. So it gets harder to find the empty terrain in your own head, that wide-open quiet that I always have needed to write a novel. You get to a point, too, where you're just not as hungry. You think: I've got four books; they're selling okay. Do I really need to write another book? All of these things figure into getting work done. Elizabeth and I still have that high school sense of "What page are you on?" That is more motivating to me than anything else.

Earlier you were talking about the difference between the beautiful book in your imagination and then sitting down to the reality of writing. What is your process like for seeing your first draft through to a final draft? What goes on through each revision?

That's really not the way I work. I do an enormous amount of thinking and planning at the beginning, while it's still in my head. I get it all where I want it to be.

Do you have the language in your head?

Yes, if I have the narration, I have the language. So I get that all set. Then I have a really hard time starting. I'll write the first fifty pages of a book twenty times, but once I get going, once I have the voice right and the narrative right, the characters in place, and the start is right, I go pretty cleanly. When I finish a chapter, I go back and polish it for a couple of days and then go on to the next one. I do not get to the end of a book and then start a second draft. Elizabeth will retype everything that she has once she gets to the end. She really does create a second draft. I don't do that. When I type that last sentence of the book, that book is extremely close to the book that you will see in the bookstores. I do it as I go along. I can't go on to the next part until the last part is right.

Do you conceive of a story in the voice of a narrator, or in key images or characters, or in events?

Not in terms of a narrator. That changes a hundred times. More in terms of character and plot. I'm a very plot-driven, story-driven writer. But who tells it, how it's told, is the thing that I have a really hard time with. That's the thing that I write over and over again at the beginning.

At what point do you decide upon a narrator?

Before I start writing it, because it's hard to write a book without a narrator. The last two things I do before I start writing a book is decide on a narrator and decide on the characters' names, and I think that because they're the last two things I do, they're the two things that inevitably really stump me, because I never want to start.

What is your process like for developing the narrator's voice, for instance, someone like John Nickel, who is so different from you?

It's not a matter of developing the voice. I develop it offstage, before the book is started. I don't develop it as I go along. All I do is think about it. I don't think, Hey, I'm going to go hang out with black men in blues bars. You just figure it out. That's the lovely thing about writing first person. You get that voice in your head, and the voice is then compelling. It's the thing that takes you along. Whereas with the third person, the voice in your head is always you, and so I'm not as compelled.

One of the themes that recurs in your novels is the idea of an unlikely group of strangers who wind up together by circumstance and eventually create some kind of a family or a society that sustains them. What draws you to this theme?

That's the theme that occurs in all of my novels. That's my theme.

You know, there aren't that many themes. I think about the theme that seems to be Ian McEwan's theme, which is that everything's fine, then something goes wrong, there's an accident, and people get on that slippery slope and it snowballs. For instance, J. M. Coetzee's *Disgrace,* which is such a good book. Somebody trips, and you think they're going to get up, but they don't. They just keep sliding and sliding. There are lots of books that are a stranger-on-the-train book. People come together by chance, and then interact. It's fascinating to me. I can trace it all back to *The Magic Mountain,* which is a book that I'm constantly trying to plagiarize. The idea of writing a book set in a tuberculosis sanitarium is *so* delightful to me. I haven't done it just because I feel that it would be too blatant an attempt at plagiarizing, not that I could ever, ever plagiarize *The Magic Mountain.* That's such an appealing scenario. A bunch of people are sick and forced to lie down together in a big room. When I read *Angela's Ashes,* I was devastated by the scenes in the TB ward, because they were so beautiful. They were just perfect. I was thinking: Why, why didn't I write this? It's not off-limits to me. Look, he did it.

How did you get the idea for *Bel Canto?*

It's based on a true story. I saw it on the news. I said, "Look! It's an Ann Patchett novel unfolding in the news." It's very much like *The Patron Saint of Liars.* A group of pregnant girls go to a house, and they're stuck together for this determined amount of time. They're taken out of the world, then forced back into the world. It's a very similar sort of thing, though hopefully no one would read those two books and say, "Wow, what a rut she's in." I loved working from the news because it gave me all of those parameters that were so warm and comfortable, such as a starting time and ending time, a duration. There were a lot of things that I took from that true story. They were teenagers, they lived in the jungle, they hadn't seen television, two of them were girls. Alberto Fujimori, the president of Peru, really was obsessed with soap operas. There were all sorts of little facts that I took from life that gave me structure. When you have a structure, it's so much easier for the imagination to flourish. People believe that the imagination is at its best when it is completely and totally unencumbered, but everyone likes boundaries, and something to push up against. I really appreciated having that structure.

Were you a big opera fan before you wrote that book?

I was not an opera fan at all. I knew nothing about opera, but I knew that I wanted an opera singer in the book, and I knew that the situation was operatic. I liked the idea of structuring the novel like an opera. I liked the idea of flirting with melodrama; you always hear that melodrama is something you should avoid. I buckled down and tried to learn about opera, and after many false starts, I found a book by Fred Plotkin, called *Opera 101*, that was the greatest book I've ever gotten my hands on. It explained everything to me and set me on my course.

What do you mean when you say that you structured the novel like an opera? How so?

I should have said I wanted to structure the novel like an opera, by which I mean that it took on the larger-than-life qualities of opera: passion, melodrama, death. Also, that there would be a lot of characters with different rankings. This book has the main characters, soprano and tenor, then the mezzo or "maid" character (second tier); then it has a large chorus. I loved the idea of writing a novel with a chorus.

This is your first omnisciently narrated novel, and it has the fullness and breadth of a vision realized. Do you feel that it was a leap for you in terms of craft?

Huge. It's what I've always wanted to do. It is exactly the thing that I have not been able to pull off in my last three books. In my last three books, every time, I was trying to do this, and I couldn't. With *The Magician's Assistant,* I finally moved into the third person, but it's a very first-personish kind of third person. In *The Patron Saint of Liars,* I have those different first-person narrators because I couldn't figure out any other way to do it. I didn't know how to do third person, and I didn't know how to do omniscient, but I did know that these characters didn't communicate with one another. The only way I could structure it was to have three first-person narrations, because they're all feeling things they can't say to the other one. Then, in *Taft,* I have those little Taft scenes that are in third person, which was like a little running jump at something. In *The Magician's Assistant,* I have the limited third person. So you can see the trajectory of where I'm going with this.

What were the challenges in writing it from the omniscient point of view?

The challenge of balance, especially when you have sixty characters, to feel like you're seeing everybody in a sweep. It's not just that you have this scene and you're in their head, and you have the next scene and you're in this other character's head. There has to be an easy flow between point of view. You also don't want to create a situation where the reader is more interested in one character than another. It's the responsibility of the narration to keep the story even in its interest.

You were saying earlier that when you're writing from the omniscient point of view, you don't have that voice in your head that you can latch onto. It's not a voice-driven enterprise. What does drive it forward?

Elizabeth McCracken accumulating pages. Nothing! That's what makes it so hard. *Bel Canto* was like a piece of knitting. I'd work on it fiercely for two weeks, and then I'd put it in a drawer for three months. Every time I finished a chapter, I felt like it was over—I didn't know where to go next. I didn't have anything that compelled me from point to point. It was just sheer will. So it took me a lot longer.

Was it difficult to create sympathetic yet realistic characters in the terrorists? How did you go about this?

I have no idea if they're realistic, because I don't know any terrorists. It's never any problem at all for me to create sympathetic characters. I'm an absolute bomb when it comes to creating villains. I have no villains in any of my books. I have a villain-free oeuvre. Carl, in *Taft*, is the closest, and I don't think anyone would consider him a villain. He's a kid who's trying and messing up. Any character I get my hands on becomes a sympathetic character. I'm a bleeding heart.

Early on in the narrative, you let it be known that all of the terrorists will die in the end. Why did you decide to reveal this up front?

Because I don't want to have the reader racing through the book wondering if they were going to live, if they were going to make it. They're not going to make it, and that's not the point. We're all going to die. We don't know how long we're going to live, and none of us will feel that it's long enough. It really isn't about quantity, it's about quality. These people have short and beautiful lives. I want the reader to focus on their life, rather than on their death. Also, it puts the reader in the same position that it puts the characters, which is, they know how it's going to end, and yet they put it out of their minds. So many readers have said to me, "I read that line, but I made myself forget it. I turned away from it." That's what the characters do. They know that it's not going to work. At the end everyone will say: "Of course this is where it was going. I didn't want to believe it." That's how we are with our own death. We know that we're going to die, and yet we willfully turn away from it every day to enjoy our beautiful life. There's something I refer to as the *Love Story* syndrome, in which Ryan O'Neil says: "This is about Jenny. Jenny is dead." So, you don't go into that movie wondering if she's going to beat the cancer. She's not going to beat the cancer, so you spend the movie looking at this beautiful girl in her average and charming life, which is all so heightened by the knowledge of her imminent death. And even then you think Jenny's going to pull through.

Why did you decide to leave the host country's identity nameless? What does your narrative gain from this?

When I was writing this book, I thought that everyone who read it would know that it was about Peru and the hostage takeover. In fact, nobody knew. Until the book was published with press materials, not one person who read the book knew that it was based on a true story. Tragedy dilutes tragedy. We only feel bad about a plane crash until there's a monsoon, or a flood in Prague, or a fire in Colorado. We go from thing to thing. I didn't want it to be about Peru, because it's not about Peru. It's about a living room, and I wanted it to be outside of time in the same way that I wanted *Taft* to be inside of time. It seemed that to ally it with a country or with a real event wouldn't really benefit the book. And it sounded so nice to say "the host country."

The operatic quality of the event, the fact that one's awareness of every emotion and experience is heightened, like in the moments before dying, is expressed beautifully through reactions to Roxane's singing. "All of the love and the longing a body can contain was spun into not more than two and a half minutes of song, and when she came to the highest notes it seemed that all they had been given in their lives and all they had lost came together and made a weight that was almost impossible to bear." That two minutes of song could contain such a depth of feeling is remarkable, but understandable given their circumstances. How did you, as the writer, maintain that pitch of emotion within yourself? Did listening to opera help you inhabit that extreme?

Opera certainly helped. When I was writing the scenes in which she was singing, I'd listen to the same aria ten, twenty times, to try to write it and get that feeling onto the paper. I didn't live at this pitch while writing the book.

But in moments you had to go there.

Yes, but that's just what the job is. You go there. As I get older, it gets easier to go there. I know more about how to get in and how to get out. When I was writing *The Patron Saint of Liars*, the scene in which Cecilia drowns felt awful. I sat at the computer and cried and cried. I don't do that now. I get a little dazed, or shaken up, when I have to write something really sad, but I don't necessarily go all the way down myself. It's a little like acting. You put on the suit and do the part, and then you get off and you take the suit off and you're still yourself.

The hostages and terrorists speak so many languages between them that communication is a constant issue. The music is the easiest way for them all to relate to one another, to become united. Comment?

In every book, I set up a problem for myself that's just for me. In this book, it was, What would you do if you had a book in which your characters don't have a common language? I started out with the translator. I took him and his work as far as he could go, and then he burns out. He can't keep up with the workload. Then slowly there's a transition between Gen's responsibility and Roxane's. Her role gets larger. I'm not talking about the part in the book, but the part of language versus music—they have a kind of exchange. More and more, people begin to conduct themselves through the music. They relate to one another through the music. At first, Mr. Hosokawa and Roxane need Gen to speak for them, but after a while they start humming to one another, and then they can just be together. How can people learn to simply be together without having to express themselves verbally, constantly? It's a three-tiered process where they go from having an interpreter, to having music, to really being able to exist in peace with one another. Mr. Hosokawa learns the art of invisibility, of true silence, from Carmen, so that he can move around the way that she does without anyone seeing him so that he can be with Roxane. At the same time, Cesar picks up the torch of singing, which means that singing doesn't belong only to Roxane. It's all flexible and connected, and hopefully it has a sensible arch to follow.

Almost the entire novel takes place in the living room of the vice presidential mansion, yet it never feels stagnant. How did you keep things moving in this small setting?
    It was a very big living room, and I always had that in mind. I pictured the lobby at the Plaza Hotel, which is not just a big room. It's like a microcosm. The lobby at the Plaza is a universe of activity. I never felt claustrophobic in that house, and the characters don't feel claustrophobic. The characters aren't longing to get out, because for so many of them that's not their county, and they don't really trust the people on the other side of the wall who have the guns. They're not feeling caged or pining for freedom. What they're pining for is for music, for beauty. Everything they want is inside the house. If the characters were pressing up against the windows all the time, it would've felt claustrophobic. The trick was to move the story from one side of the room to the other, to have a conversation next to the piano, then a conversation in the hallway going to the kitchen, then a conversation on the sofa. Keeping it flowing was the harder part.

Many characters take on roles or discover parts of themselves previously hidden. For instance Kato, a businessman, becomes Roxane's accompanist. "He made what he felt to be wild presumptions in handing

over his suggestions, but what did it matter? He was a vice president in a giant corporation, a numbers man, suddenly elevated to be the accompanist. He was not himself. He was no one he had ever imagined." One terrorist shows a talent for chess, another a gift for singing. What intrigues you about these undiscovered aspects of character that come out under dire conditions?

That goes back to *The Patron Saint of Liars*. There's a line in there that says something about somewhere there's a child drawing with a stick who would've been Picasso if he'd ever had any training. I've always been so fascinated with that notion. All of these artistic geniuses arise in countries that promote education and health and have more money and more time. Art is a leisure activity. If you have to scramble for your food every second of the day, you're not going to make art. Art is a luxury of time. I'm fascinated by the idea that in the Sahara there are people who would be Chopin, and people who would be Picasso, and people who would be Balanchine, but they don't ever in their lives get anywhere close to having the luxury of time to discover those talents. The terrorists who have been living that kind of life, a life that is about poverty and struggle and food and survival and then they suddenly have this beautiful home in which they have all their needs met and all the time in the world—how do they develop? All that genius—the law of averages says that everyone gets an equal shot at it—all that genius is there. It's time and comfort and security that allows it to emerge.

From the first page there is both love and beauty set against a threat of violence. This counterpoint continues and builds throughout the novel, the presence of beauty in the midst of a violent, and inevitably the fatal, standoff between the terrorists and the authorities. This dichotomy is also present in individual characters, such as the general, who shows concern as well as a very real threat of violence. What drew you to this dichotomy?

Isn't that just life? Isn't that just reading the newspaper each day? It's the front page and the arts section. It's really, really horrible things, and really beautiful things, every single day, right there next to each other on the pages. In your own life, it's part drudgery and part love. You can blow it up. It can be brought to passion and melodrama, to true, true love and death. But if you reduce it in the same way that you would reduce fractions, take it to the smallest common denominator, it's the same thing, whether it's small or it's large. It could be the juxtaposition between going to the grocery store to get dinner, and then getting to have dinner with the person you love—what's boring, what's charming. If you took that to its highest level, it could be making a truly great piece of art, and some little girl in Virginia getting kidnapped. Everything in life exists next to each other, and hopefully exists in some kind of balance. Maybe the trick is to keep it in balance, to keep pitching for truth, and beauty, and love, because the other things are there in great abundance. That's an interesting thing about art for me. This is a very violent and sad novel. I feel like it's my responsibility to keep making the case for the beauty and the art.

It seems so obviously about beauty and love, especially the ending with the beautiful women walking toward the men. I love that.

I was trying very hard to plagiarize the ending of a John Cheever story, "Goodbye My Brother," when he sees his wife and sister walking out of the ocean. I was *really* trying, really just reading that ending over and over again and trying to get that feeling of hopefulness and goodness of these two beautiful women walking towards him. You should read it. If you want to see beauty, it's phenomenal. It's all about plagiarism really. I'm trying hard to plagiarize *The Brothers Karamazov* right now.

This novel hosts a huge cast of characters, yet each is distinct and leaves his or her own impressions on the reader. How do you create unique characters without running the risk of one character blending into the next, or falling out of the reader's consciousness during the story?

I read a lot of Chekhov. Honestly, there is nobody who does a better job with a one-sentence walk-in character having a complete and distinct personality than Chekhov. It's something that I've studied for years and years. He never lets anybody fall through the cracks, no matter how tiny. If it's just a postman bringing a letter to the main character, you know that postman. No one is a throwaway character. You don't have to present a full life history—we're all distinct. We're distinct at a glance, and your characters should be distinct at a glance. That's the trick to that. I will say that I kept a list of the characters by my computer because I couldn't keep all their names straight, and also because I would always be looking over and thinking: He hasn't been in the room lately. It's time to bring him back around.

In his quest to express his love to Roxane, Fyodorov declares, "Some people are born to make great art and others are born to appreciate it. Don't you think? It is a kind of talent in itself, to be an audience, whether you are the spectator in the gallery or you are listening to the voice of the world's greatest soprano. Not everyone can be the artist. There have to be those who witness the art, who love and appreciate what they have been privileged to see." How do think this idea relates to the world of literature and writing?

I think it comes out of literature and writing. I think about it in terms of M.F.A. programs specifically. There's no way that everyone who comes out of an M.F.A. program is going to make it as a writer, not by a long shot. So the question is, Do you use that time to become a great reader and a great appreciator of art, or do you just feel a constant disappointment in yourself and in your life if you go through one of those programs but never go on to be somebody who creates great art? It seems that M.F.A. programs are kind of tragic if they're just creating a whole lot of people for very few spots on the job. But if it can be that people have a chance to express their own creativity, and to genuinely appreciate more fully the creativity of others, then it doesn't seem like a waste of time. It does seem very sad to me that M.F.A. programs leave so many people feeling that they've failed.

Did you know ahead of time that two of the terrorists would be young women, or did that come out in the writing? What were the challenges of making that aspect of the narrative believable?

In that sense, it's very, dare I say, Shakespearean. I like that. The young man is the young woman, and the two couples who wind up with the other partner. Reading Shakespeare for a long time, it just seemed perfectly normal that the young women would masquerade as young men and be believed.

Why were Mr. Hosokawa and Carmen shot by the same bullet?

Because that's their pairing. In the same way that Gen and Roxane are paired in life, they are paired in death. Mr. Hosokawa and Carmen were very similar. In the same way that Gen and Roxane were the communicators, Mr. Hosokawa and Carmen were the silent strength. They both had this great talent for being invisible. Neither one of them could've gone on in the world. It wouldn't have worked. If everything had ended peacefully, Carmen never could have gone into Gen's world, and Mr. Hosokawa couldn't have gone into Roxane's world. What would he do, divorce his wife? Would she have moved to Japan? It wouldn't have worked. He couldn't live with her, and he couldn't live without her. Also, there's a scene in which Beatriz pulled a gun on Mr. Hosokawa, and Carmen instantly jumped in front of him. It's the same thing. It's who they both were. They would always protect the other. I like to think of them dying together.

What drew you to write about a magician's assistant? How did *The Magician's Assistant* unfold in your imagination?

The book is so not about magic or a magician's assistant. I wanted to have a profession in which you have a primary and secondary member of a relationship in which the secondary person believes that they couldn't possibly do what the primary person does. In other words, it could have been a story about a surgical nurse and her surgeon who worked together every day, and then the surgeon died and the surgical nurse realizes that in fact, just by having been there and watching all those years, she can perform the surgery as well. But she never knows that about herself until the surgeon dies. This is basically the relationship of a lot of marriages. In those long relationships, everyone picks up different roles, and they believe that there are things that are their responsibility that they know how to do, and they believe they couldn't possibly do, because their partner did that thing. Then if the partner leaves or dies, the person has to come to terms with the fact that they can do all sorts of things. That's a really interesting transition to me. The magician and the assistant were the flashiest, most metaphorical jobs that I could give them and put them in the best-looking outfits. What was funny about that, though, was that when I was about halfway through the book, I sent it to Elizabeth, who said that it was appalling, that I knew nothing about magic. She wanted me to do some research, so I did. I had never really given it much thought, but what I discovered when I started doing my research, with half the book written, was that I hated magic. I had literally given it no thought outside of the pretty costumes, the doves, the stage, the pink lights. When I started going to magic shows and reading books about magicians, I saw that it's so sleazy. It's carnival sleazy. I never would've written that book if I'd done my research ahead of time.

Did you get anything useful out of the research?
    Nothing. Of course, anything you want to know about magic, you can't find out in a book about magic. What I discovered was that magic was all about authority. I read one book by Harry Blackstone, Jr., in which he said—and not in any condescending way—was that the reason there are virtually no female magicians is that a woman cannot command the authority in a room. There are always going to be men and women who won't give their total suspension of disbelief to a woman the way that men and women will give it to a man. Magic is about dominance in a way. Unless you have complete authority over the room, and every person believes you—because they're fighting it, everyone is looking for the trick—unless the magician can dominate the whole room, the magician can't succeed. And women can't do that, because there are both men and women who will never take women seriously. That was such a fascinating thing to me. I realized that writing is a lot like magic. It's about dominating your audience, and making them believe what you say is true. What I

ended up having to do was write the scenes in which Sabine is performing the acts with such confidence that it would be reasonable to the reader that she was not saying to herself in her narrative: "And now I'm doing this. Now I'm doing that." When you're reading it, you're thinking that she just totally knows what she's doing. That's the way writing is. You have to command the reader's belief, which I completely believe that women can do in books. It makes a perverse kind of sense to me that they can't do it onstage as magicians.

Parsifal is very much a main character, even though his death marks the first page. We get to know him through Sabine's memories, until his mother is introduced and his story slowly unfolds and deepens. What did you want to show about intimacy and secrets by having Parsifal's hidden life come out only after his death?

In the same way that the trick of *Bel Canto* is, What if you have a book in which nobody has a common language? the trick of *The Magician's Assistant* is, What happens when your main character dies in the first sentence of the book? I had to relay the information about the character using very few flashbacks, working mostly through conversation. Kitty and Sabine each have half the puzzle, and we don't get to see the full picture, and they don't get to see the full picture, until they come together and they exchange their information through talking, through convincing one another about the half that they have. And in that, Parsifal becomes whole.

At first Parsifal's mother loses integrity in the eyes of the reader, because she tells Sabine that she had her son sent to a reformatory because he was gay. Only when she reveals the truth of why he was sent away, readers see her as protecting her son by not unveiling his history all at once. This interplay between the sympathetic and the not-so-sympathetic aspects of character comes up in your other books as well. What interests you about this?

I don't agree with that, really. I think that when Dot tells that lie, she is sympathetic in that moment because she's saying that she did a terrible thing, she made a terrible mistake. I may be wrong, but I don't think the reader is coming down on her. Her grief is in the fact that she let him get away after all that happened, that she didn't do more to mend the break. Her remorse is real. A good lie is always a lie that is based in truth. Her lie is believable because it's so close to the truth—she knows that she made the wrong choice, and she's been punished her whole life with the loss of her most beloved child. So I don't think that the reader condemns Dot, but maybe just I don't condemn her because I have such a hard time with villains.

One reviewer said that "perhaps a struggle with credulity is precisely what she [Patchett] wants to encourage. Improbable relationships can flourish; strange havens do exist. Becoming accustomed to sad endings may be more naive than believing, now and then, in happily ever after." Do you agree with this?

I don't struggle with credulity. I was raised Catholic, and things that seem magical to other people do not seem magical to me. I went to Catholic girls' school for twelve years. I went to mass every day. I grew up loving the saints. I grew up reading *Lives of the Saints*. I grew up believing that Saint Lucy's eyes were both in her head and on the plate at the same time. I buy that. In the convent outside of the chapel there was a table of holy relics, which were little tiny bits of cloth and little tiny bits of bone from different saints. That was unbelievable to me, that there was this little one-eighth-inch scrap of a sheet that had touched the Shroud of Turin and wound up in a girls' school in Tennessee. That's phenomenal. The notion that what is real exists only on one plane, which is what you can see with your eyes in your life, is nothing that I've ever bought. I love this interview with Gabriel Garcia Marquez that I read a long time ago in which he says that people always say he writes magic realism, but he says he doesn't write magic realism. "These things happened in my time. Everyone remembers the beautiful girl who rose up to heaven with the sheets." I totally understand that. I believe that. I have a looser grasp on reality than most. I don't ever sit down and think that I'm going to write magical realism.

Sabine says, "People long to be amazed, even as they fight it. Once you amaze them, you own them." Your narrative seems to prove this theorem, in that many of the events that on the surface seem incredible, feel perfectly organic and natural. The magic of these events is thrilling, and uplifting, and it leaves readers wanting more. Were you aware of the interplay between your characters, who are magicians, and the style of the narrative, which contains one rabbit pulled out of a hat after another?

No, I was not, but this is a book about the balance between real magic and faked magic. It's about the difference between magic and tricks. I love the end of that book, the scene at Birdie's wedding when Sabine does the card trick that she's brought back from her dream, and the only one who gets it is the little girl who's helping her. After all of these tricks, there are moments of real magic that defy understanding, which I think ultimately, back in California, is what Sabine and Kitty are going to have, this real, genuine magic of love. So many people have said to me that they just think they're falling for each other because they both loved Parsifal. But no, they've really found what they'd been looking for their whole life without knowing what they were looking for. They finally find themselves; they get into that other dimension, which is real love. That's up against all these tricks that we do, the show of it, to get through life or to make a living.

Let's talk about *Taft*. How did you arrive on John Nickel, a black bartender in Memphis, Tennessee, as the narrator for this novel?
I was in a bar in Memphis flirting with a drummer. I just started thinking about this person. He was an incredibly compelling guy, a great musician, and I sat in the bar all night and listened to him, and I was wondering about his story, where he was from. So I started making up a story about this guy. I'd been trying to write a book about some people in East Tennessee who were snake handlers, and it just wasn't working. When I saw this guy, I suddenly realized that all the people from East Tennessee would come to West Tennessee, and they would have to be in his world. East Tennessee seems like Bangladesh, it's so far away when you're in Memphis, and those two worlds would never meet, that kind of Appalachian poor white, and a very savvy urban black man—never. What if they were thrown together? So I took the characters from this book that wasn't going anywhere and put them into his world. I tried for a long time to have the white characters narrate the book. First, Fay and Carl's mother was the narrator, then Fay was, then Carl was, and none of it worked. Finally I had Nickel be the narrator, and that worked. He was the only character in the book who was trustworthy. The others were too unreliable, and I don't like unreliable narrators. That just wears me out. He was the only reliable person around to tell the story. It was in no way a conscious effort to write from the point of view of a black man.

How did you decide to include the sections about Taft, and what does the narrative gain from these glimpses into the past?
It's really about writing, because I'm making up a character who's making up a character. Nickel is engaged in the writing process. He is using his imagination to try to answer a question for himself. Who was this person? How did these children get here? And of course, he's always wondering about his own child. There's a scene in the beginning in which Franklin falls on a Coke bottle and he sees that whole scene play out realistically, so he's someone who problem-solves through imagination.

How did you decide to end with Taft rather than John Nickel? What did your story gain from this?
I was dating a guy a long time ago, and he read the manuscript of the book. It ended with the scene of John Nickel, but Mark said it should end

with a scene of Taft, a boring scene in which nothing happens, a really straight life-scene when the kids were little. It made perfect sense to me, because what Nickel was saying at the end when he's in bed with Franklin was, "I choose you. I'm going to protect you. You're my priority." Taft said the exact same thing when he was a young man with young children, and he was unable to do it. Nickel's not going to be able to do it either. It's the great myth of parenthood. We want to protect our children, and we can't. But we have to keep trying. I don't know if that ending registered with most people. It's a very melancholy ending.

What was the experience of writing a screenplay for *Taft* like?
It took me three days. Alfred Uhry wrote the screenplay for *Taft*. He wrote the screenplay for *Driving Miss Daisy*, and he and Morgan Freeman are friends, and Morgan Freeman paid him a lot of money to write the screenplay, which didn't work out so well. Morgan and I had a long talk about it, and he said that he wanted it to be much more like the book, so I went back and wrote a screenplay that was much more like the book. He didn't like that either, so the project was dropped. I was able to do it quickly because I wasn't working from scratch. I had the characters, their voices, the story. It seemed logical and straightforward to me.

How has the success of *Bel Canto* impacted your writing life?
Not at all. When I do interviews after I've won prizes, people want to know how it will affect my writing. Sadly, it doesn't affect anything. It's sort of like someone asking, "How does that great new haircut affect your writing?" Sentence to sentence, it doesn't do anything for me. I'd like to say that it's terrible, that I have this terrible burden to live up to. It's not even that. It's nothing. When you're alone with your computer trying to write a novel, nothing helps, nothing hurts. It's just you and your dog, alone.

What are you working on now?
I'm on page nine of a new novel. Because I'm on page nine of a novel, I've become an extremely intrepid little journalist this past week or two, and I've been writing all sorts of articles. Consider the fact that it is now three o'clock and I still don't have any notion of what my *New York Times* piece, which is due tomorrow, is going to be on. Isn't that a problem?

Can you say something about what your new novel is about?
It's about politics. Believe me, if I'd told you I was writing a book about South America, terrorism, and opera, you would've thought it was awful. They all sound so horrible. I'm writing a book about a dead, gay

magician. Doesn't sound great, does it? But seriously, if *Bel Canto* is a book that is redeemed by art, then this is a book about somebody who is trying to redeem himself through politics. It's *Brothers Karamazov* meets Joe Kennedy. There's a father with three sons who's trying very hard to raise one of the sons to be a politician and striking out.

What would you say to new writers working on their first stories or novels?

Finish them. That's a huge thing. It's amazing to me how often people call me and say, "I have a great idea for a novel. I'm looking for an agent." Put business out of your mind and write because you love to write. People get so caught up with the notion of publishing or selling something, and it's an incredibly backwards logic. If you love to write, if you write passionately, if you work at it hard, which involves a lot of reading and rewriting, the other thing will come. It is incredibly cart before the horse to say, "I want to get an agent because I have an idea," or "I wrote a story and I want to try to sell it." If you were taking a course in glassblowing, and you blew your first glass, and you said, "I want to go to Tiffany's and sell this glass," that would be crazy. Yet, people write one story and want to send it to the *New Yorker*. That's just not the way it goes. You write a story, then you throw it away. You write a story, you throw it away. Or you file it away. You write and you write and you write for a long time because you're learning how to do it, because there's pleasure in doing it. People need to work harder at writing and work a little less hard at publishing.

Conducted: August 2002

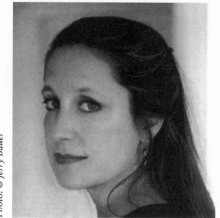

JAYNE ANNE PHILLIPS

Taking Cues from the Work Itself

Jayne Anne Phillips's first book of stories, *Black Tickets,* won the Sue Kaufman Prize for First Fiction. *Machine Dreams,* her first novel, was a *New York Times* best-seller, was nominated for the National Book Critics Circle award, and was chosen by the *New York Times Book Review* as one of twelve best books of the year. She is also the author of a second book of stories, *Fast Lanes,* and a novel, *Shelter,* which was awarded an Academy Award in Literature by the American Academy and Institute of Arts and Letters and chosen one of the "Best Books of the Year" by *Publishers Weekly.* Her most recent novel, *MotherKind,* was nominated for Britain's Orange Prize. Ms. Phillips is the recipient of a Guggenheim Fellowship, two National Endowment for the Arts Fellowships, and a Bunting Fellowship from the Bunting Institute of Radcliffe College. Her work has appeared most recently in *Harper's, Granta, Doubletake,* and the *Norton Anthology of Contemporary Fiction.* She has taught at Harvard University, Williams College, and Boston University, and is currently Writer in Residence at Brandeis University.

How did you get started writing?

I was always a reader, the kind of kid who read constantly. Very early on, reading seemed a way to be bigger than I was, know more than I should know, travel more than anyone I knew had traveled. I came from a small town in West Virginia, and people there were very stationary, much less mobile than the rest of the country. Most of the people I knew—and I think it's still true of that place—tend to move in and out for jobs much less than people from other places. They tend to be really connected to the land and the region, and they tend to have had several generations of their families there. It was a very isolated, intense world. Early on, I saw reading as a way of both escaping that and deepening it. Reading seemed very subversive, and writing later became an extension of the same knowing, mysterious secrecy. Reading led to writing for me. I started out writing poetry in high school, and by the time I was nineteen or twenty, I'd started writing short prose pieces. Those developed into the one-page fictions in my first book, *Sweethearts*, which was published by a small press. I taught myself to write fiction by writing very compact, spiral-shaped pieces that moved according to language rather than plot or idea.

Pieces that had the intensity of a poem.

Yes. I've always written line by line, with a real sense of the sound of a sentence and the rhythm of words against one another. My early sense of narrative had more to do with trying to get across perception itself rather than telling a conventional story. That very short form was a good way to intensify and deepen language. They were narratives, but they moved out from an image and worked very much according to sensory association. I'm still a very language-oriented writer.

What inspired the shorter form of story you use throughout *Black Tickets*?

I've worked from short forms to longer forms. That's been my trajectory. Short forms suited me early on because I was working from a more jagged consciousness. That's where I was at the time. As I moved into more conventional story lengths (though I've never really been a conventional writer), I grew more interested in having a longer relationship with the material and working with it for years, which is what I do with a novel. I went from writing those short pieces that were complete in one page to writing stories that worked like one piece of glass pressed against another: stories in alternating sections, stories that found their own form, monologues, and series of monologues telling the same story from different points of view. I found voices that let me work with scary or intimidating or spiritual material inside more conventional forms, so that readers take the words into themselves before they realize what the book's about.

This is one of the interesting things about fiction as opposed to poetry: When we read a poem on the page, we're aware that we're reading a poem because of the shape it has. When we pick up a story it's in paragraphs, just like the news or the directions for how to operate an appliance. The reader takes the voice into her mind before she has time to erect barriers against it. That's true for the writer, too. Many times you're not aware of what you're working with until you get deeply into the material. The material itself instructs, compels, mesmerizes the writer—just as the resulting book teaches the reader how to "read" the world of that book.

Would you call yourself a minimalist writer in *Black Tickets*?

That's funny, because I found myself featured as the definition of minimalism in one book that came out few years ago. It really depends on what I'm writing. I feel strongly that, at least for me, the material dictates form rather than the other way around. I write my way into the material to find out what it is and what form it should take. There are stories and pieces I've done that are minimalist, and there are other things I've done that are very lyrical. It really depends on the voice in which the work resides. Most writers work at trying to find the right voice. Stories often occur to me complete with voice. That's all they are in the beginning. It's a question of being faithful to that voice and staying inside it and sustaining it until the end of the piece, whether it's a story or a novel.

How do your stories come to you?

Fortunately, that's a mystery. Stories and novels often occur to me in their first lines or their first paragraphs. I've had the experience of writing a first paragraph that's very language-oriented but very cryptic in terms of the story or a narrative act. I'll hold on to the words in a notebook for years before I find my way into the book that the paragraph describes.

And when you write the book, is that paragraph included?

Oh yes, usually as the beginning. I don't throw much away. I'm a very self-censoring, slow, painstaking type of writer. I find it difficult to write. I have to overcome a lot of resistance, but the resistance is part of the pressure that makes the writing work. It's all a matter of one's relationship to the work. It has to do with people finding a way to do what they need to do. Writing has always seemed to me to be an art in which there are no guarantees at all—it's meant to be extremely risky. I've always tried to write about what's most compelling or frightening or attractive to me, what is least understood by me. I don't require a knowledge of what I'm entering into. That's part of the writer's bargain. That's part of the risk we must take in order for there to be any risk apparent in the work.

What interests you about the lives of the disenfranchised in *Black Tickets*, and how are you able to inhabit them so completely?

In the same way that presence is sometimes defined by absence, that is, you don't know what something is until it's gone, until it's absent from you, until you miss it. I think outlaws, outcasts, the disenfranchised, those who are outside the Ozzie and Harriet stereotype often define the values of a culture and a civilization. Literature is the conscience of a culture, and that conscience should deal with what the culture is trying to reject or what the culture is not aligning itself with. In the past, people who read were upper-class people and educated people. Now, even upper-class and educated people don't read. It's like the canary-in-the-coal-mine idea. They take the bird into the coal mine, and when it falls over they know there's not enough oxygen. Literature inhabits that same territory. Many times, I don't see these disenfranchised characters as being that far from the mainstream. For instance, in this country, the top 5 percent of people whose incomes are highest control most of the wealth and wield most of the influence. I sometimes feel that I'm writing for those who won't write for themselves. I'm articulating thoughts and feelings, or losses, that people can't articulate for themselves. That's a kind of spiritual and political necessity, and art must do that.

How do you create realism in these gritty contexts?

"No ideas, but in things," as the Pound dictum states. No matter what the voice or style or technique of a piece, my work is always grounded in very physical, sensual detail. Physicality has to be present because the work tries to go so far spiritually, and the reader can't move inward without being extremely grounded in sensory reality. The piece can't move off without first being completely real and convincing. We're all concerned with what reality means. Does it mean anything? Is there anything besides this moment or this room? What are these dimensions that we inhabit in our thoughts, which are not physical, or in our dreams, or in our memories? Literature is operating in that territory, in a dimension that isn't real, yet it can connect with the real in a way that's sensory. It can trigger memory that is actually sensual, memories of smells or feelings or tastes. You work your way into a psychic understanding through the real world. You do it every day in your life, and you do it in your art.

Is this something you have to keep in mind as you're working?

No. I don't make any decisions while I'm working. Some people comfort themselves with decisions and work into the interior of the piece, but that's just a different way of doing it. I want my work to have an organic organization, to feel and appear to the reader as if it opens out of itself like an organic thing, like a flower or a piece of fruit. So, I don't make decisions about it at the outset. I try to take my cues from the work itself, because if I make decisions, I'm going to limit what I can do.

Do you believe that writers should "write what they know," as the adage states?

Yes, I do, but you don't always know what you know, and the more practiced you are as a writer, the more that might be true, and the more you might be able to do. You have to start with what you know, and that gets back to the question of physical detail. The reader has to start with something the reader knows. "My mother left home." Everyone immediately relates to that sentence. Everyone has had a mother, and everyone has been separated from their mother at some point. Language is operating in deep subconscious territory, and words set up associations. The writer doesn't have to be conscious of those associations; language communicates them.

Several of your stories take place on the border between Mexico and Texas, and depict the intersection of American and Latina cultures, such as in "El Paso" and "Mamasita." Did you live in that part of the country? What interests you about these intersections?

Again, that's an outlaw question. Any time you have an intersection of one thing smacking up against another, whether it's age versus youth, wealth versus poverty, one culture versus another, something is going to happen. Just as various religions arise from various cultures, various ways of handling language arise within cultures, and that is a very rich subject matter. I did spend some time in Mexico and Texas, and some of those ideas and details came from visual instances. "Mamasita" is set in New York City. You can find anybody anywhere.

Many of these stories are preoccupied with specific family events that shape or permanently shade characters' lives. For instance in "Home" you have the absence of the father and the mother's illness. What draws you to writing about family?

Family is endlessly fascinating. It's the psychic map that we use all our lives. We start out with this first pattern, much of it unconscious in the beginning. The mother and father, or the absence of the mother or father, or the people who stand in for the mother or father, are these colossus figures in the beginning, like the sun and the moon. They have that mythic power. They have very much to do with how we first see ourselves, with how we relate to men and women, with what we want, with what we don't have, and with what we have to provide for ourselves. Then, as we get a little older, identity is formed in relationship to siblings, to place, to the culture we're in, and all of that is reflected again in the microcosm of family. Each of us is separated from one another inside our identities, and we only really overcome that separation in certain moments: in sexual moments, in moments of passions, physical passion, athletics, art. We move beyond identity when we forget time and lose our boundaries. That blood connection to another person is something we feel with family. We inherit our parents' physical characteristics and mannerisms. We also inherit their unresolved dilemmas, unresolved losses, dreams that didn't happen. All these things are subliminally communicated inside families and relationships. That's why myths are so powerful. Myths have to do with identity and who we are in relation to the people who made us. So, writing about family is like writing about weather—it's such a big part of the world.

Who are some of the writers who've influenced you?

A whole gamut of people. Initially, and still, most of them are writers who broke the rules in one way or another, or who made their own rules. Writers like Faulkner, Burroughs, Bruno Shultz, Flannery O'Connor, a lot of the southern writers for their connection to the physical world, and for their enslavement to it. A lot of the central European writers, such as Kafka, for his anomie, that almost existential separation from the world, and a lot of language-oriented writers, such as James Agee, just because language was my way into writing. Spiritually, I'm attracted to writers who seem to have gone somewhere, who've been to the other side, and come back to bear witness to that event, that is, writers who can represent other dimensions of being in language, like Katherine Anne Porter, William Maxwell. A story like Cheever's "The Swimmer," in which a metaphor represents a whole journey into death, compresses time almost miraculously.

You also write about people coming of age in the context of family, how children often outgrow the constrained and limited world of their parents, and yet cannot fully come to terms with the wider world beyond the family—in the story "Fast Lanes," for example. There is a desire for safety, yet an unwillingness—or inability—to accept or create safety of one's own. Comment?

I don't believe in safety. People struggle with wanting to grab safety and hold on to it. When we're children, if our parents do a decent job, we think we're safe. We don't actually know that our parents don't control Ebola or mad cow disease. If we grow up inside some kind of safety, there's a period of time in which we struggle with realizing that there was never the kind of safety we thought we lived inside. Then we come into the situation of trying to provide safety in our lives for our partners, for our children, for our families, for ourselves. The stories in *Fast Lanes,* and a lot of other work I've done, have been about the struggle to accept the fact that there is no safety. It's interesting to look at the ways that different cultures represent the way the world is supposed to be. For instance, the Buddhist idea that life is suffering is one way of looking at it, that what we're here to do is to learn compassion. It's not about getting as much as we can get. It's about finding out what things mean and connecting one thing to another, and deepening the spiral into meaning. This is not a random universe; life is not random. Art stands against the notion that this is simply where we find ourselves and it's meaningless. Art makes its own meaning. It evokes the connections between us, and the existence of a dimension bigger than us, a dimension that holds time inside it, which is something we cannot understand. We now know how many genes there are, but we have no idea how they work. How language and speech operates inside a culture is just as various as the information genes hold and where they hold it.

What is the role of autobiography in your fiction?

It's a starting point, much in the way that physical details are a starting point for writing about meaning and time and dimension. The reader should think that whatever you write is autobiographical, because they should be convinced intensely of the reality of the piece. They should feel that it comes from somewhere very deep in the writer. But the minute you work in language, the minute you work in fiction, there's a translation that occurs, like the translation from one language to another, from book to film, thought to speech. Life and art are such different forms of being. One fears death; the other subverts it.

When you're writing a short story, what do you look for in an ending?

I look for a stepping-off-into-space kind of feeling, a rightness, a surprise, or the feeling that something has been set into motion and suddenly, at the end, it all becomes clear. Novels can work in a lot of different ways because it's a much bigger canvas. Novels work with patterns, whereas stories must succeed with words alone.

What was it like to go from writing short stories to writing your first novel, *Machine Dreams?*

I see all my work as a continuum. One book opens out into the next in a very natural way. I've often thought about books for years before I've written them, and known about the material. I've written each book as I was ready or able to write it, psychically. There's a natural timing to how writers write. They may resist it, or dislike it, but timing is one element of writing that I trust. I'd been writing stories, and the characters in some of the stories were recognizable as characters in the novel. It was set in what I remembered about my hometown, although by the time I wrote the book, my hometown had vanished. That's another thing about autobiography. By the time you write about something, it no longer exists. Memory is so faulty and so selective; memory is the proverbial blind man and the elephant. There may be a certain piece that's very similar to what you remember, but the whole is a very different reality than anything that ever happened.

Black Tickets was about a kind of anger and mobility. The intense energy that survivors have is in itself an incredible form of life, the optimism of energy itself, that pell-mell forward motion of it. With *Machine Dreams,* I started with that energy and then looked back at what created it, and looked at that world. Writing is very political. You're political in what you choose to write about and the way you choose to write about it. *Machine Dreams* was my looking at the world that had enclosed that small town where I first became aware of identity in myself and in others. I think of *Shelter* as being about the politics of family and the absence of family. I think about the story "Lechery" and *Shelter* as being connected. In "Lechery," a child makes a family out of what she can find, and she operates out of instincts that have been fractured by the world she lives in. In *Shelter,* four children with secrets find themselves in an extremely isolated, sensual, lush, fierce setting without families. It was a passion play, a group of children moving through an underworld, a rite of passage into a survival they created for themselves. It was a book about jarred dimensions, one reality existing alongside another, how perception alters reality.

In *Machine Dreams,* why did you choose to write from each character's point of view rather than a third-person or omniscient narrator?
In all my books I use time in a particular way. In *Machine Dreams,* the family in the book becomes familial to the reader. You encounter the same characters after lapses of time, and suddenly see them at a different point. I wanted readers to inhabit the minds of each character, to have a sense of recognition each time they encountered one of these characters.

Was it difficult to differentiate each voice in these chapters?
No. But it depends on what you're trying to do. In both *Shelter* and *Machine Dreams,* I wanted readers to circle through the world of the book, whereas in *MotherKind,* I wanted readers to remain inside Kate's

mind, because that is, in fact, where she stands in the book, in this iso-lated yet very intensely sensory space.

Why did you decide to write the war chapters—both Mitch's experiences in World War II and Billy's in Vietnam—as a series of letters between characters?

In West Virginia, particularly at that time, men and women lived in very different worlds. Men were defined by the work they did, and women were defined by family, even if they worked outside the home. I grew up in a world in which men weren't expected to be articulate, and were suspect if they were articulate. When I was writing *Machine Dreams*, I was given a box of my father's letters from World War II. They were letters in which this very plain-speaking voice says very plain, simple things. But they're made eloquent by distance and time and the situation, and the fact that he was speaking for thousands of men. I wanted to work with the contrast in language and tone that there would be between men in similar situations, yet very dissimilar, because the world had changed so incredibly. The letters were a natural way to do that.

In *Machine Dreams* your characters, rather than becoming drifters, settle into makeshift relationships, seeking comfort in familiar routine. Mitch and Jean's relationship is an example of this attempt to settle. But even family can't provide safety or respite from the wider world. In this case, the life of the family collides with history—the Vietnam War. What interests you about this collision?

There's always a collision. It could be the Vietnam War. It could be Wall Street. It could be anything. That war was a turning point, and was important for the generations that have inhabited this century. People make decisions that have political consequences, and there's a ripple ef-fect. Decisions made at a high level move down until they affect your son or your daughter, and then suddenly it's a matter of life and death. That's what *Machine Dreams* is about. It's about paying attention. And now we live in a world where it's even easier not to pay attention. Kids aren't on the line, unless they're poor kids who join the army.

You stay focused on the personal, intimate effects of war and create a novel that could be called political without actually exploring politics. Comment?

The personal is political. There's no point in commenting on the polit-ical in a novel in a straightforward way, because that's not the basis of the narrative. If you're going to comment directly on the political, you should be writing speeches or running for office. Also, you want to address yourself not just to what is happening at a particular moment but to all of it. This, again, comes back to questions of identity itself. Sometimes books that are extremely personal become political, because they are set in language, and they're bound between covers, and they suddenly have a different significance. *MotherKind* is an extremely personal book in that it's about one woman's life, one death, one birth, one year. It's set in a typical East Coast, New England family—typical now being that there's been a divorce, there's a stepfamily with lots of kids, there are baby boomer people taking care of aging parents and raising young kids at the same time. Yet, the stories of our lives are intimately political, though we often don't have time to notice as we're getting up in the morning and rushing through the day. *MotherKind* is not obviously set in a particular time, but it's clear that's in the eighties and that it represents a time when women were, as now, expected to do everything. They expect it of themselves. They have to be successful, and to be parents, and to be fabulous mothers who are working with reading and writing with their three-month-old child. How do those expectations measure up against the ageless rituals and questions about how death should happen, how people separate after a lifetime of relationship, what death means, how death can occur in a society like ours and retain any meaning for those involved in it? It's interesting that we now hire help to do or to move through the most basic transitions that family and community used to support, whether it's birth, labor, death, illness. These important junctures have traditionally been handled by women or by feminine sensibilities, and now we often hire hospice workers, or midwives, or baby-sitters, or au pairs—all the people we have to call on to support the way that people live now. And those people are still, by and large, women. I find that an interesting juncture of cultures. One of the big questions in *MotherKind* is, How is this transition going to happen in this new world? In that book, what is really eternal about female sensibility manifests itself in a surprising way, or in a way that is surprising to Kate. And it works. Together, the women move according to more ancient rules of identity and communication. Women who have experienced and been through labor can truly see death as a similar process. I'm teaching *A Death in the Family*, James Agee's novel, and "They Came Like Swallows," William Maxwell's story which was based on his mother's death. In both of those books, and in numerous other instances, the labor metaphor applies not only to giving birth but to certain touchstones of identity or life passage. There is a process of labor that comes along with any massive realization or transition. Any major transition or realization is a birthing process, even if it has to do with grief. It's a movement into a larger identity that can hold more realization, more sorrow, more understanding, and more meaning.

How was writing your second novel, *Shelter,* different from working on the first?

As John Irving says, none of the novels knows that you've written any of the other novels. It's always like working without a net. It doesn't get easier. I think it's actually easier in the beginning because you don't know what you're wading into.

When you first start working on a book like *Shelter,* how much do you know about the story before you begin writing?

I never know very much about the story, because I don't conceive of things in terms of story. *Shelter* was a situation in which I'd written that section that appears in italics at the beginning years before I started the book. I knew the entire book was inside that paragraph, but of course I didn't know what the parameters of that world were. I've always been interested in bonding between girls, and in a child's point of view as a consciousness inside a book or inside a world. I wrote my way into those characters through their points of view, through their voices, their perceptions.

When you say that you don't conceive of a book in story, do you mean that it comes to you in a voice?

Or a certain image. In that first paragraph of *Shelter,* there's a real sense of a world. There's a denseness. *Shelter* was written in a very specific type of voice that was difficult to sustain. It has to hold the reader inside it in the same way that the physical world of Camp Shelter holds these children, to isolate the reader from the world that he or she really lives in and pull them into this world until the book has finished its arc.

In *Shelter,* the loss of innocence that is a necessary end to childhood has dangerous and tragic outcomes. What interested you in exploring the inner world of violated children and the degrees to which they understand that violation?

I think all children are violated. That's part of childhood. I don't mean violated physically. Children, because they're powerless and extremely impressionable, and part of their identity is interfacing with the world, are bound to feel violated. I don't see *Shelter* as a tragedy. I see it as a situation in which these children manage to save one another and come out of it. What would have happened if Carmody had just kept going?

I was working with the idea of damage, in the same way that *Machine Dreams* was working with the ripple effect of political damage, decisions that are made far away from ordinary lives that ripple down to completely obliterate those lives. I was working with the ripple effect of damage inside a character who has been so damaged that he's in the process of exploding. He's like a psychic suicide bomber who's almost disassociated. He creates the politics of the planet for the people he's living with or near. How do the relatedness and the connections between these children finally protect them, and what do they do with that later? What do we do with secrets? I don't have an answer, but the book poses the questions.

Both Alma and Buddy carry unbearable secrets, and while Alma needs a spiritual unburdening—she "wanted a series of screams that opened out until the earth shook"—Buddy needs a physical salvation. He needs to be left alone by his stepfather. What drew you to exploring the different dimensions and manifestations of this issue in these two very different characters?

We all stand at the apex of our own lives. Lines are intersecting, and we're standing at the center of our own circles. Alma has been a confidante and a witness. She's the writer in the book, obviously. And Buddy has a kind of everychild sensibility. Alma's working with the burden of her mother's life, the burden of the secret, while Buddy's working not only with the burden of the secret but with the burden of needing to save his mother—pretty impossible at age seven or eight, yet he manages to do it. These characters are standing at different points along the same spectrum. That's how books should work. They let the reader inhabit different stages, different movements through a spectrum, through an arc, concurrently. The reader takes an entire journey that is like different facets of light coming into a point.

Buddy is reminiscent of the marooned boys in William Golding's *Lord of the Flies*. Were you aware of this while you were writing him?

I thought of it more as a *Lord of the Flies* having to do with girls. I thought of it as a female version of a marooned group of children. They're not marooned physically, but they're marooned far away from the war of their parents' lives, the war of their parents' relationships, in the same way that World War II is going on way outside the confines of this island where the children are in *Lord of the Flies*. But I think that *Shelter* is a much more optimistic book. Instead of finding a group of children who take on the macho games that have created the war that's going on across the ocean, you find in *Shelter* a group of children who begin to think each other's thoughts, who begin to work in tandem in a layered and primal world. There's the sense that the physical world is an ally, and that it provides a set of rules that are more ancient and fair than the rules they're leaning inside family.

What's your process like when you're working on a novel?

It's the same as my process no matter what I'm working on. I work according to language. I work starting with language, so that my process is simply to work my way into the next sentence. Sustaining the voice of a book is level one, where I have to stay to move forward. I work very slowly, until I find my way into the middle of the book. I know what to write next by reading what I've already written.

Do you do a lot of revisions?

Not really. I ceaselessly go over what I've written, but I'm not making major changes. I'm just fixing it by making minor changes that might have a big effect. I don't write reams of material and then throw it out.

Now that you've successfully written both short stories and novels, do you find that you prefer one form over the other?

In the past fifteen years, I've preferred novels because I like the sense of living in relationship with the material for a long time and being able to descend more and more deeply into it.

***MotherKind* is a departure from your earlier, darker novels and stories, and takes as its setting the domestic scene. What precipitated this shift in subject matter?**

I think it's just as dark as my other novels, and just as bright—they all work their way into the open. I wanted to look at very dark material, like death, but inside a very accessible surface. I wanted the language of *MotherKind*, unlike the language in, say, *Shelter,* to be superficially simple, clear, and familiar. I wanted to look at the ancient, mythic dimension of both birth and death as spiritual transitions and departures inside a very ordinary world. That was a difficult voice to sustain, too, for different reasons.

Kate is a poet in the book, so she is more reflective and language-oriented than your average person, but she's living a very normal life. How does identity function in that world? It's a total surprise to her that she feels what she feels toward her child, even though she's grown up considering parenting from a daughter's perspective. When giving birth really happens, it defies conventional explanation or definition. What does it have to tell her about her extremely strong connection to her own mother? All through my work, there has been this sense of the confidante inside the parent-child relationship, that double burden of being the one who is chosen or selected for special attention, for secrets, for confidences, the one who holds everyone else's life story. It's the writer-in-the-family idea. Kate thinks that she's rejected her mother's life. She's tried hard not to be like her mother, though she respects and loves Katherine. She's tried to escape the limits of her mother's time. *MotherKind* is an exploration of where women really are, what they really have, what they've lost and what they've gained.

Were there challenges you faced in writing this novel that were particular to writing on the domestic scene?
The challenge was really in the reception of the novel. The minute you write a book that's domestically oriented, you automatically cut your readership, or your serious readership, in half. There's a ghettoization of subject matter that has to do with women's lives. It's the writer's responsibility not to pander to an audience or to a culture or to a publishing climate. You just have to do what you need to do and let the rest of it happen.

In *MotherKind*, did you draw on personal experience more than in your other work?
No. It seems that I did. People assumed so, but in fact I didn't really remember what it was like to have a baby or an infant! There's a selective amnesia that happens. I felt as though I was creating a world that I had visited a hundred years before. There were certain things, like the paper that lined the baby's drawers, that were real, but a lot of it was created inside the writing, just as it was in *Shelter* or *Machine Dreams* or in any of my stories.

What are some of the common problems you find in your students' work?
They just don't read. Even if they think they read, they really don't read much. They don't come to writing with a various background in reading. They haven't read a spectrum of writers, or they haven't read all the works of six or seven writers. Now more than ever, they're very sound- and print-oriented, that is, very popular-culture oriented. They have less and less of a sense of history, and less and less interest in history. Kids who are twenty now grow up in a world in which emotional literacy is discouraged by the culture they live in. I don't hold them personally responsible. Somebody's got to come along and convince them that it's important to read.

What would you say to someone working on their first novel or stories?
They need to remember that it's a privilege to do the work. The point for others may be what you produce, and whether it's good enough, but the point for you, the point for the writer, is doing the work.
Conducted: February 2001

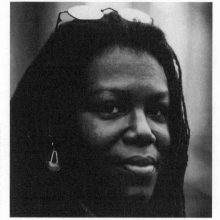

Photo: © Frank Stewart

A. J. VERDELLE

Managing the Whole Fictive World

A. J. Verdelle is the author of *The Good Negress*, which was awarded the Harold
D. Vursell Award for distinguished prose fiction from the American Academy of
Arts and Letters. It was a finalist for the PEN/Faulkner Award, the Los Angeles
Times Book Award, and the International IMPAC Literary Award. Verdelle re-
ceived the prestigious Whiting Writer's Award and the Bunting Fellowship from
Radcliffe College at Harvard University. She teaches creative writing at Princeton
University.

Your first career was in statistics. How did you go from such a left-brain activity to writing fiction?

I always loved writing, even though writing felt like a leisure activity. (This was before I started writing seriously, before I knew the truth about the work involved.) I was raised to try to find a definite and lucrative career. That was considered success in my family. I planned to become a lawyer. During an internship at the American Bar Association, I found out that not only do lots of lawyers secretly wish to be writers, but several attorneys I met had novels they had written, lingering in their drawers. I started to feel suspiciously like I was only drawn to law because I secretly wanted to write. So I leapt from that locomotive. Since research was my second love, I got a graduate degree in quantitative research, which is statistics applied to human social behavior. I had learned through political science studies that there was all of this data being collected nationally. Statisticians analyze data. I know it sounds like another world, but I wanted to protect my writing energy. I wasn't looking to accidentally choose a career that would seize the novelist in me and disappear her. Novels in my drawer seems like a nightmare, a hell of incompletion, the state of being perpetually undone and unrevised. Statistics and research turned out to be a good career choice: I could work for myself, and it paid well. As soon as I took control of my time, I used big blocks of time to write.

As to your question about left and right brain—everybody uses both their left and right hemispheres. I did my twelfth-grade science fair project on left- and right-brain activity. I took my mother's wig head; I cut it in half, displayed brain area functions. I wrote a whole survey for right- and left-handers. You see, I started working on statistics and data collection in high school.

Can you talk about your development as a writer?

I experimented for a while, mostly allowing myself to write in multiple genres. I felt liberated because no one was ever going to read this early work. I believed that we all have to do early work, so I might as well not delay. I wrote a lot of "poems, stories, essays" and realized that I didn't know what I was doing. I didn't like what I was writing—but I didn't know how to cross the Rubicon. I started reading and trying to understand what aspects of other texts appealed to me. I returned to the the books that I loved to try to figure out why I thought they worked, what compelled me. I have had favorite writers all my life. I started trying to study and to name what I admired in their works. This is how I taught myself to write. About the same time I started looking for an audience of readers: people who felt like reading the work but who don't care about me one way or the other. Since you get a captive audience of students and teachers, the idea of an M.F.A. program started to tempt me like a mirage in the distance. I went to the program at Bard, which meets in the summers and is multidisciplinary. There were writers, composers, painters, sculptors, filmmakers, photographers. We all studied together and critiqued each other's work. We worked dialogically all summer, and we were left the full academic year to improve ourselves without interference. There are lots of low-residency programs, but at Bard I got a whole summer of concentrated work rather than the more typical low-residency strategy of two weeks, twice a year. Eight weeks of multidisciplinary studio experience really inspired me. When you want to be an artist, you have step up to inspiration every time.

What were the most challenging aspects of learning to write fiction?
Being willing to work with the *whole* world your fiction brings. My shorthand for this is "360 degrees." The fewer degrees of a character's life and world that you deal with, the thinner the narrative. You have to deal with a character's physical environment. You have to write the physical self in some way that's not clunky or obvious, but that's present and not overbearing. You have to strike a balance between too much and not enough. Then there are emotions, desires, pains, parents (living or dead or absent), ex–broken legs and ex-boyfriends and ex-girlfriends, vehicles or horses or trains or jets, siblings (real or imagined), thoughts, selected memories, the children and when they were born and what happened to them. When you choose a character and you decide to write a book rather than a story or a novella or poem, you have to manage the whole fictive world. Life is big and so is fiction, especially since fiction renders life condensed.

I know that you also write poetry. How does your experience writing poetry inform your fiction?
My poetry is about abbreviation and nothing else, really. I can be poetic sometimes, but I'm not a poet. In general, I don't feel that I cover ground enough with my poems. But I do have one published poem in *Ploughshares,* which I'm very proud of. If I hadn't done the experimental writing in the beginning, I may never have written a poem. I used to make greeting card poems for my family when I was younger. That's how bad my poetry is.

But there's a poetic drive present in your prose as well.
The poets speak most succinctly. The best poets make enormous statements with small turns of phrase. That's the ultimate challenge, the poem,

or next to that, the song, which has a huge advantage in the support of fine music. But a song is a poem, and a poem is succinct and concise and compressed and crisp. That's the degree world of language I'm managing. In a novel there are some aspects of a character's life that are presented broad-swipe and some aspects that are presented quickly or nimbly, in a compressed, remembered way. You have to be able to be poetic to compress and still be compelling. I appreciate poetry. I do not shy away from poetry when the novel demands neat, sweet words that are not necessarily narrative. But until now, I haven't really written poems.

You write nonfiction pieces about photography as well. How does studying and writing about the visual arts feed your creativity as a fiction writer?

Visual is a big part of any art, including writing. I look hard and directly at the images put before me. Because we live and write in a technological era, the film, the photograph, the moving image, the frozen advertisement—all of these are part of the world of my age. Sometimes, a writer just needs a face, and photography, more than any other medium, offers as much. Suspicion, contentment, despair, plaintiveness, disgust, unawares—all these expressions can rise from a photograph. From the picture straight to the text. Do not pass go, do not collect two hundred dollars, do not dally so you end up in jail.

How did you get the idea for *The Good Negress*?

I wanted to write a long story. (My friend Nikky Finney, the poet, calls the novel the n-word. I like her turn of phrase, her appropriation.) I was somewhat preoccupied with the differences in how boys and girls are raised. I had this notion that girls have less freedom and it makes them more adaptable as adults. I view this as a reasonably good thing. Boys are given loads of freedom as children, which makes them less adaptable as adults, which turns out to be a bad thing. So many boys are brought up to think that everything is available to them. In my culture, even as their families give boys as much freedom as they can, prison looms large and harrowing for the African-American boy who feels entitled. Many boys in my culture can't constrain themselves enough to even finish school. And on the richer, whiter side, boys/men often can't constrain themselves enough to be honest, to share the boardroom, and to be participative and open and compete with people across the board, not just invent games they keep secret, that only they can play. Excessive freedom disservices everybody. There are all sorts of in-betweens, not only extremes, but those were the extremes; I wanted to write about those and the betweens.

So I sat down to write the book, and this little girl was separated from her brothers to highlight the differences in her raising. That permitted separation was part of the difference in how boys and girls are raised, that the mother could separate herself from her daughter and not from these two boys. Strange, but normative. Denise rejoined her family as a teenager and was startled to see the men that her brothers had become. Once in Detroit, Denise got involved with this teacher—which I hadn't imagined at all. James Baldwin (one of my hands-down all-time favorite writers) said, "You don't get the book you wanted. You get the book you get." You have to have the confidence and the willingness to pursue the imaginative gifts you get. So I let this teacher become who she became. Many people think that the book is more about the story with the teacher than the story that I set out to write. Both stories are there. I'm happy with either way the book is read.

What was your process of revision like for your first novel? What went on through each draft?

Because I didn't know what I was doing, and I couldn't find anyone to teach me revision, I developed my own notions of revision. In this very meticulous, almost statistical way (which is very obnoxious to some people), I figured out how I could take specific steps toward revision stepwise and thoroughly. In statistics we have this method we call stepwise regression. If I hadn't learned that, I never would have learned to revise. It may be mathematical, but it works for me. I went back to that notion of what impresses me in writing. In revision, I revisited each element I appreciated in the texts and tried to make each element the best I could in my manuscript, one element at a time. I defined for myself what I wanted from scenes, from dialogue, from sentences, nouns, verbs, extra language. I considered each element and tried to improve the work they performed in my story. I revised the entire manuscript six or seven times, and then I revised the beginning and the end together. But whatever you can do to improve your writing, you should. It doesn't much matter how you accomplish your revisions. However you can get there is fine.

My specific theory about writing and revision is that you can separate the two tasks. Draft with as much abandon as you can, and then try to stretch your inventions. Be even more imaginative. We never know how much we can stretch. So I draft with abandon; then I look at the manuscript and see what's in the manuscript that I didn't expect. I see what makes sense—or, I try to make sense of it. I look at how central each piece is to the draft, and then I start revising. I try to make a new book based on the combination of what I planned to do and what has evolved. I look at verbs. I look at action. I look at agency. Have I given my main character enough power? I consider clarity, which as an element is not negotiable. The writing must be clear. I look at each mistake to see if it rose from my unconscious. I usually consider how my mistakes might fit within the narrative before I delete them. Many mistakes I expand, rather than delete. My strategy is very time-consuming and requires a high tolerance for chaos. I give myself credit, but at the same time it takes a long time and a lot of meticulous work—some people might think ridiculous work—to get my manuscript to be lilting, cohesive, ordered. The other side of this pain is that so much of what thrives in the manuscript would not have been there if I had required myself to be ordered all along. Order is an imposition. In this book that I'm writing now, I have this big wedding. I can't imagine that I was thinking about this wedding in the beginning. This book did not have a wedding in it. Now it has a wedding. Weddings carry huge cultural weight, and there's so much that goes on around them, it's just amazing. If I'm writing about culture, then how am I going to shake off a wedding? So I'm not shaking it off. I'm working on it. I'm grateful to have imagined it; now my job is rendering.

Can you say more about that first draft, which you write with abandon? What is the role of that draft?
    None of my notions about revision make sense if you don't accept that the writing of the draft is the time to turn on the dream—let the draft be fanciful, fully fictive, surreal if you want. Revision is when we get technical, crafty, practical, and require that every standing person have a floor beneath their feet. If we know that's coming, then we may as well have our major characters born out of the sun. At least if we allow it, we can consider what that means to our narrative, and maybe make our new, revised, constrained character have sun-bleached hair so remarkable that everyone notices—almost every witness in the story responds sweetly to such celestial hair. If you never turn on the dream, then no matter how religiously you revise, your story will be thin and your narrative mostly unsurprising. The sun will never be watched, its birthings will not be witnessed. Reaching for imagination is the way to go. This is my opinion anyway.

I took a workshop with you at the Provincetown Fine Arts Work Center called "Making Your Manuscript Sing: The Art of Revision." You shared many techniques for revising a manuscript. The first exercise we did was circling all of the verbs in our piece. How is this useful as a tool in revision?
    In her diaries, Virginia Woolf talks about how difficult it is to read the manuscript through without changing it. As long as you keep changing it,

you're thinking about small aspects of the manuscript. You're thinking about words. At some point you have to read the manuscript for itself, which is bigger than words. You have to know (to decide) what you want to work on with the manuscript largely considered. She's right. It's nearly impossible to work on a manuscript, to read it through, without diminishing this and heightening that. The way I got around this was to tell myself that I wouldn't change anything. I'd only circle the verbs. Big bombshell for me. Huge (accidental) lesson about writing. It's all in the verbs. Every motion in fiction requires a verb to make a move. Fiction is dependent on action, and all action happens by way of verbs. We bury our verbs in our nouns and adjectives. Verbs are the velocity of fiction. There is motion in emotion. The word "is" is small and mostly ineffectual.

I learned to do global searches on forms of "to be." You go through your manuscript and come up with 3,452 uses of "is," then right away you know you have a problem. No manuscript can sustain that. Verbs attract my attention (as a result of this accidental effort in restraint). I thank Virginia for inspiring me, and I seek specific, active verbs.

You also had students underline all of the prepositional phrases. Why?
Language starts to lose its spark, and sentences their meaning, when readers have to consider too many objects in one place, especially objects of prepositions. Two or three prepositional phrases in one sentence, repeated through a manuscript, starts to become obnoxious. Many student writers can't remember the definition of preposition, much less recognize them as weeds in the work.

What are some of the other things you consider during revision?
Make sure your sentence has a subject. So many of them have a pronoun for a subject, which is not a subject as far as I'm concerned. It's confusing and weighty. Make sure the main actions are not stuck in a sentence with other, less important actions. Learn how to set off what's important that's going on instead of covering it up with long sentences and adjectives. Make sure readers get to see the action of the narrative. Let your writing be transparent, at least most of the time. Vary the pacing in the text. Know that there are parts of your narrative that are going to be quick and choppy, say, if there's a murder or an abduction or a rainstorm. Then there are parts that are going to be leisurely, such as a sex scene or a walk in the park. Writers need to learn to manage speed in writing, pacing. Learn when to end a section or paragraph. Learn how to use a pause.

I love the beginning of *The Good Negress:* "I knew I was sleepin too long. And as I have come to know myself, I think I felt her leavin, the door clos-

ing behind the belly at the end of my rope." What do you look for in a beginning of a novel?

I don't worry about the beginning until I get to the end of the book.
Ultimately, I choose a point in the narrative that's not at the beginning of
the story, and that has enough drama to draw. Storytellers from old times,
from caves, started stories in a way that signifies the story to come. The
most ancient stories start with "once upon a time" or alternately, "our
father in heaven." Either start is going to bring on a story of strong feats,
man against nature, of ills and plagues, of prayers for redemption. So too
our beginnings have to signify the story to come. That means get the
drama heaving right away. Let the reader see something happen, and then
let the reader decide if this is a happening that they want to follow. You
have to signify, and you have to drive the action. You have to help the
reader make the decision to take the ride.

The beginning of *The Good Negress* is about that moment of lying in
bed being half-conscious, knowing that you're missing something, and
then rising to find what you've missed is monumental.

**You talked earlier about editing the beginning and the ending of the novel
together. How do the two inform each other, and what do you look for in
an ending?**

The beginning and ending refer to each other, and there is some balance between them. I'm not talking about rectangular or square balance.
It can be triangular. You could even make the decision to have it be off
balance. But you have to make the decision. You have to observe how
you've handled the beginning, which you may want to refer to nimbly in
the end or resolve fairly bluntly. For Denise, in *The Good Negress,* the beginning was about our willingness to be only half-awake, about missing
an event that changed her life irrevocably. In the end Denise is again half-
conscious, but she's witnessing. She has sworn off being half-asleep and
inactive forevermore.

Narrative signifies its endings as well. Oftentimes they signify by starting to refer to the story's start, however lightly or with however much extension. Beginnings and endings create the frame for the book, so it
makes sense to work on them together. Again, I'm deciding on my beginning after I've finished the book. Part of it is selecting where the beginning
is going to be. Then working it up to the pitch that a beginning needs to
be, and making sure that the ending matches (or silences) the scream (if
your drama takes you there) you've begun.

**The *New York Times Book Review* said of *The Good Negress* that "[Ver-
delle] illuminates the way language itself can both reflect and circum-
scribe a person's character and experience." In Denise's case, language**

reflects her down-home, backcountry upbringing, and can potentially limit her opportunities in Detroit by making her sound uneducated. How did you arrive at this as a theme?

That's not how I think about that part of the story. Denise is a genius. Denise comes to Detroit, which is a huge city compared to where she's lived. She has a very vague memory of it. She thinks she's supposed to be at home there. She goes in and starts trying to wash herself into the apartment. She doesn't know what else to do. She doesn't feel at home. She has no room. She does the cleaning to try to psychologically infuse herself on the apartment. Then she goes to school, and she has to get through this tempestuous and thick cloud of language, which she doesn't expect at all. Even inside the household, which tells you something about the household, there's not much said about the way she talks, and she talks the same way she does at school. She's got a huge hill to climb, and she and the teacher figure out how to manage it, and she totally manages it. By the end of the book, you forget that that was an issue. It's gone.

Thematically, the issue arose when Denise spent five years in rural Virginia, living with her grandmother. Between this reality of her upbringing and the blunt though loving teacher, Miss Pearson, the language issue demanded to be part of the story. I had only to oblige, and work the language until it worked.

For Denise, the ability to learn and grow and become educated is her salvation and a source of comfort during difficult times. For instance, in the end of the novel, when she goes to get Luke Edward, she says, "I have to take my mind to think on something soothing. Even as I stumble up the road. I recall myself learning. I remember when that sky opened up." People draw comfort from all kinds of things—a secure and happy home life, making money, having friends, or love—but Denise finds comfort in learning, which says something about her as a character and the woman she may become. Comment?

For the few years that Miss Pearson pays hovering attention to Denise, Denise comes to understand life and its possibilities and its demands—to a greater extent than she ever perceived possible. Denise has had a major epiphany in her understanding, and she recognizes the power of her awakening. Denise believes her new knowledge will permit her new and broader directions than those she would formerly have had access to. She is right in her judgment.

Let's talk about the novel you're working on now. I know that it's a historical novel. Can you tell me about it?

It's supposed to be a love story that I'm still working to get the lan-

class and then leaves. There's a really brief residency. A lot of times the teachers don't have any kind of background or support, so they don't feel confident in taking what the poet presents and using it year to year. Because it's a one-shot deal with no long-term follow-through, I thought that if I took the job, I wanted to give them opportunities to really learn how to teach poetry. I go in and teach, and I watch them teach, and we work it out so that they can teach poetry on their own. It's the first time I'm working with the little ones, and they write fabulous poetry. It's so honest, and sad, and poignant.

Your work alters our view of Hawaii. It offers a look behind the proverbial curtain at how some Hawaiians live in the midst of a tourist industry that strives to hide anything that doesn't fit a mainstream idea of paradise. You've given voice to a marginalized population, which has made you both a hero and a villain. Comment?

The native Hawaiian population is an indigenous people. They have their very political, social, and economic battles that have gone on for generations. I am not the person that speaks to that. My husband is native American, but I am not. I'm Japanese-American. Just one generation ago, the generation before me was told that we would never produce a novelist from Hawaii, because we're too early in our journey away from our mother country. Maxine Hong Kingston would say that "I haven't even really been an American for that long," because we attained statehood in 1959. They said we'll write short stories and poetry, but that's as far as we'll go.

The second generation off the plantation, the ethnic groups that formed the workforce, were really determined to have their children go to college. In my father's generation there were thirteen children, and the children have to help the parents pay off the debt to the general store, because they're only being paid a dollar a day. The debt to the general store was enormous. My oldest uncle had to pay off that debt and take care of his younger brothers and sisters. By the time my father came along, he was number seven—he could go to college because they were going to put him through. If he ever decided to be an artist or writer, that would be it. They had to have a more traditional job like teachers or accountants. Our generation comes along, and if I decide to be an artist, they cringe. They still are not as adamant, but they want you to have a degree to fall back on.

The problem here is that we're an adolescent literature, and everyone's trying to find their place. People start pointing fingers. "How come you didn't write about ———?" "Why did you write about Filipinos?" "How come you're writing about Koreans? You're not from Korea." And on and on. I've been trying to advocate: instead of the crab-in-the-proverbial-bucket metaphor, we are spokes on a wheel. If we keep plucking the spokes off, we're not going anywhere. Everybody's story is vital to the movement of that wheel.

What do you think enabled you to have the confidence to write in your true voice and in your native language of Hawaii Creole English?

I wanted to be a lyric poet. I wanted to be more mainstream. Our models out there, people who had succeeded, were poets writing lyric poetry like Cathy Song, who won the Yale Prize. That's what I wanted to be. I'm so ashamed, because we had to do a chapbook at the end of the semester and a couple of years ago Morgan gave mine back to me. I thought, I'm going to burn this ugly thing. It was so overwritten. At one point, I wrote one line in pidgin in a poem, and she said that that was my authentic voice. I said, "No it's not!" and we had a big disagreement. She wanted to know why I wouldn't write in pidgin, and I told her that everyone in the workshop who I admired would think I was stupid. They were all from private schools on Oahu. "They're very smart people," I told her, "and when we talk like that we're dumb." All our lives we try to hide the dialect, hide the inflection, and we never are able to do good job at it.

When you sat down to write in pidgin, did you have to struggle with your own feelings about it?

Morgan made me read women poets like June Jordan, Ai, Thulanie Davis, Jessica Hagedorn. I read all these women who were doing work in voice, and I was eating it up. Morgan told me that I was not any different, that I was on the tail end of women doing work in voice, women from all over the place involved in the same tradition. It gave me a kind of freedom. Then when I started to write in pidgin I couldn't stop. There are so many stories linked to our voice. I've come to understand the process about how the first language is the language of your heart, and when you write good poetry or good stories you want your heart to speak, not your head. If you process through your head you start censoring and denying, but if you speak through your heart your family is attached to that, your life, your feelings.

There's been a lot of controversy surrounding your work, including critics and scholars who condemn the use of pidgin. Why do you believe so strongly that it is important to write in pidgin?

I don't know if it's so important to write in pidgin anymore. The characters dictate the way the story should be told. The characters know the sound of their own voice. I really try to trust that now. People say that with my last book I sold out because there's no pidgin, but that book is set in urban Honolulu and people don't speak like that. Language is not so separate with pidgin on one hand and English on the other. Our teachers taught us, not in a mean way but by their gestures, that pidgin was bad, and it was so insidious that by age twenty-seven I hated myself, I hated who I was, why I was. I didn't feel that I was good enough. They gesture with their right and left hand: here's pidgin down here, and here's Standard English, and they raise their hand higher. I tell my students that language is a wheel—it's round. Ilocano, English, and pidgin are three parts of a pie that are equal, and we're so smart that we know how to get what we want. If you're asking your grandmother for money, you speak in Ilocano because she thinks it's so charming. If you go to a job interview and you speak pidgin, they'll think you're so dumb. That's how I teach it. Language is so whole for me.

Other controversy arises among local Hawaiians who complain that your work shows only the harshest aspects of native Hawaiian life and culture. How do you respond to these kinds of comments?
You cannot expect one person to tell the story for everybody. I've never lived any other way than the small slice of life that was given to me. That's all I'm representing. I'm not trying to represent anybody else. I tell people to write their own story. If they want help, I'll help them.

Your work really causes us to consider the role of art and the artist. It seems false to expect writers and other artists from marginalized populations to have to speak for their specific group and always uplift or say positive things about that group.
That happens, and it turns into another type of stereotype that leads to other trouble. Real life just isn't like that. The scary part for me is that people cross the line between characters speaking and me speaking. I try to be as truthful as I can to the integrity of my characters. But that's not me. I don't think that way and feel that way. I don't agree with all of my characters. In the real world, I didn't agree with a lot of things that were said to me and done to me. Some people don't know how to distinguish between me and the character in the book.

Who are some of the writers who've informed and influenced your work, and who are you reading now?
I've mentioned some, but the books that I read have to do with the book that I'm writing. I'm having a hard time with the book I'm writing

now because I had different purposes for the book. I was reading William Faulkner, because I realized that when I was in college I was so slow-minded with reading that I read Cliff Notes and I'd never read William Faulkner. So now that I'm working on a historical novel I decided to read his work. It had the opposite effect on me that I hoped for. After I read *The Sound and the Fury*, I thought I had to quit writing. I thought, I'm doing amateur theater here—I've got to quit. In the presence of this genius, I felt embarrassed. Amateur night at the Pahala Theater, good night everybody.

You mentioned Maxine Hong Kingston.

Maxine Hong Kingston is such a great influence and such a great person. Early on with *Woman Warrior* she was put on the chopping block, and she was so gracious. That happens to every ethnic group—the women tend to be published more widely, and the men are critics. This is such a generalization, but I've seen it with Amy Tan, Alice Walker, Sandra Cisneros. I feel like at least I'm in good company if I get chopped up.

How do your novel ideas come to you?

Novel ideas come to me all in different ways. *Blu's Hanging* came to me because I had a friend who was Blu and another friend who's life was Blu. The book was about love and how we can kill each other with love that is so intense. Your love for somebody can actually kill them. I'm like that. With my sister, I have that feeling of wanting to make her life better. I'm going to love her to death. The novel helped me to learn the importance of letting go. The book I'm working on now I started because my house is haunted. I've had spiritualists and healers, and my autistic son hears the ghosts and the dog hears the ghosts, so finally I did research on who they were and what they were all about.

Was it difficult to strike a balance between writing accurate pidgin and finding an eloquence and intelligibility that would make the narrative accessible? Were there any challenges you encountered in getting the voice right?

There are grumblings that I didn't make it true pidgin, it's too accessible, it's generational. It's all true. My consideration when I sit down to write it is soundwise. "Da dog dat I love came home" gets hard to read after pages and pages, and "The dog that I love came home" is not so different, yet easier to read. The words that are more important are the words that are really in the dialect, the words that have more impact. If you get into changing all the little words—"more," "for," "your," "or"— it gets ridiculous. I had to draw the line somewhere. People don't agree with everything I did, but I don't agree with what everybody else does either. The discussion about this isn't around so much anymore. People are not so uptight about it now.

Lovey's teacher at school warns the students that if they speak pidgin, no one will give them a job. "You sound uneducated. You will be looked down upon. You're speaking a low-class form of good Standard English. Continue, you'll go nowhere in life." His racism makes him invalidate his students' true voice and discourages them to maintain their own identities. Do you think it's important to speak Standard English, and what do you think is lost when children are discouraged from speaking pidgin?

It has such a tragic effect on your psyche. It still goes on in some classrooms, but there is a little more tolerance now because the books are being sold in a national market. People are starting to see the dialect in print. But only when we got validation from outsiders did people start to see using pidgin as artsy or acceptable. People are still reluctant to have children write or speak in dialect. They don't want to encourage it.

Let's talk about some of the other themes that recur throughout your work. There is a sense of shame about local traditions, which often is expressed in a character's fascination with pop culture. Lovey says, "I don't tell anyone, not even Jerry, how ashamed I am of pidgin English. Ashamed of my mother and father, the food we eat, chicken luau with can spinach and tripe stew. The place we live, down the house lots in the Kicks Homes that all look alike except for the angle of the house from the street. The car we drive, my father's brown Land Rover without the back window." She secretly wishes to be *haole* with a name like Betty Smith. In *Name Me Nobody*, Emi-Lou is named after the singer EmmyLou Harris. How did you arrive at this theme in your work?

Because we were Asian growing up in Hawaii in the seventies and eighties, there weren't a lot of faces in the media that were our faces; there weren't a lot of faces in print that were our faces. A writer friend of mine said that until you see yourself in print or in the written language, you don't exist. It's true. You read storybooks or adolescent literature, and you don't see yourself. You don't exist. That's the power of the written word. We didn't see that. We notice the difference between Japanese and Chinese, so when we did see ourselves in movies or on television, everyone was playing everyone else's role because there were such limited parts. Even people like Shirley McClain were taking our roles. They just do the heavy eyeliner. Even Juanita Hall (Bloody Mary) was African-American. It's interesting the way that the media represented us. Today it's different. Kids see themselves in magazines and on television and in the movies. They still play roles that aren't ethnically exact, but it's something.

You also write about the intense desire of the young second- and third-generation immigrants to pass for *haole*: to sound *haole*, to look *haole*, and to have *haole*-sounding names. What's underneath this wish to pass?
    It's the same kind of thing. It's better to be white and have a white name. People that were biracial or *hapa-haole*, half-white, who had light hair or light eyes. They weren't so Japanese or so Asian, but that comes with its own issues.

***Name Me Nobody* is told in the voice of thirteen-year-old Emi-Lou. When you started this novel, did you have the young adult audience in mind, or did the voice simply lead you in this direction?**
    I had the young adult audience in mind. I wanted to do it quickly as an in-between project, and it turned out to be the longest book I ever worked on, about five or six years. To get the story out, which I knew was for young adults, I wrote it all in pidgin so I could write the story fast. Then I wanted to translate the narrative back to English and leave the dialogue in pidgin. It was so hard to translate the pidgin into English. There's so much humor attached to the way that you say pidgin, and when it's translated to English you loose that. I'll never do that again.

Are there challenges in writing from the point of view of a thirteen-year-old or for a younger audience?
    The challenge is not writing from the point of view of a thirteen-year-old. The challenge is in writing for a younger audience, so you put on your censor's hat at some point. You realize that you can't have characters say and do certain things. That book was the hardest book I've done.

You depict the racism among Japanese-American, Korean-American, *haole*, and gay people. "They don't want to say the words *lesbian* and *butchie*. But it's all around us in town, at the high schools and intermediate schools, ball games, the mall, the beach . . . tough aunties with pretty girlfriends, uncles with soft voices and buffed bodies. . . ." Nobody figures out that they're all in the same position or, like you said, part of the same wheel. It's sad and difficult, but you write about it with candor and humor that makes it very accessible. Comment?
    We live here in this small, small place, and our lives are so connected and so complicated and so wonderful and so disastrous. There's a lot of humor in there, a lot of poignancy, a lot of stories that can be told with great honesty. Or, we can cover it over and call ourselves a melting pot

like everybody else calls us. Anyone with a brain knows that this is no melting pot. My father's generation was discouraged from marrying out of their ethnic group, because of the plantation mentality. The plantation owners didn't want their contract workers to intermingle, because they didn't want them to unionize. They kept each ethnic group separate— Japanese camp, Filipino camp, Chinese camp—and then they spread rumors about each other that have filtered through three or four generations. In my father's generation, you don't see marriage outside the ethnic group. Our generation is more tolerant. You see more intermingling. It's still very complicated because we fall back on those old stereotypes. "Your old uncle, he so *chang!*" Because he's Chinese he's penny-pinching.

Heads by Harry **displays your poetic gifts right from the first page. "A roseate sky envelops Mauna Ke'a on the Big Island of Hawai'i, youngest in the chain of Hawaiian Islands, and the only home I have known." What do you look for in the opening to a novel?**

Somebody wants to tell a story. That's the hardest part because when you're starting a novel, everyone wants to tell a story. For the first 50 to 75 pages you're floundering because you don't know who should tell the story, who has the most compelling voice. I didn't know if Sheldon was going to tell that story, or the father. With *Father of the Four Passages,* I had a character Mia telling the story, and she was passive and stayed home. She became so boring. I wrote about 170 pages and had to trash the whole thing. When I finally realized that I wanted to have Sonia tell the story, that's when that voice came out from the first page: "Sonny boy, son of Sonia. . . ." Where was she? She had been wanting to tell the story, but I had allowed 170 pages of another character telling the story.

What do you look for in an ending?

You know how you said the story begins telling itself? Once this happens, I can start approximating an end. I know where I want to take it toward, and for the most part I've been able to hit that mark. I know how it ends. When I hit that last period on the manuscript, I stop, I lean back, I start crying.

Your characters are very vivid and real. How do you create characters that come alive and stand on their own, especially when there are numerous characters? How do you keep them from blurring together?

Not all characters are major characters. Major characters are three-dimensional. The minor characters who are pushing the characters forward are two-dimensional characters. Uncle Paolo in *Blu's Hanging* was a minor character. I wasn't going to flesh him out more than I did. But people placed all kinds of meaning and interpretation and intent on that. He was moving the narrative forward; he wasn't central. The three-dimensional characters cannot be all good or all bad. Even the antagonist characters cannot be all evil. There has to be balance, even when they do terrible things.

I know that your character Uncle Paulo in *Blu's Hanging* caused a lot of controversy. You were accused of racism for showing a Filipino man as abusive. How did you respond to this, and how did it affect your writing?

I got really terrified. I thought everyone was going to love me when *Saturday Night at the Pahala Theater* was published. People in the workshop loved it; then I was criticized for the first poem, which makes a comment about a Filipino. And then with other books I had some mediocre reviews. By the time *Blu's Hanging* came along, I'd had to learn to accept criticism for my work. Morgan really helped me with this. I had to learn to let go of the books. A healer told me that I hold on too tightly. She told me that when a book is done and I put it in the FedEx box and it crosses my threshold, it's like sending my child into the world. I don't know how my child will be received. At that point I have to say good-bye. I have to let it go. Now I have my ritual. I have my friends on call, liquor available, then friends who come after work with liquor and food, and I play the sound track—I always create a sound track for each book—and we say good-bye. It's sad to let go. I get really attached to some of the characters.

In *Blu's Hanging,* the children protect their identity by speaking pidgin English, a dialect only they can understand. Language becomes a form of resistance and protection. Comment?

It's in reaction to the teachers and the Department of Education here—because we're so short on teachers, they've gone into recruitment on the mainland. So these young *haole* girls and men come down here and expect the picture-postcard version. They land, and everyone in their classroom is brown, and the landscape is arid and dry, or they end up in a teacher's cottage with holes in the screen and the mosquitoes swarming. The kids don't really protect themselves with language. In real life, they kill your spirit, so the book was a reaction to that.

In *Father of the Four Passages,* how did you decide to use letters written by Sonia to her three aborted fetuses as a means of expressing her feelings about these aborted births in the face of giving birth to number four, Sonny Boy?

My dad left us after he retired. He was so bohemian. He was the true artist in our family. He wanted to travel, so he went and taught in Japan and didn't come back for two years. He wrote me these letters that were so magnificent, things that I'd never seen, because I didn't leave Hawaii until my first book tour, when I was thirty-five. But I always wanted to leave, and my father's letters were a way for me to see the world that I thought I would never see. After he made a little bit of money, he mapped his way through the world. With his letters I followed him through Calcutta, Burma, and Katmandu, where he stayed for a month. It was so fascinating, the things he wrote about, the foods and traditions. So that's how the letters came into the book.

You also include letters from Sonia's father Joseph, and letters that Sonia writes to Mark. What are the letters able to express that a straight narrative cannot?
The father in the book is emotionally and physically unavailable, but in the letters he can express the music of his soul. That was the only way he could do it. In person, he couldn't be a father. There are things she writes to her aborted babies that she cannot say, that she couldn't express even in a prayer.

The letters, in addition to offering a glimpse into Sonia's psyche, often act as transitions between narrative sections. Did you plan this, or did this arise in the writing of the story?
I knew that I would use the letters of the father in other ways. Then, because the narrative is so internal that it gets overwhelming, I had to look at where I could create transition and break up the narrative so that she didn't overwhelm the text.

"Sonny Boy, son of Sonia, the only one I did not kill." This is the first sentence to *Father of the Four Passages*. It's interesting that she thinks the word "kill," and not abort, or deny, or some softer version of the truth. Why does she see her decision to abort as murder, and why is this so important to the story?
That's the church. I knew that that would play in, that there would be that kind of backdrop to it. It's a choice that Celeste makes to take care of her pain. I know plenty of people who go running to the church, and it ends up creating a creature that is so holier-than-thou that they become frightening with that kind of knowledge and belief system. That's what happened with Celeste, so I knew where it came from. With Sonia, she had to try to understand that kind of Bible-speak and try to make sense of it for herself and for what she's done. That book is a conversation about

God and about who God is, and what things mean when we make our choices, and how much God really loves you in the end no matter what you do. You can always be forgiven. Sometimes it's easy to think what we've done is so horrific that we cannot be forgiven. But we can.

Another theme that comes up again and again is namelessness. Characters often have no mother or no father, and hence no real name. How does this theme arise in your work so often?

What I'm really writing about is the emotional abandonment, which is more scary than being physically abandoned. In writing books, I can look at it from everybody's point of view and why it happened, and then I can forgive people for their limitations. It wasn't that they loved me less. It meant that they had a lot of their own issues and they brought it into their life with me. I saw it as generational, so it helped me to consider how I am with my child and be a better mother. Putting words to it is powerful.

Even the parents you write about who don't know what they're doing when they do harm—they have good intentions.

That's what I mean by a three-dimensional character. Mr. Harvey in *Wild Meat and the Bully Burgers,* the teacher, didn't have bad intentions. He wanted to do his best job and help his students become job-ready and prepare them to be in the real world. So he's not a bad guy. He's well intentioned. But the kids get hurt. That's what makes it so sad.

I know that you're part of a writing group that includes Nora Okja Keller, among others. Can you say a little bit about your group and the role of this group in your writing life?

One time I called us a dysfunctional family because we disagree, we criticize each other, we say things that we shouldn't say, but I've never had a more loyal group of friends who've been supportive of me and my work. They haven't liked everything I've done, but they support me. It centers around Wing Tek Lum, Darrell Lum, and Eric Chock, the heavy hitters, and when they got mad at me for calling us a dysfunctional family I called them Grandpa Wing Tek, and Darrell is our old Chinese uncle. But it's a great group, thick-and-thin kind of people.

What would you say to new writers working on their first novels or stories?

When I work with college students I say, "Writing is 10 percent talent, 90 percent passion. When I look around the room, I see us all in the same boat with talent, but I don't see the passion." Nora Keller is a young writer with a fire burning in the middle. That's a story you were born to tell. It's eating you up. You're going to be burned. You're going to be ash. But what a lot of young writers do, instead of jumping into the flame, is they do a little dance around the flame. Every story has to do with some part of the flame, but they never get enough courage to jump into the fire. They're hiding from the truth. They don't want to hurt people, but those concerns become invalid once you jump into the fire.

Conducted: September 2002

Bibliography

Andrea Barrett

Servants of the Map: Stories. New York: W. W. Norton & Company, 2002; paperback, 2003.
The Voyage of the Narwhal: A Novel. New York: W. W. Norton & Company, 1998; paperback, 1999.
Ship Fever. New York: W. W. Norton & Company, 1996; paperback, 1996.
The Forms of Water. New York: Pocket Star Books, 1993. Reprint, Washington Square Press, 1994.
The Middle Kingdom. New York: Pocket Star Books, 1991. Reprint, Washington Square Press, 1992.
Lucid Stars. New York: Delta, 1989.

Aimee Bender

An Invisible Sign of My Own. New York: Doubleday, 2000; Doubleday, 2001.
The Girl in the Flammable Skirt. New York: Doubleday, 1998; Anchor Books, 1999.

Amy Bloom

Normal. New York: Random House, 2002.
A Blind Man Can See How Much I Love You. New York: Random House, 2001; Vintage Books, 2001.
Love Invents Us. New York: Random House, 1999; Vintage Books, 2001.
Come to Me. New York: HarperCollins, 1993; HarperPerennial, 1994.

Elizabeth Cox

Bargains in the Real World. New York: Random House, 2000.
Night Talk. St. Paul: Graywolf, 1997; Griffin Trade Paperback, 1998.
The Ragged Way People Fall out of Love. New York: North Point Press, 1991. Reprint, Baton Rouge: Louisiana State University Press, 2002.
Familiar Ground. New York: Scribner, 1984; Avon, 1986.

Chitra Banerjee Divakaruni

Fiction
The Vine of Desire. New York: Doubleday, 2002; Anchor Books, 2003.
The Unknown Errors of Our Lives: Stories. New York: Doubleday, 2001; Anchor Books, 2002.
Sister of My Heart. New York: Doubleday, 1999; Bantam Doubleday Dell Publishing, 2000.
The Mistress of Spices. New York: Anchor, 1997; Doubleday, 1998.
Arranged Marriage: Stories. New York: Anchor, 1995; Anchor Books, 1996.
Poetry
Black Candle: Poems about Women from India, Pakistan, and Bangladesh. St. Paul: Consortium Book Sales, Reprint 2000. Reprint, St. Paul: Calyx Books, 2000.
Leaving Yuba City: Poems. New York: Anchor, 1997.
The Reason for Nasturtiums. Berkeley, Calif.: Berkeley Poets' Workshop & Press, 1990.
Childrens' Book
Neela: Victory Song. Middleton, Wisc.: Pleasant Company Publications, 2002.

Maria Flook

Nonfiction
Invisible Eden: A True Story of Love and Death on Cape Cod. New York: Broadway Books, 2003.
My Sister Life: The Story of My Sister's Disappearance. New York: Pantheon, 1998. Reprint, Broadway Books, 1999.
Fiction
Open Water. New York: Random House Value Publishing, 1997; Ecco Press, 1998.
You Have the Wrong Man. New York: Pantheon, 1997.
Family Night. New York: Pantheon, 1993.
Dancing With My Sister Jane. Bristol, R.I.: Ampersand Press, 1987.
Poetry
Sea Room. Middletown, Conn.: Wesleyan University Press, 1990.
Reckless Wedding. New York: Houghton Mifflin Co., 1982.

Lynn Freed

The House of Women. New York: Little Brown & Co., 2002.
The Mirror. New York: Crown Publishers, 1997; New York: Ballantine Books, 1999.
The Bungalow. New York: Poseideon Press (Simon & Schuster), 1993; Story Line Press, 1999.
Home Ground. New York: Summit Books (Simon & Schuster), 1986; Viking Penguin, 1987; Story Line Press, 1999.

Friends of the Family. New York: New American Library, 1982; Story Line Press, 2000.

Gish Jen

Who's Irish? Stories. New York: Random House, 1999; Vintage Books, 2000.
Mona in the Promised Land. New York: Knopf, 1996; Vintage Books, 1997.
Typical American. New York: Houghton Mifflin Co., 1991; Plume, 1992.

Nora Okja Keller

Fox Girl. New York: Viking Press, 2002; Penguin USA, 2003.
Comfort Woman. New York: Viking Press, 1997; Penguin USA, 1998.

Jill McCorkle

Creatures of Habit. Chapel Hill: Algonquin Books, 2001.
Final Vinyl Days and Other Stories. Chapel Hill: Algonquin Books, 1998; Faw-
    cett Books, 1999.
Carolina Moon. Chapel Hill: Algonquin Books, 1996; Fawcett Books, 1997.
Crash Diet. Chapel Hill: Algonquin Books, 1992; Fawcett Books, 2001.
July 7th. Chapel Hill: Algonquin Books, 1992; paperback, 1992.
Ferris Beach. Chapel Hill: Algonguin Books, 1990; Fawcett Books, 1993.
Tending to Virginia. Chapel Hill: Algonquin Books, 1987; Crest, 1991.
The Cheer Leader. Chapel Hill: Algonquin Books, 1984; HighBridge Company,
    1992.

Elizabeth McCracken

Niagara Falls All over Again. New York: Dell Publishing Co., 2001; Delta, 2002.
The Giant's House: A Romance. New York: Dial Press, 1996. Reprint, Avon
    Books, 1997.
Here's Your Hat What's Your Hurry: Stories. New York: Turtle Bay Books, 1993.
    Reprint, Avon Books, 1997.

Sue Miller

The World Below. New York: Knopf, 2001; Ballantine Books, 2002.
While I Was Gone. New York: Knopf, 1999; Ballantine Books, 1999.
The Distinguished Guest. New York: HarperCollins, 1995; paperback, 1999.
For Love. New York: HarperCollins, 1993; paperback, 1999.
Family Pictures: A Novel. New York: HarperCollins, 1992; paperback, 1999.
Inventing the Abbots and Other Stories. New York: HarperCollins, 1987; paper-
    back, 1999.
The Good Mother. New York: HarperCollins, 1986; Reprint, Delta, 1994.
Anthology
Best American Short Stories 2002. New York: Mariner Books, 2002.

Sena Jeter Naslund

Ahab's Wife; or, The Star-Gazer: A Novel. New York: William Morrow & Co., 1999; HarperPerennial, 2000.
The Disobedience of Water: Stories and Novellas. Boston: David R. Godine, 1999; HarperPerennial, 2000.
Sherlock in Love: A Novel. Boston: David R. Godine, 1993; HarperPerennial, 2001.
The Animal Way to Love. Bristol: Ampersand, 1993.
Ice Skating at the North Pole. Ampersand, 1989.

Ann Patchett

Bel Canto. New York: HarperCollins, 2001; HarperPerennial, 2002.
The Magician's Assistant. New York: Harcourt, 1997; Harvest Books, 1998.
Taft. New York: Houghton Mifflin, 1994. Reprint, Ballantine Books, 1999.
The Patron Saint of Liars. New York: Houghton Mifflin, 1992. Reprint, Ballantine Books, 1996.

Jayne Anne Phillips

MotherKind. New York: Knopf, 2000; Vintage Books, 2001.
Shelter. New York: Houghton Mifflin, 1994; Vintage Books, 2002.
Machine Dreams. New York: Washington Square Press, 1991; Vintage Books, 1999.
Black Tickets. New York: Vintage Books, 2001; Delacorte Press, 1989.
Fast Lanes, New York: Vintage Books, 2002; E. P. Dutton, 1987.
Out-of-print, Small Press Editions
The Secret Country. Winston-Salem, N.C.: Palaemon Press Limited, 1982.
How Micky Made It. Minneapolis: Bookslinger Editions, 1981.
Counting. Ancram, N.Y.: Vehicle Editions, 1978.
Sweethearts. Weston, Conn.: Truck Press, 1976 and 1978.

A. J. Verdelle

The Good Negress. Chapel Hill: Algonquin, 1995; HarperPerennial, 1996.

Lois-Ann Yamanaka

Fiction
Father of the Four Passages. New York: Farrar Straus & Giroux, 2002; Picador, 2002.
Heads by Harry. New York: Farrar Straus & Giroux, 1999; Bard Books, 2000.
Blu's Hanging. New York: Farrar Straus & Giroux, 1997. Reprint, Bard Books, 1998.

Wild Meat and the Bully Burgers. New York: Farrar Straus & Giroux, 1996. Reprint, Harvest Books, 1997.
Young Adult
Name Me Nobody. New York: Hyperion Press, 1999; paperback, 2000.
Poetry
Saturday Night at the Pahala Theater. Honolulu: Bamboo Ridge Press, 1993.

1 7/06